Diversifying Open Source

An Open Standards Playbook for Inclusive and Equitable Tech Projects

Paloma Oliveira

Apress®

Diversifying Open Source: An Open Standards Playbook for Inclusive and Equitable Tech Projects

Paloma Oliveira
Berlin, Germany

ISBN-13 (pbk): 979-8-8688-0768-8   ISBN-13 (electronic): 979-8-8688-0769-5
https://doi.org/10.1007/979-8-8688-0769-5

Managing Director, Apress Media LLC: Welmoed Spahr
Acquisitions Editor: James Robinson-Prior
Development Editor: Jim Markham
Coordinating Editor: Gryffin Winkler

Cover image designed by Freepik (www.freepik.com)

Distributed to the book trade worldwide by Springer Science+Business Media New York, 1 New York Plaza, New York, NY 10004. Phone 1-800-SPRINGER, fax (201) 348-4505, e-mail orders-ny@springer-sbm.com, or visit www.springeronline.com. Apress Media, LLC is a Delaware LLC and the sole member (owner) is Springer Science + Business Media Finance Inc (SSBM Finance Inc). SSBM Finance Inc is a **Delaware** corporation.

For information on translations, please e-mail booktranslations@springernature.com; for reprint, paperback, or audio rights, please e-mail bookpermissions@springernature.com.

Apress titles may be purchased in bulk for academic, corporate, or promotional use. eBook versions and licenses are also available for most titles. For more information, reference our Print and eBook Bulk Sales web page at http://www.apress.com/bulk-sales.

Any source code or other supplementary material referenced by the author in this book is available to readers on GitHub. For more detailed information, please visit https://www.apress.com/gp/services/source-code.

If disposing of this product, please recycle the paper

To George, Felix, Nova, and Tofu, whose purrs and me-ows remind me to measure life not by hours worked but by sunbeams and full bowls. To Mateus, my house, the ground beneath every step of this book.

Table of Contents

TABLE OF CONTENTS

About the Author

 As a free and open source advocate, software developer, community organizer, artist, curator, climber, and base jumper, **Paloma Oliveira** is a wholehearted explorer who navigates various social, professional, and investigative endeavors connecting people, ideas, and passions. This book emerges from years of collaborative culture work—building together with great minds toward more kind, socially just, and regenerative ways of working and being together. She focuses on technologies that enable autonomy, equity, and care for humans and the more-than-human world, recognizing that our digital futures are inextricably woven with ecological wellbeing.

About the Technical Reviewer

 **Dr. Dawn Foster** provides consulting services around open source strategy, contributor strategy, improving project governance, and similar topics. She also works as the Director of Data Science for the CHAOSS project where she is a board member, working group lead, and maintainer. Dawn is an OpenUK board member and was previously a co-chair of the CNCF Contributor Strategy Technical Advisory Group. She has 20+ years of experience at companies like VMware and Intel with expertise in community, strategy, governance, metrics, and more. Dawn has spoken at over 100 industry events and has a BS in computer science, an MBA, and a PhD. In her spare time, she enjoys reading science fiction, running, 3D printing, and traveling.

You can learn more about Dawn by visiting `https://fastwonder.com`.

Acknowledgments

This book, like any free and open source project, is a collaborative effort. It is stitched together from countless conversations, readings, and gestures of support. Writing is solitary only on the surface; every paragraph carries echoes of people who nudged me forward, challenged me, or reminded me to keep going.

My deepest gratitude goes to the free and open source communities, for making collaboration and sharing a way of life.

My editor, James Robinson-Prior, made this book possible, guiding me patiently through the process. Chris Hiller, Tobey Langel, and Dawn Foster shaped its direction with their brilliance and generosity.

Angelo Pixel, Armağan Amcalar, Christian Bromann, Felipe Fonseca, Josh Goldberg, Katharine Jarmul, Luciano Ramalho, Paulo Schor, Pedro Medeiros, Thomas Steenberg, Tobie Langel, Jordan Harband, Malcom Bain and Eric Deeds shared their time and experiences so I could, in turn, share them with others.

Jessica Greene has been a force of inspiration, showing me how to change the world from exactly where I stand.

The fellowship program came alive thanks to Jason Baum, who gave me both the means and the freedom to set it up. It thrived because of the extraordinary mentors—Marija Stupar, James Tacker, Diego Molina, Clara Ko, Bee Sharwood, and Jessica Litwin—and the courage of fellows who welcomed my experimental, transdisciplinary ideas: Rajene Harris, Danielle Madry, Janackeh Blackwell, Django Skorupa, and Esther Cotton.

From activists, artists, and scholars I learned the most important lesson of all: technology is never neutral. Every technical decision carries values, exclusions, and possibilities, and to talk about equity in open source is to talk about equity everywhere. From musicians and writers, I borrowed rhythm and atmosphere; when prose faltered, their pulse carried me forward.

Most of all, I thank Mateus Knelsen, my partner in life and in edits, for giving me emotional and intellectual support, being my constant point of reference during indecisions, and reminding me why this book needed to be written. He has also designed an incredible cover I wish you all could have enjoyed. Some day.

This is also a thank-you to everyone who has ever put in the work, reflected, documented, and shared. You left traces I could not ignore. This book is my remix of your contributions.

If your name is not here, please forgive me. This book contains far more influences than can be credited in a single list. I hope, though, that you recognize something of your spirit in these pages.

May it be forked, remixed, argued with, and carried forward by others.

Introduction

I write wondering how this book will make its way into your hands. Maybe you share the worry that open source is "eating the world" and want to understand how to take a bite, or maybe it's the other way around. Maybe you're concerned about who is making the decisions about the technologies everyone relies on. This book is made for both of you.

This book is a mixtape. Every chapter is a track, each with its own rhythm and mood. Like any mixtape, you don't have to listen in order. You can skip around, play one track over and over, or leave some for later. I hope one day we'll meet maybe at a conference, a sprint, or a community gathering, and you'll tell me what your version of this mixtape sounds like.

Here's my setlist:

Chapter 1—**The Journey Begins** feels like "Me Gritaron Negra" by Victoria Santa Cruz: raw, awakening, revealing, reclaiming. I have broken it down into separate parts to facilitate digesting it, but it may take you a while, as I borrow from many thinkers to build this big picture for you. This chapter reveals how technology and open source work in a global, intangible, complicated geo-political world today just for you to see that neither technology nor open source is neutral. It carries politics and power, and that naming those truths can be a form of liberation, of a possible rewriting.

Chapter 2—**Impressions of Open Source** carries the restless layering of Hiromi's "Kaleidoscope." It's all shifting patterns and multiple voices. Here we expand what open source means beyond code, hearing from people who've lived it in business, politics, medicine, art, activism, and education. Every turn shows a new perspective based on interviews and stories.

Chapter 3—**Unraveling Diversity and Labor Issues** is a dense one. You may feel it like a punch in the stomach. It's Calle 13's "Latinoamérica": strong, unapologetic, and grounded in the issues we don't want to see exist. This is where we face contradictions, invisible work, and systemic exclusion that open source still reproduces. It's not easy listening, but necessary.

Chapter 4—**Making It a Standard** sounds like "Beep Box" from Snarky Puppy: structured but playful, grooves within complexity. Here we talk about standards, governance, and best-practice templates, all things that look bureaucratic but are pragmatic ways to shift power and create room for equity. Well, that's the whole hypothesis of this book.

Chapter 5—**Models for a Sustainable, Diverse Open Source** bursts into Anat Cohen's "Happy Song": joyful, full of possibility. You'll meet people and projects already building alternatives: fellowships, pirate-inspired organizations, grassroots initiatives that prove change is already happening. This chapter is meant for you to be immersed in hope and feel inspired.

Chapter 6—**Weaving the Commons** closes on "To Build a Home" from The Cinematic Orchestra: grandiose, reflective, like watching the sunset over an infinite horizon. Instead of wrapping up, I open up, connecting open source with ecology, solidarity, and more-than-human intelligence. It's bigger than us.

That's my mixtape. Yours will sound different. You might swap out the songs, feel other moods, or even add a new track. That's the point: this isn't a fixed playlist; it's an invitation for a continuous remix.

But here's why it matters. Open source isn't just about lines of code; it's about remix. The way musicians sample and recombine, this movement allows us to take what exists, adapt it, and create something new together for the benefit of the commons. That spirit of remix belongs as much to coders as it does to ethicists, educators, artists, and activists. If you're a developer, the standards and practices here will help you build more resilient projects. If you're from the social sciences, you'll see how technology can be studied, questioned, and reshaped through ethical commitments and technical decisions. If you're an activist, you'll find tools here for fighting inequities, redistributing power, and demanding accountability.

Because technology doesn't live apart from society, it's entangled with our struggles, our dreams, our histories. The demand for fair labor, the urgency of climate justice, the fight for inclusion: all of these flow into and through the tools we build. Technical systems and ethical questions aren't two separate tracks, but part of the same song.

So welcome. Take what resonates, leave what doesn't, remix the rest. Read it cover to cover or one chapter at a time. This book is my mixtape, but it's also yours to remake. And maybe, if we're lucky, we'll cross paths someday and you'll share your version with me. Because in the end, it's not just about the music or the code; it's about how we use them to build a world worth living in, together.

CHAPTER 1

The Journey Begins

What if there existed a template that could be integrated into any open-source project, one that, when utilized, could bring more equity, awareness, and diversity? This book proposes just that: a straightforward, pragmatic, almost magical way for anyone to address and patch the systemic issues we strive to solve but always seem to fall short of. However, "magic" might be the wrong term. While I wish for the implementation to be as effortless as the wave of a magic wand, you'll realize that the magic lies in the awakening of consciousness, continuous trial and error, and the act of making rather small and consistent improvements in the way you do and govern projects. The magic is the courage to touch upon wounds that seem complicated and to tackle one problem at a time.

I'm not gonna lie; I could be a witch with a potion of cat's whiskers and salamander tails promising to fix everything that's broken in tech with a single spell. But that's not how transformation works. Instead, I'm offering something more subtle yet powerful: standards that gently guide us toward better practices, like feeling that exact spot where the muscle aches after you've been coding all day, pressing on it, and suddenly feeling ready to jump back in and squash that elusive bug.

With time, I came up with my own definition of open source. Most people are familiar with the Open Source Initiative's definition, which focuses on licensing criteria—free redistribution, source code access, permission for modifications and derived works. This technical definition has served as the industry standard for decades. But as I will repeatedly communicate in this book, open source is much more than these

© Paloma Oliveira 2025
P. Oliveira, *Diversifying Open Source*, https://doi.org/10.1007/979-8-8688-0769-5_1

technical requirements; it's a real possibility for achieving equity, breaking down hierarchical structures, and harnessing the potential of collective organization. It builds upon the OSI definition by extending into the human dimensions—the collaboration patterns, communication structures, and community dynamics that truly determine a project's success and impact. It's about fostering collaboration, creating spaces for flowing ideas, and fostering a sense of belonging in a truly global community. While some may perceive me as a naive idealist, my journey through the open source world is fueled by the understanding that I am not alone in this belief. This movement is not just about sharing code; it's about sharing, whether it be ideas, aspirations, or a vision for a more equitable future. Chapter 2 is dedicated to expanding our notions about what that term means in different contexts.

Open source, as I've come to understand it, isn't just about visible code repositories or licenses. It's about creating commons—spaces where knowledge flows freely, where diverse minds can contribute without predetermined hierarchies. I see these spaces like an atoll—distinct islands with their own ecosystems, connected by flowing currents that carry ideas, practices, and innovations between them. No single island dominates; each contributes to the richness of the whole.

Picture us sitting in a bar, me probably drinking some weird herbal concoction while you have something you like (it's your imagination, you get to choose what you want). I'd lean in and say, "Look, I've been in this open source thing for years, and I love it, but damn, we keep missing something big, ya know?" I'd take a sip, maybe wipe some foam from my lip. "We talk about meritocracy and collaboration, but have you noticed it's mostly the same kinds of people building the same kinds of solutions? And then we're surprised when tech doesn't work for everyone!"

You might nod or raise an eyebrow, so I'd continue, "What if I told you we don't need a revolution? What if we just need better plumbing?" I'd laugh at my own terrible metaphor. "Seriously though, what if small changes in how we document, govern, and credit work could actually shift who gets to participate and what gets created?"

2

This book traces a journey that mirrors Victoria Santa Cruz's powerful "Me Gritaron Negra"—that moment when she transforms an insult into affirmation, claiming her identity with pride. Our first chapter confronts us with uncomfortable truths about who's driving that Progress Express train and who gets left at the station. To this beat of awakening, we examine how technology isn't neutral—it carries our biases, our histories, our values, whether we acknowledge them or not.

Then our melody shifts to "Kaleidoscope" by Hiromi—complex, multilayered, opening to new patterns with each turn. We'll travel across different interpretations of open source, meeting folks who've shaped these commons in unexpected ways. Open source as code, as infrastructure, as a counterforce—each perspective adding richness and depth, widening our horizons beyond technical definitions.

The rhythm becomes more intense with Calle 13's "Latinoamérica" as we roll up our sleeves and dive into labor and diversity issues— the invisible work sustaining projects, the myth of meritocracy, the exploitation disguised as volunteerism. This might feel like digging into uncomfortable territory, but finding these roots is essential before new growth can begin.

Just when you might be thinking "OK, but what do we actually DO?", our soundtrack shifts to the structured patterns of "Beep Box" by Snarky Puppy, as we pivot to practical solutions—detailed templates, checklists, and governance frameworks you can implement today. This is where small changes in daily practices accumulate into significant cultural shifts.

Before wrapping up, we'll find inspiration in people and projects already creating change, accompanied by Anat Cohen's "Happy Song"—a celebration of what's possible when we commit to equity and inclusion. These models show paths forward, lighting the way toward more sustainable, diverse open source futures.

Throughout this journey, I'm drawing from Michel Foucault's approach in "The Archaeology of Knowledge." I'm offering you fragments and inviting you to assemble them in ways that resonate with your own experience. Some parts might feel academic—I can't help myself sometimes—but I've tried to make sure there's something for everyone, whether you're a coder, an activist, or just curious about how tech and society shape each other.

The language we use matters deeply. Words like "diversity," "sustainability," and "inclusion" have been tossed around in meetups and corporate blogs until they've lost their edge. They've become comfortable pillows we rest on rather than tools that cut through complacency. Throughout this book, I'll invite you to reconnect with these terms, to feel their weight and possibility again.

When I talk about diversity in open source, I'm not just talking about having more women on a team (though that's important!). I'm asking: Who gets to shape technology? Whose problems are deemed worth solving? What knowledges and perspectives inform our solutions? These questions extend beyond human relationships—they encompass how our technology relates to all living systems, to the more-than-human world we share this blue planet with.

The main assumption here is that we can achieve great improvements through the use of standards. I argue that by using open standards, an open source project improves its quality and shareability since such guidelines exist to foster better communication among all creators, maintainers, and consumers. Most importantly, open standards can guide technology development by gently enforcing space for diversity and equity.

This book is organized to follow our journey from awareness to transformation. We'll start by exploring what open source means and why it matters. Then we'll investigate problems with the current culture and why it's crucial to achieve more diverse community representation. Next, we'll explore existing standards and how they can be improved. Finally, we'll conclude with practical propositions on how to take action to improve the ecosystem.

In 2025, as layoffs sweep through tech companies and polarization deepens, open source emerges as a counterforce with renewed importance. Like water finding cracks in parched earth, collaborative creation continues to find ways to flourish despite corporate consolidation.

I strongly believe it's fundamental to think critically about the world around us so we can make our existence a step forward in the search for a more equitable world for all beings with whom we share this planet. Open source is, for me, a possible way of changing things for the better, but it's only possible if we recognize its failures. And this is my contribution.

So grab another drink (metaphorical or actual) and let's continue this conversation. This journey may not always be comfortable, but the destination—a more equitable, inclusive, and sustainable open source ecosystem—is worth it. By the end, we'll return full circle to where we began, but transformed, equipped with tools to build something better, as the Cinematic Orchestra might soundtrack our heroic return.

The following sections, Code It, Use It, Live With It, are fictional examples.

How Open Source and Social Issues Shape Each Other

What does your open source project have to do with a social problem?

The short answer is: everything. However, looking at the broader perspectives of technological development and its impact on society is important to understand this relationship fully.

Imagine the Industrial Revolution as the moment when humanity decided to hop on the Progress Express, thinking it was a train that moves forward automatically, powered purely by the sheer genius of technological advancements. This mindset reflects technological determinism—the belief that technology develops along its own inevitable path, independent of social influences, and that society must simply adapt to these technological changes. It's like saying, "Hey, society and nature, shape up or ship out because we're making this tech whether you like it or not!"

This perspective treats technology as an autonomous force that drives us toward a better future without requiring anyone to steer it or consider important questions like resource limitations or who gets left behind. It's akin to believing in a fairy tale where the forest never runs out of trees, the mines never run out of minerals, and all creatures, great and small, cheerfully adapt to whatever changes these inventions bring.

However, just like in those stories where the hero discovers the beautiful castle is actually in need of serious repairs, this view overlooks the complexities of living in a world where actions have consequences. It forgets that our Progress Express is rumbling through a landscape of finite resources, and not everyone is enjoying the ride. It's time to peek out of the window, see the bigger picture, and maybe start asking, "Are we there yet?" in a way that includes everyone's well-being, not just the passengers aboard the techno-train. So, while the idea of unstoppable progress is enchanting, it might be wise to remember that even magical trains need tracks to run on, and it's up to us to lay them thoughtfully.

Open Source, but Not As You Know It

The technological determinism we see in broader society also appears in open source communities. When projects focus purely on technical excellence without considering accessibility, they create implicit barriers. Documentation written only in English, community discussions held during North American business hours, or development environments that require high-end hardware all reflect choices that determine who can participate—though these choices often remain unexamined.

Consider how open source tools shape daily life. The Linux kernel powers everything from smartphones to supercomputers, but its development community remains predominantly male and Western. This isn't because others lack interest or ability, but because the community's structure, communication styles, and expectations often reflect the cultural norms of its dominant participants.

Code It, Use It, Live with It

Miguel maintains a mid-sized open source data visualization library. For years, his team prided themselves on their "technically focused" approach. When usage statistics showed minimal adoption in Africa and South Asia despite high technical quality, Miguel was puzzled.

Through community outreach, he discovered that their documentation assumed familiarity with specific data science concepts taught in Western universities but approached differently elsewhere. Their installation process required sustained high-bandwidth connections, making it nearly impossible to use in regions with intermittent internet. Their examples featured Western datasets and scenarios, leaving developers from other regions to figure out how to adapt the library to their contexts.

These weren't conscious exclusions but reflections of the team's limited perspective—a textbook case of how technology embeds its creators' worldview, despite claims of neutrality. By redesigning their onboarding with global accessibility in mind, Miguel's project began to see growing adoption across previously underrepresented regions.

Colonial Patterns and Its Intersections

In the so-called Age of Discovery, which might be more aptly named the Era of Uninvited Guests, explorers from Europe embarked on journeys to "find" lands that were, amusingly, not lost, inhabited by peoples rich in culture and history. This era marked the beginning of a global tradition of showing up unannounced, taking things that weren't offered, and leaving a mess in the process.

Fast forward to the Silicon Valley saga, where the tech elite's quest for innovation has sparked a modern-day gold rush, transforming cities into playgrounds for the well-paid tech crowd. In San Francisco, for example, the cost of living has skyrocketed, with median rents increasing dramatically, causing an exodus of those who can't afford to share their city with the tech giants' campuses. Berlin, known for its vibrant culture and history, is experiencing its own version of this story as the tech boom threatens the fabric of its diverse communities.

The plot thickens with the tech industry's voracious appetite for resources, leading us to the mines of the Democratic Republic of Congo (DRC). Here, the quest for cobalt and lithium—vital for our beloved gadgets—paints a stark picture of exploitation reminiscent of colonial ventures, with over 40,000 children working in hazardous conditions, a modern-day echo of historical conquests but with smartphones.

And let's not forget the final frontier—space. Our cosmic junkyard orbits above us, a testament to our exploratory zeal. With millions of pieces of space debris, we've managed to extend our footprint to the heavens, a clear sign we're all about leaving our mark, literally everywhere.

Open Source, but Not As You Know It

This pattern of discovery, extraction, and disruption is mirrored in the open source ecosystem. Large tech companies often "discover" valuable open source projects, extract their value without proportional contribution, and sometimes leave behind a wake of maintenance burdens. Companies build billion-dollar businesses atop open source infrastructure while original maintainers struggle with burnout and lack of compensation.

The devices we use to write open source code depend on supply chains that often exploit vulnerable populations. When our projects optimize for the latest hardware or fail to support older devices, we implicitly participate in accelerating consumption patterns.

Meanwhile, open source serves as both victim and enabler of gentrification dynamics. The same tools that power tech giants' expansion—Kubernetes, Python, and Linux—were created through collaborative effort, yet their success has accelerated economic disparities in tech hubs. Many open source maintainers cannot afford to live in the very cities where tech companies profit from their work.

Code It, Use It, Live with It

SolarFuture, a Silicon Valley startup, launched their "Open Energy Initiative" with much fanfare. The project open-sourced designs for advanced solar panels and battery systems, with a mission to "bring light to those living in darkness." The company selected a cluster of villages in rural India for their pilot implementation, investing significant resources in hardware, documentation, and a deployment team.

The company's engineers spent months adapting their designs for what they imagined were local conditions, making everything available under an open license and creating detailed technical specifications. Company blog posts celebrated how their technology would "transform lives" and "leapfrog traditional infrastructure limitations." Not a single team member had visited the region before implementation.

Six months after installation, the company's follow-up team arrived to document their success story. Instead, they found most of their sophisticated solar arrays disconnected or repurposed for parts. The villages, however, weren't without power.

Three years earlier, engineering students from a regional university had worked directly with village residents to develop simple, low-cost wind turbines built from locally available materials. These systems required minimal maintenance, could be repaired by community members, and had been quietly providing sufficient electricity for the villages' most critical needs.

The university project had involved community members from the beginning, adapted to seasonal weather patterns (including the heavy monsoons that had damaged the solar panels), and created a local maintenance network. While the solution wasn't as technologically advanced as SolarFuture's system, it was resilient, sustainable, and—most importantly—developed with rather than for the community.

When interviewed, village elders expressed appreciation for SolarFuture's intentions but explained that what they needed most wasn't cutting-edge technology from abroad, but rather support for expanding their existing systems that already worked in their environmental and social context.

Intersectionality in Open Source

In the midst of our evolving narrative, Kimberlé Crenshaw's intersectionality theory stands as a powerful beacon, cutting through the fog of historical and ongoing injustices. It doesn't whisper; it speaks boldly, challenging us to confront the reality that the journey of exploration and innovation has been navigated on terms set predominantly by white, able-bodied male perspectives.

Imagine standing at a busy crossroads where multiple roads intersect. Some travelers cruise through with ease, while others find themselves stuck at complicated crossing points, navigating traffic from all directions simultaneously. This is Crenshaw's brilliant insight—that some people don't experience discrimination as a single lane of obstacles but are caught at dangerous intersections where multiple forms of bias converge.

The theory emerged from Crenshaw's observation that Black women were often invisible in both feminist movements (centered on white women's experiences) and racial justice efforts (focused primarily on

Black men). They weren't just facing a double dose of discrimination; they experienced something unique at that intersection that couldn't be understood by looking at racism or sexism separately.

Think of it this way: a tech conference might remove financial barriers to help low-income attendees and provide childcare to support parents— both excellent initiatives. But what about a single mother who also needs evening childcare because she works during the day? What about an immigrant developer whose visa doesn't allow them to accept the travel stipend? The experiences at these intersections create challenges that one-size-fits-all solutions miss entirely.

This crossroads metaphor has become especially relevant in our digital age. As we witness attempts to ban books about diverse experiences and legislate against teaching structural racism in schools, Crenshaw's framework helps us see how technology often inherits these blind spots. Those facial recognition systems that fail to recognize darker skin tones? Those machine translation tools that reinforce gender stereotypes? They're not just technical glitches—they're signposts showing whose experiences were considered when building these systems and whose were overlooked.

By engaging with intersectionality, we're not raining on the technology parade; we're making sure everyone gets to enjoy it. It's like realizing your neighborhood block party hasn't considered wheelchair access or that your potluck menu excludes several cultural dietary needs. Addressing these oversights doesn't diminish the celebration—it makes it truly wonderful for everyone.

Crenshaw's work invites us to create a world where progress isn't measured by how fast the express train moves, but by whether all passengers can board it in the first place.

Open Source, but Not As You Know It

While proprietary technology can perpetuate biases without accountability, open source stands as one of our most powerful tools for countering technological hegemonies. Its core premise—that code should be freely accessible, modifiable, and redistributable—offers a radical alternative to opaque-box systems controlled by profit-driven corporations.

But here's the twist: open source is only revolutionary when it's truly open to diverse contributors. The promise of "anyone can contribute" falls flat when "anyone" really means "anyone with substantial free time, high-speed internet, advanced technical education, and fluency in English." Without conscious effort to address these barriers, open source can unwittingly reproduce the same exclusionary patterns it aims to disrupt.

This matters profoundly because open technologies shape our digital infrastructure. When facial recognition struggles with darker skin tones or voice recognition falters with certain accents, these aren't merely technical failures—they're governance failures. An open source project should not have the luxury of overlooking diverse users; its very design should incorporate perspectives from the communities it serves.

Unlike proprietary systems where profits might incentivize narrower user targeting, open source's strength lies in its potential for global, collaborative problem-solving. But this potential remains unrealized when governance structures and contribution pathways mirror Silicon Valley's homogeneity rather than the world's diversity.

Code It, Use It, Live with It

Ana grew up in a favela in São Paulo, where she witnessed firsthand how surveillance technologies were deployed in her community—often without consent or oversight. After studying computer science through a scholarship program, she became determined to create privacy-respecting alternatives to the facial recognition systems increasingly embedded in urban infrastructure.

She founded PrivaSense, building an open source facial recognition framework with privacy at its core: locally processed data, user consent controls, and transparency about how images were analyzed and stored. From the beginning, she structured the project to include voices typically excluded from technology development.

"I knew that to build technology that truly serves diverse communities, those communities need to help shape it," Ana explains. "But I also knew that contribution takes resources many people don't have."

She allocated 30% of her initial investment to create stipends for contributors from underrepresented backgrounds, established flexible contribution pathways that didn't require constant internet connectivity, and launched an education program in the favela where she grew up. This program taught technical skills while explicitly connecting them to community needs and ethics.

Ana's approach paid dividends beyond social impact. While her Silicon Valley competitor faced mounting lawsuits for privacy violations and struggled to enter markets with strict data protection laws like the EU and Brazil, PrivaSense thrived. The diverse contributor community had naturally built solutions that worked across different regulatory frameworks and cultural contexts.

Three years later, PrivaSense became profitable as governments and organizations worldwide sought facial recognition technology that respected privacy and worked reliably across diverse populations. The project's success challenged conventional wisdom about who creates technology and how it's developed.

"Open source isn't just about accessible code," Ana reflects. "It's about accessible creation. When we remove barriers to contribution, we get better technology that serves more people—and that's good for business too."

Ana's story demonstrates how intersectionality applied to open source development isn't just morally right but strategically advantageous. By centering those typically excluded, she created technology that avoided the pitfalls of systems designed from limited perspectives, building a globally competitive company while strengthening her community.

The Decolonial Politics of Objects

Decolonial theory challenges us to examine how historical patterns of domination continue to shape our technological present. While often associated with European maritime colonization, this perspective applies equally to all contexts where one group's knowledge and practices were forcibly supplanted by another's—from the Americas to Africa, from Asia to the Pacific Islands. At its heart, decolonial thinking asks: whose knowledge counts? Who gets to define progress? And how do power imbalances determine which technologies flourish and which are marginalized?

Though rooted in the critique of colonial imposition, decolonial thought expands toward the recovery of knowledge as manifold— technology not as a single arc of progress, but as a constellation of practices shaped by diverse ways of being and knowing. Each of these systems has its own validity and value, often containing insights that dominant technological paradigms have overlooked or dismissed. When we limit ourselves to a single tradition of technological development, we miss out on the full spectrum of human ingenuity.

Decolonial theory shares concerns with intersectionality, though it approaches them differently. While intersectionality helps us understand how individuals experience multiple, overlapping forms of discrimination, decolonial thinking focuses on how entire knowledge systems have been subjugated. Together, they reveal how power operates at both personal and structural levels, shaping not only who participates in technological development, but which problems are recognized as meaningful to solve. This is where the notion of bridging becomes more than metaphor. It recalls Langdon Winner, a political theorist who, in his seminal 1980 article "Do Artifacts Have Politics?", explored how technological forms can embed and enact specific arrangements of power. Still foundational in the sociology of technology, Winner's work challenges us to consider not just who builds tools, but how those tools structure social life.

Starting from the principle that what we call technology is about ways of constructing order in the world, Langdon assumes that such artifacts are essential in everyday life and will, therefore, order human activities for a long time. This order, which influences how we communicate, work, transport, consume, and relate to each other, determines inequalities among individuals, being unequal in terms of power and awareness of such relations. This view could be a reading of socio-determinist theories of technology. Still, Langdon tangles the issue by noting that the questions must change according to the context and the type of artifact.

In some cases, the nature of certain technologies will unavoidably lead to rigid contextual changes that require political and social accommodation. In his most known example, nuclear power, he will say that a hierarchical and authoritarian political relationship is built into this artifact since this type of technology requires control and surveillance. This seemingly rational pure technological choice will bring, as a consequence, authoritarianism to the subject communities around such an artifact.

In other cases, technology can allow an organic open redesign driven by its community and usage, leading to more equity in its relations of use. For example, the solar energy system is modular, nondangerous, and nonpervasive, allowing its potential to be adopted by communities in a decentralized and nonhierarchical way.

In other words, technology is more than merely a technical choice.

However, it is essential to reinforce that this potential will only emerge through the organization and will of the communities.

In 2016, during the inaugural technological rewriting meeting in Mexico City, Eugenio Tisselli and Nadia Cortés explored what they termed "technological rewriting." This concept revolves around finding ways to challenge dominant systems in technology, looking for gaps that enable broader participation and social involvement in creating technology.

Tisselli points out a fundamental issue: the design and production of most modern technological systems are in the hands of specialists. These experts often work in isolation, far removed from the eventual users of these technologies. He suggests that a critical task in our technology-saturated era should be to re-envision these devices as tools of mutual benefit, designed to meet actual needs rather than to introduce unnecessary innovations. To make his point clearer, Tisselli uses the cell phone as an example, noting how many of its features are not about meeting user needs but rather about offering innovations that users never asked for.

On the other hand, Cortés emphasizes that our interaction with technology shouldn't be about merely adapting to it to alter how it's used. Instead, it should be seen as a form of resistance against imposed values that don't align with those of certain communities. However, we must recall that, according to Langdon, this form of resistance might not be feasible with all technologies. To Cortés, this resistance comes from our own social and political configurations, and those technologies should be tools to reflect on how we constitute ourselves as a community, not the other way around. To this end, the author reinforces, as does Langdon, that we must assume that—what the author calls—a technological experience does not take place in isolation, nor in a unidirectional way, but within a web. And it is this web capable of transforming and rewriting the values inscribed in technological artifacts.

Open Source, but Not As You Know It

For open source communities, decolonial thinking means questioning fundamental assumptions: Why are English-language projects considered "universal" while non-English projects are seen as "localized"? Why do we privilege certain development paradigms while marginalizing others?

The decolonial approach challenges the notion that technology should follow a single, Western-defined path. Instead, it recognizes that technological innovation emerges from diverse cultural contexts and knowledge systems, each with its own validity and value. In open source, this means creating spaces where multiple knowledge systems can coexist and cross-pollinate.

Unlike proprietary technology, which often imposes a single worldview, open source has the potential to incorporate diverse perspectives precisely because its creation is distributed and collaborative. However, this potential remains largely unrealized when project governance, communication norms, and technical requirements implicitly center Western experiences and knowledge.

By addressing these structural biases, open source communities can transform technology from a tool of homogenization into a vehicle for cultural sovereignty and diverse innovation. This isn't just about translation or localization—it's about fundamentally rethinking how decisions are made, whose problems are prioritized, and how solutions are developed.

Code It, Use It, Live with It

In the Amazon rainforest, a collaborative project between Indigenous Kuikuro digital artists and open source developers created "ForestOS," a community-governed environmental monitoring system that challenged conventional approaches to conservation technology.

Traditional conservation software typically relied on satellite imagery analyzed by distant experts, with minimal input from forest communities. This approach often failed to incorporate crucial local knowledge and left communities as passive recipients of external conservation directives.

ForestOS took a radically different approach. The system was co-designed from inception, with Kuikuro elders and youth working alongside programmers to integrate Indigenous cosmological understanding of forest cycles with sensor networks and data visualization. Rather than imposing Western scientific categories, the project's governance structure ensured that Indigenous ways of knowing guided the technical architecture.

"Our ancestors have monitored this forest for thousands of years," explained one Kuikuro contributor. "We don't separate the 'technical' from the 'spiritual'—these are Western divisions that don't exist in our understanding of the forest as a living entity with its own intelligence."

This philosophy transformed the resulting software. Instead of organizing data around Western scientific taxonomies, ForestOS incorporated circular time models reflecting Indigenous calendars. Its alert system integrated indicators that Western science often overlooked— subtle changes in insect sounds, plant flowering patterns, and animal movements that preceded larger ecological shifts.

The project's documentation was equally revolutionary, with code comments and architectural decisions explained in both Portuguese and Kuikuro language, often using metaphors from Indigenous storytelling to clarify technical concepts. Contributors could participate through voice recordings rather than text-based communication, removing barriers for community members with limited literacy or internet access.

What made ForestOS particularly successful was its adaptability. Other Indigenous communities across the Amazon began forking the project, adapting it to their own knowledge systems while contributing improvements back to the main codebase. This created a federation of related but distinct projects, each honoring local expertise while benefiting from collective technical development.

When compared to conventional environmental monitoring systems, ForestOS detected early warning signs of ecological disturbances weeks before satellite-based approaches, giving communities crucial time to respond to threats. Its success challenged the assumption that technological sophistication requires Western scientific frameworks, demonstrating that Indigenous knowledge systems offer not just alternative but often superior approaches to complex problems.

For open source communities worldwide, ForestOS became a case study in true participatory development—not just inviting contributions from diverse communities, but allowing those communities to fundamentally reshape how problems are conceptualized and solved.

Digital Stratification: The Stack As Techno-Political Architecture

While many open source practitioners—particularly those working within corporate environments—may view their contributions as purely technical or utilitarian, the very architecture of open source ecosystems inherently shapes power relations and governance structures. When a corporate developer submits code to an open source project, they participate in a system that redistributes control and access, regardless of whether they frame their work in political terms. As Langdon Winner reminds us, artifacts have politics whether we acknowledge them or not. The design decisions, governance models, and contribution patterns within open source communities all embed values and power dynamics that transcend the purely technical realm. Understanding these dimensions becomes crucial for all participants—from independent activists to corporate contributors—if we are to build truly equitable technological futures.

Benjamin H Bratton, a sociological, media, and design theorist, calls this web The Stack. In his book *The Stack: On Software and Sovereignty*, Bratton explores the ways in which technological systems are shaping our world and the implications of these changes. The term stack is used to describe the layers of interconnected technology, from the physical infrastructure of the internet to the software applications that run on top of it. Bratton considers how the stack redefines political sovereignty, economic power, and social identity through a wide-ranging and interdisciplinary analysis, including philosophy, political theory, urbanism, media studies, and computer science. He argues that the stack has created new forms of control and surveillance and that it presents

19

both challenges and opportunities for democracy, citizenship, and human rights. This system operates as a sovereign authority with its own politics, form of governance, and system of control. It affects our lives, shaping the political, economic, and social spheres of society.

Although not an easy book to read, it offers us a very important message: by understanding the power at play, we are offered the possibility to redesign or, as Tisselli and Cortés simply propose, rewrite the world we inhabit.

The author further elaborates on the layers of technological systems concerning societies by refining categories to account for such complexities using two main arguments to elaborate his theory. Bratton argues that the genres of planetary scale computation, such as smart grids, cloud platforms, mobile apps, cities, and the Internet of Things, form a coherent whole when aligned layer by layer into a vast, incomplete pervasive system. This stack becomes an irregular accidental megastructure that is both a computational apparatus and a new governing architecture.

Nadia Eghbal's acclaimed research "Roads and Bridges: The Unseen Labor Behind Our Digital Infrastructure" offers a complementary perspective to Bratton's theoretical framework. Where Bratton examines the macro-political implications of technological stratification, Eghbal illuminates the practical realities of how digital infrastructure is maintained—often through unseen, uncompensated labor. Her analysis reveals how the sustainability crisis in open source reflects broader political tensions within The Stack, as critical infrastructure components that power billion-dollar industries frequently depend on the voluntary efforts of individual maintainers. This invisible maintenance work forms the practical substrate upon which Bratton's theoretical layers rest, demonstrating how abstract technological sovereignty materializes through concrete human labor. The connection between these perspectives—theoretical and practical, macro and micro—helps us understand open source as both a political architecture and a lived human practice.

It goes without saying how evidently our lives have been changed by the use of computer systems in the last 40 years since Langdon wrote his article. However, it is interesting to remember his approach to technology as something broader than high-end digital systems, as we tend to understand it today, but technologies are ways of building order in our world. Bratton's arguments seem somewhat in line with this line of thinking, although he will no longer question whether artifacts are embedded in politics or not. He will instead explore the intricate dance between technology and geopolitics and come out of this loop to understand how they are intrinsically affected and being affected by one another.

In his first argument, he will say that *what we call planetary scale computation has both distorted and deformed traditional Westphalian logic of political geography and in doing so has also created new territories in its own image* (Bratton, 2018). In other words, the exploitative logic exercised by hegemonic States continues to reflect and replicate the hierarchical, authoritarian, and dominating colonialist grounds present since the time of the maritime expeditions.

For a better understanding of how the cartography of the globe is still the stage for power disputes between different cultures, I recommend reading the book *Prisoners of Geography* by Tim Marshall. Although the reference is beyond the scope of this book, it is a helpful reference to understand more about the divisions mentioned by Bratton.

In his second argument, Bratton contends that the disparate manifestations of planetary-scale computation—from smart grids and cloud platforms to mobile applications and the Internet of Things—are coalescing into a coherent, albeit incomplete, totality. When these elements align in stratified layers, they form what he terms "the Stack"—an irregular accidental megastructure functioning simultaneously as computational apparatus and nascent governing architecture. This structure, neither fully designed nor entirely spontaneous, becomes

a technological palimpsest upon which new forms of sovereignty
are inscribed and contested, often beyond the purview of traditional
nation-states.

The layers, or Stack, are organized in the book in the following
categories: Earth, Cloud, City, Address, Interface, and User. The Earth layer
is about ecological flows, physical places that house cloud computing
sites and become sites of sensing and quantification, and governance that
stimulates various platform economies, creating virtual geographies in
their own image. This layer also generally refers to the physical foundation
and infrastructure that supports the entire stack architecture, including the
material basis for digital technologies and their environmental impacts.
It emphasizes the geopolitical and ecological aspects of technology's
physical underpinnings.

The Cloud layer conceptually represents the data processing and
storage infrastructure that supports global computation. It's a critical level
where information is centralized, managed, and distributed across digital
networks, impacting how services are delivered and accessed worldwide.
This layer embodies the shift toward virtualization, where the cloud
becomes a key site of control, data sovereignty, and infrastructure power,
redefining traditional notions of territory and governance. It sometimes
absorbs traditional core State functions and vice versa. The implications
for politics and geopolitics are profound, but the conversation to date
has failed to address what this new normal really could mean directly.
Bratton argues that we need to rethink some basic assumptions instead of
reimposing old political maps directly onto platforms.

*Cloud platforms have absorbed many modern States, and the
public in well States themselves are co-evolving the implications for politics and geopolitics are profound, to say the least,
but the conversation to date, I think, has failed to directly
address what this new normal really could mean and I think
we need to rethink some pretty basic assumptions. Instead of
reimposing old political maps directly onto platforms we need*

to measure what has shifted and imagine and design what comes next, including what are the boundaries of a public in a platform, what they could be, and what they should be.

—Bratton (2018)

The City is the layer where discontiguous networks weave their borders into virtual addressing system escape routes, locating billions of entities on unknown maps. This layer conceptually addresses how urban environments integrate with and are transformed by digital technologies. It explores the intersection of physical space and digital infrastructure, envisioning cities as hubs of connectivity that blend architecture with information networks. This layer examines the impact of technology on urban planning, governance, and the lived experience, suggesting that cities function as crucial nodes within the Stack's broader ecosystem, where the digital and physical realms coalesce to shape contemporary and future urban landscapes.

The Address layer delves into the crucial aspect of how entities within the Stack—be they objects, locations, or individuals—are uniquely identified and located. This layer underpins the organization and accessibility of information, enabling precise interaction across the Stack's other layers. It's about the fundamental systems of naming, addressing, and thereby controlling digital and physical entities, reflecting on how these processes influence the structure and dynamics of connectivity and accessibility within the Stack's architecture.

Interfaces are the layer that presents augmentations of reality, a form of extended knowledge. The Interface layer explores the critical juncture where humans interact with digital technologies. It focuses on the design, functionality, and impact of user interfaces in mediating the relationship between the digital and physical realms. This layer emphasizes how interfaces shape our perceptions, behaviors, and interactions within the technological ecosystem, underlining their role in guiding user experiences and facilitating access to digital services and information.

Lastly, the User layer consists of those humans and nonhumans who populate this tangle of devices. This is an exceptional understanding of "users," which are often synonyms for "people." In this case, the author understands users as a relationship of interdependence between artifacts. One example is the relationship between the QR code and the camera. This layer refers to the entities—again, both humans and nonhumans— that interact with and are impacted by the layers above it, from Earth to Interface. This layer emphasizes the diverse roles and identities that users embody within the digital ecosystem, highlighting the importance of considering how individuals and collectives engage with technology, influence it, and are shaped by its structures and outputs.

For the author, there is no layer where the interaction between software and sovereignty is more truly and adequately localized and then radiated. Sovereignty, which is fundamentally a governance problem (replication, repercussion, and enforcement), becomes multiplied and dissolved among several layers. Contested and produced in each of these layers makes it complicated for thinkers to identify beforehand the problems and consequences around such problems.

However, there is a problem with this proposition, and it is primarily a design problem, which the same author raises. If design means reinventing a possible future, which Cortés and Tisselli also aim for, we need to understand what the future is. For any serious system design, 50 years ahead are already being designed, but we are doing it, according to Bratton, in a very bad way, short-sighted in a utilitarianism based on the "presentism" of the dominant interested parties, which do not allow to be permeated by further abstractions. If we keep acting in this eternal presentism, thinking in the long term becomes an unattainable privilege. Therefore, we will create superficial futures stuck in an autobiographical time of life, death, and wish fulfillment. In inadequate models of design, we must assume that subjective user experiences of cause and effect are necessarily flawed and insufficient as direct models of good design directly and, therefore, look elsewhere.

For which bodies are we designing it and why?

Bratton notes secessionist withdrawal in traditional territories and consolidation domains in stacked hemispheric, the continuing expansions of nebular sovereignties, and the reform of conventional States into regional platforms. Through a more radical abstraction of sovereignty, the author indicates the already existing shapes previously unthinkable, such as States without people, since the absence of a population would make it easier for an army to protect the wealth of sovereignties and industrial resources. If this sounds like a dystopian future, what should we call the informal economies, which are estimated to be one-fifth of the global economy?

From a State economy without people to a social economy without a State, both obscure, how do we redesign the present and the future we wish to be in?

Perhaps Cortés is, in the end, correct in intuition that all technology allows for fissures to intervene and modify in resistance to hegemonies that seem to be invisible, intangible, and unstoppable.

After all, if we have managed to demystify even the train of modern progress, why can't we jointly re-create a present and a future that suits us?

> *Against the present moment may be that the job remains still towards our successive generations to build on and against previous accomplishments to automate and democratize processes for escaping our intuitive and arbitrary biases not reinforcing their chauvinism. The world itself is a model open to design and designation not by false mastery but because our planet uses humans and other things to know itself and to remake itself. We are in short the medium, not the message.*
>
> —Bratton (2018)

Navigating the complex cosmos of digital sovereignty, Bratton's Stack invites us to reimagine governance in the age of planetary-scale computation. This exploration, enriched by Tisselli and Cortés's advocacy for participatory technological development and resistance against imposed values, echoes Langdon's broader definition of technology as an order-building tool. Together, these perspectives underscore the potential for open source as a spacecraft—commandeered by a diverse crew of developers, theorists, and users—to navigate through and redesign the stacked layers of Earth, Cloud, City, Address, Interface, and User, crafting a future that aligns with communal values and social justice. This narrative weaves a rich tapestry where technology's impact extends beyond utility, embedding itself within the very fabric of societal evolution and offering a blueprint for a more inclusive, equitable world.

A practical example of how to steer this spacecraft is how open source has grown increasingly vital, attracting numerous highly intelligent individuals who have organized themselves politically. Their goal is to ensure sustainability and secure spaces along with government funding, aiming to make open source synonymous with essential infrastructure. The pivotal question we face is whether we will continue to build bridges that exclusively accommodate cars, invoking the critique by Winner, or whether we will integrate this fundamental infrastructure with a conscious awareness of its sociocultural impacts.

The open, sharing culture has always been aligned with this ideology. It emerged precisely from this desire to stop this train by giving space for action, participation, and collaboration from other bodies. However, by doing this without asking ourselves what bodies and how we are designing these processes, we end up replicating the same dominant exploitative logic. The Interrelation of Open Source and Social Issues, or connecting standards with equity, means understanding that technology is not neutral but rather that it reflects the values and interests of those who design, develop, and control it.

It is past time to understand the complexities around what we call the culture of openness, and that is exactly what this book tries to bring, weaving together the understanding of what we are creating so that we can, together, design in a not innocent nor superficial way a present and a future where the ecosystem benefits equitably.

I repeat here the question I started this chapter with: what does your project have to do with a social problem?

Loading… A Prelude

The term FLOSS—free, libre, open source software—emerged in the late 1980s as a radical proposition: technology should be accessible to all, legally guaranteeing anyone the right to copy, modify, and redistribute software. What began as a specific legal framework has evolved dramatically over four decades, expanding from niche programmer circles into a culture of sharing that now underpins political movements, scientific research, artistic creation, and a multi-billion-dollar technology industry.

Today, open source forms the invisible foundation of our digital world. The 2024 Synopsys Open Source Security and Risk Analysis report confirms this ubiquity: approximately, 96% of codebases contain open source components. This means virtually everyone who uses technology—from smartphones to hospital equipment, from banking apps to government websites—relies on open source software, whether they realize it or not.

This omnipresence carries profound implications. Open source has transformed from a technical methodology into a complex ecosystem with multiple dimensions: a concept, a system of collective work, an ideology loaded with political meanings, an epistemological shift in how we legitimize creation, and a business approach that has fueled countless careers and companies. The collaboration model pioneered by open source has inspired fields far beyond software—from open science to open government, from open education to open hardware.

Yet as open source has grown, so have its contradictions. The same ecosystem that theoretically values diverse contributions regardless of contributor identity has become strikingly homogeneous—research indicates less than 5% of contributors come from underrepresented groups, with the remaining 95% identified as white northern males. The movement founded on principles of freedom and accessibility has inadvertently erected barriers that reinforce existing social hierarchies.

Projects and their communities have evolved into complex ecosystems that extend far beyond code. They encompass governance structures, decision-making processes, power dynamics, and labor relations that mirror—and sometimes amplify—broader societal inequities. Simply placing code in a public repository achieves little if the community surrounding it remains exclusive or inaccessible to "the other" who should, by design, participate actively in decision processes.

This growing recognition of open source's complexity and contradictions provides the foundation for our journey through this book. We'll explore the multifaceted nature of open source, unravel its labor and diversity challenges, propose practical standards to address these issues, and showcase models that demonstrate more equitable approaches already in action.

The soundtrack of our journey begins with Victoria Santa Cruz's powerful "Me Gritaron Negra," a declaration of identity reclamation that parallels our first step—acknowledging systemic inequalities within open source communities. From there, each chapter builds toward a vision of transformation, culminating in The Cinematic Orchestra's hopeful "To Build A Home"—because ultimately, this book aims to help construct more equitable digital spaces where all contributors can thrive.

In Chapter 2, we'll explore open source through multiple lenses, much like Hiromi's "Kaleidoscope" reveals new patterns with each turn. We'll travel from Richard Stallman's foundational philosophy to Brazil's government-backed digital inclusion initiatives, examining how open source manifests differently across cultural contexts while uncovering both its liberatory potential and its limitations.

Chapter 3 is forged in urgency and rage, echoing the defiant spirit of Calle 13's "Latinoamérica." It interrogates the myth of meritocracy and how, when applied without critique, this ideal becomes a mechanism of exclusion—disguising structural inequality as individual failure. In the open source ecosystem, this dynamic plays out through a reliance on unpaid contributions and invisible labor. These forms of participation are often framed as passion or dedication, but in practice, they generate untenable burdens for those already navigating racial, gendered, economic, or geopolitical disparities. This rage is not nihilistic—it is clarifying. It names what is often ignored: that the sustainability of our technological commons depends on care work, emotional labor, and community stewardship that are too often erased from view. If open source is to be more than a site of extraction dressed up as collaboration, it must reckon with this imbalance. This chapter asks how we might channel that rage into practices of redistribution, recognition, and repair—transforming participation into something not only possible, but just.

The structured composition of "Beep Box" by Snarky Puppy guide Chapter 4, where theory transforms into practical application. Here we'll provide concrete frameworks for governance, recognition of diverse contributions, and embedding equity directly into project architecture— standards that create pathways for participation while addressing historical exclusions.

Chapter 5 resonates with the joyful possibilities of Anat Cohen's "Happy Song," showcasing real-world models already creating change. From fellowship programs to liberation spaces, these examples demonstrate that more equitable open source communities exist beyond theoretical frameworks—they're being built now by visionaries who understand that diversity drives innovation.

Through this journey, the book serves as both critique and blueprint—exposing the contradictions within open source while providing practical tools to transform these spaces. By the conclusion, you'll possess strategies to take immediate action in your own environment, recognizing the social implications of even the smallest contributions to the open source ecosystem.

The revolution in open source will emerge through conscious application of standards that recognize all contributors, address historical barriers, and build genuinely inclusive communities. This transformation has already begun—and you have a vital role in shaping its future.

CHAPTER 2

Impressions of Open Source

After an introduction rather heavy on academic references and concepts, in this chapter, I want to take you, dear reader, on a journey through the diverse realms that open source has to offer. Through interviews with several individuals who are integral to my personal history and the very inspiration behind this book, this chapter unfolds like a well-structured design methodology—distilling and then expanding upon defined concepts. It amplifies voices, concepts, and, most importantly, interpretations from those who are the hands-on practitioners of what we strive so earnestly to understand and define: open source. These contributors, engaging from various fields and perspectives, enrich our understanding of open source as culture.

Defining Open Source

What actually is open source? Maybe that's the question that brought you here, and it's totally understandable. The definition of open software has evolved so much over the past 40 years, as well as the fast-evolving technological changes around the globe. It's not surprising that there are misunderstandings and misconceptions about it, considering the diverse audience it reaches and the societal aspects it touches. That is to say that if you feel lost or lacking words to define it, you're not alone.

P. Oliveira, *Diversifying Open Source*, https://doi.org/10.1007/979-8-8688-0769-5_2

So let's understand it together starting at the source, the free software movement. The principles of free software are grounded in the notion of user freedom and community respect. At its essence, free software grants users the liberty to run, copy, distribute, study, change, and improve the software. This freedom is fundamentally about liberty, not price, and campaigning for these freedoms is a collective act because everyone deserves them. With these freedoms, the users control the program and what it does for them. This statement represents a deeply political stance, recognizing how central and ubiquitous software would become to everyone's lives. It's a poignant reminder of the power dynamics hidden within the technology we use daily. As we navigate through our digital routines, it's crucial to pause and consider not just what our software can do, but also the fundamental freedoms it affords or restricts. This insight pushes us to think beyond the immediate utility of our apps and programs to the broader implications they hold for personal autonomy and collective agency.

Another point that emerges vividly from the quote is the frequent misconception about what free means—nothing is truly free. Everything has a cost, be it structural, energetic, or labor related. This becomes particularly salient when we discuss open source within the context of business. On one side, there's a notable temptation for businesses to exploit the "free" nature of open source to cut costs. This perceived advantage is often a key selling point when businesses pitch the idea of open source. However, in a world where open source has grown into a billion-dollar industry, treating it as a cost-free option can gravely threaten the sustainability of the ecosystem, leading it to a well know "tragedy of the commons."

The open source movement, whose name was coined by Christine Peterson in 1998, emerged with a definition derived from free software criteria, though with slightly more permissive boundaries. While technically similar in many cases, the philosophical underpinnings differ significantly. Where free software emphasizes ethical imperatives of user freedom, open source often highlights practical benefits like collaborative development.

FOSS or "free software" emphasizes the ethical and political dimensions of freely using, studying, modifying, and sharing software. It's a movement deeply rooted in the belief that software freedom is a fundamental right. Although the "free software" movement encompasses more than just technical aspects, it has often been associated with niche technological spaces. The movement itself carries a strong political ethos challenging proprietary software restrictions. This political stance emphasizes the importance of software freedom as a matter of liberty and ethical practice, not gratis.

To illustrate this conceptual difference, let's use a reductive metaphor: imagine a community garden and a public park. The community garden represents "free software." It's a space where every gardener has a say in what gets planted, everyone contributes to the upkeep, and the harvest is shared among all who work there. The rules are strict because they are based on deep ethical beliefs about collective ownership and mutual benefit. This garden thrives on the principle that all gardeners should have the freedom to cultivate, modify, and share their produce. However, because of its stringent rules and the dedication required, it can be less accessible to those who are not as committed or knowledgeable about its principles.

Now, consider the public park as "open source." It's open to everyone, and while there are guidelines for its use, the focus is more on the enjoyment and utility of the space rather than on who maintains it. People can use the park freely, organize events, and enjoy the amenities without needing to deeply engage with the underlying principles of its management. This inclusivity allows for a broader range of activities and contributions. However, it can also lead to issues where the park's resources are exploited and all the garbage left behind—who wants to deal with the garbage? Much like how some open source projects can be used by corporations without contributing back and leaving all the maintenance work behind.

The terms free software and open source often intertwine in discussions, yet, as just seen, they are not the same. I particularly align myself with and advocate for the free software movement, because I understand any power relationship as political. Software is not just a tool; it's a form of expression, an industry, and products that wield significant power in today's world. However, "open source" has become the more commonly recognized term, capturing a broader range of practices and appealing to a wider audience. For this reason, I will use "open source" throughout this book to reflect its prevalence and acceptance in the wider cultural discourse.

This choice reflects the reality of the movement's evolution—from a niche group of enthusiasts to a global phenomenon that encompasses everything from small, grassroots projects to major corporate enterprises. In making peace with this terminology, I acknowledge the roots of free software in shaping what we now celebrate as open source, while also recognizing the term's role in engaging a diverse and expansive community. This balance allows us to delve into the complexities and widespread impacts of open source, ensuring that we respect its origins and embrace its growth.

In many ways, open source has created a crack that facilitates further exploitation, all occurring in the absence of adequate legislative support and a noticeable lack of self-awareness from the ones in positions of power and decision. The original intention was to dismantle entrenched systems that could harm users' freedoms. This approach seemed practical for a period—perhaps its success could have continued had it maintained a smaller, niched scope. However, the execution was haphazard, neglecting to safeguard fundamental rights and uphold principles of fairness and equity, ultimately leading to unintended consequences that could have been avoided with more careful planning and consideration.

There is a fundamental tension between the desire for a free culture and the systemic problems that have generated unwanted and unforeseen effects contrary to the initial ideology.

The music industry offers an illuminating example for reflection. In the late 1990s and early 2000s, Napster's emergence as a peer-to-peer (P2P) file-sharing platform dramatically disrupted traditional music revenue streams. This shift profoundly impacted musicians, particularly smaller and independent artists, who saw their incomes drastically reduce as their music was distributed without compensation, and many artists struggled financially as a result.

Following the legal battles that led to the shutdown of many P2P services, the industry gravitated toward streaming platforms like Spotify, Apple Music, and Pandora. These services provide royalties to artists under the guise of legitimacy, but the compensation model has been widely criticized for creating a new form of exploitation. The pro-rata model—where subscriber money is pooled and distributed based on share of total streams—often results in very low per-stream payouts, particularly affecting independent artists with smaller audiences compared to mainstream acts.

This era of digital music distribution has reshaped consumer expectations, with many now preferring access over ownership and showing reduced willingness to pay for music. This shift has forced many musicians to seek alternative revenue streams such as live performances, merchandise, and fan-supported platforms like Patreon. The promise of free access to music, while democratizing in many ways, has also had long-term detrimental effects on musicians' ability to earn a sustainable income, highlighting the complex consequences of free culture in the music industry.

Ultimately the breach to allow this movement to happen is a legal matter. The first software released under a copyleft free software license was the GNU Emacs text editor, which was released in 1985 by the GNU Project, which Richard Stallman launched in 1983 to create a completely free and open operating system. The GNU Emacs license, known as the GNU General Public License (GPL), was pivotal as it allowed modifications and redistribution of the software as long as the same freedoms were preserved in derivative works. This principle of "copyleft" fundamentally shaped the legal framework within which open source software could be freely used, studied, modified, and shared.

Copyleft is a licensing concept that allows creators upfront to allow other to use their creations. It's a clever play on the word "copyright," flipping its typical restrictions. This license is not only applicable to software. Creative Commons (CC) is an American non-profit organization devoted to educate and expand the range of creative works available for others to build upon legally and to share. These licenses are straightforward: they allow creators to clearly state which rights they reserve and which they waive for others' use. Creators keep their intellectual rights and use CC licenses to simplify the typical complex negotiations over rights between copyright owners (licensors) and users (licensees), negotiations that are necessary under an "all rights reserved" copyright law. Founded in 2001, CC has an important role contributing to rethinking what "commons" is in the Information Age.

Although software can be seen as a technical mathematical product, under copyright law, it is considered a form of creative expression and, therefore, subject to intellectual property laws. Maybe this is why the FOSS movement has been fostered not only by computer scientists but often by artists. Hackerspaces, makerspaces, and artistic movements such as live coding, circuit bending, and digital media arts helped translate and bring together a public that was once laymen in the technical-creative making and produced an effervescent scene around the world, especially in the early 2000s.

Remix culture encourages the creation of derivative works by combining or modifying existing materials to produce something new. This concept has been a common practice among artists throughout history, and it has gained renewed popularity in the digital age. Kirby Ferguson's *Everything is a Remix*[1], the 2010–2012 four-part web series which discussed issues of fair use and how creative works derive inspiration from existing works, highlights how all creative works build

---

[1] You can see the original and remastered material in the official website https://www.everythingisaremix.info/blog/everything-is-a-remix-remastered

upon existing works, and remix culture encourages this process. The impact of the documentary extends beyond its initial scope, showcasing the influence of open source culture on creativity and acting as a catalyst for important discussions around copyright and digital freedoms. This project exemplifies the power of open source principles to transcend traditional boundaries and foster a more inclusive, participatory culture.

Collaboration As Culture

This is not about the "digital age." Long before the contemporary pillars of free and open source software, there was a rich tradition of collective intelligence that improved decision-making and problem-solving.

Consider the African concept of "ubuntu," which encompasses the philosophy that "I am because we are." This ethical framework, prominent in sub-Saharan African cultures, emphasizes communal relationships, shared responsibility, and collective decision-making. Ubuntu principles have historically guided community governance, resource allocation, and knowledge sharing across generations, creating resilient social structures that prioritize the wellbeing of the collective over individual advancement.

In Native American traditions, practices of collective stewardship and communal resource management have long embodied principles that resonate with modern open source ideals. The Haudenosaunee (Iroquois) Confederacy's[2] governance model, with its emphasis on consensus-building and seven-generation sustainability planning, represents a sophisticated system of collaborative decision-making that has influenced democratic thought worldwide. Traditional agricultural practices among tribes like the Hopi and Zuni feature collective farming methods where

---

[2] Their official website https://www.haudenosauneeconfederacy.com/who-we-are/

knowledge of seed preservation, planting techniques, and irrigation systems was freely shared within communities, ensuring food security through distributed expertise rather than privatized knowledge.

Asian agricultural communities, particularly those centered around rice cultivation, have developed intricate systems of cooperative labor to manage the intensive work of planting, maintaining, and harvesting rice paddies. In Japan, the "yui" system creates reciprocal labor exchanges where farmers assist each other during critical agricultural periods. Similar systems exist throughout Southeast Asia, where the complex requirements of terraced rice farming necessitated collaborative approaches to water management, with communities developing sophisticated irrigation systems maintained through shared knowledge and distributed responsibility.

At the State government level, Brazil under Minister of Culture, Gilberto Gil (2003–2008), was making a bold statement for the global scenario. By advocating for open-source software and rejecting the stringent IP regimes championed by wealthier nations, Brazil was carving out a path not just for itself but as a leader for other developing nations. This wasn't just about technology; it was about asserting a national identity, one that values creativity, accessibility, and autonomy over corporate profits and rigid control—what today Europe is trying to achieve and calling it Digital Sovereignty. Gil's efforts were emblematic of Brazil's broader aspirations to reshape national and global policies on technology and intellectual property. Brazil designed a model where knowledge and technology were viewed as public goods, accessible to everyone rather than locked behind the gates of profit-driven corporations. It was from the deep understanding of the importance of stopping a well know pattern of colonization and breaking free of it. This stance was particularly poignant in a world where access to technology increasingly dictated social and economic opportunities.

These cross-cultural examples illustrate that collaborative models for knowledge-sharing and resource management have deep historical roots across diverse societies. Each tradition demonstrates that the principles underlying open source—transparency, shared stewardship, distributed expertise, and collective benefit—have manifested throughout human history as adaptive responses to complex social and environmental challenges. By recognizing these historical precedents, we gain a richer understanding of open source not as a novel invention of the digital age, but as the contemporary expression of enduring human wisdom about how communities can effectively organize knowledge and resources for common prosperity.

In the open source world, the establishment of trust networks serves as a critical foundation for successful collaboration. Unlike traditional organizational structures that rely on hierarchical authority, open source communities operate on distributed trust—a web of relationships built through consistent contributions, transparent communication, and shared values. These networks function as both social and technical infrastructure, enabling strangers from across the globe to collaborate on complex projects despite often never meeting face-to-face.

Seeking to know whether this is effectively true, James Surowiecki's 2004 book *The Wisdom of Crowds* researches how diverse, decentralized groups make better decisions than individual experts when four conditions are met: diversity of opinion (different perspectives), independence (uninfluenced by others), decentralization (local knowledge), and aggregation (mechanism to turn private judgments into collective decisions). Open source tries to embody these principles—contributors working independently on specific problems, bringing knowledge that's integrated through version control systems and governance processes. But...where is the diversity in it?

Surowiecki offers examples to proof how this diverse common intelligence is wiser as a group of narrowed one. When British scientist Francis Galton discovered a crowd at a livestock fair collectively guessed an ox's weight with near-perfect accuracy in 1906, he demonstrated how averaging independent estimates outperforms individual expert judgment—similar to how open source bug reports from various users often pinpoint issues more effectively than a single designer's perspective. Similarly, prediction markets like the Iowa Electronic Markets consistently outperform polls and pundits in forecasting elections by aggregating the distributed knowledge of participants—much as open source communities collectively prioritize features more effectively than centralized planning could.

For open source practitioners, these aren't abstract theories but lived daily experiences. The movement thrives precisely because it harnesses collective intelligence across global networks, where each contributor adds a unique perspective that strengthens the whole. This distributed collaboration, anchored in trust networks and effective aggregation mechanisms, produces innovations that centralized development simply cannot match, providing tangible evidence of collective wisdom's practical power in technological creation.

The Infrastructure and Business Of Code

For this collective knowledge sharing and cooperation to happen, it is necessary to have some sort of infrastructure in place. In the case of software development, platforms like GitLab, Bitbucket, and GitHub have transformed complex version control systems into comprehensive full feature environments for collaboration, facilitating how developers interact and contribute to projects. These platforms provide essential tools for issue tracking, code review, and communication, making managing open source projects more efficient and accessible—more importantly, improving the life of the maintainers of the project.

Nadia Eghbal, in her acclaimed book *Working in Public: The Making and Maintenance of Open Source Software*, shares a valuable methodology to research open source and tells the story about how platforms have become central hubs for developers, offering a space where they can easily find, join, and contribute to projects. Her work brings attention to the invisible scaffolding that supports this culture. She observes how platforms mediate not just access to code, but access to recognition, support, and continuity. The structure of a repository, the logic of pull requests, the visibility of issues—all these elements shape who gets to contribute and how long a project can endure.

Eghbal gives us inside knowledge about the changes that led GitHub to become a synonym for open source for people starting their journey in the movement. It has become a starting point for many new contributors, offering user-friendly interfaces and extensive documentation that guide users through their first contributions. This ease of entry has significantly lowered the barrier to participation, encouraging a diverse range of people to get involved.

Still, this infrastructure is not neutral. The convenience of centralized platforms can conceal dependencies and amplify inequalities. As James Surowiecki reminds us, the wisdom of crowds depends on diversity, decentralization, and independent judgment. When these conditions are undermined—through homogeneity, centralization, or performative alignment—the crowd loses its capacity to think, and begins instead to echo. Therefore, although GitHub has indeed become a great platform, it must not become a monopoly, neither a synonym of open source. It is owned by Microsoft, a long defender of private software, a private for-profit company with its own interests in mind that are using the power of the commons for its own profit.

Wait. Commons and profit in the same sentence? Do you think that the wisdom and power of the crowds could be applied to a profit-driven business?

The short answer is: imperfectly, but purposefully. The apparently contradictory impulses—the drive to create sustainable economic value and the desire to share knowledge freely—meet business in some ideological battle.

While a full treatment of open source as a business model might deserve a book of its own—one I have no intention of writing—it's worth unpacking some of the premises that frame this ongoing negotiation. Emilie Omier, a consultant who has carved out a niche helping open source founders make sense of this hybrid terrain, offers a pragmatic definition in her widely circulated blog post "What is an open source company?"[3] She identifies two criteria that must be met:

1. The company must maintain an open source project, under an OSI-approved license, that provides genuine standalone value to users. In other words, the project must be usable, useful, and meaningful without requiring users to purchase a commercial product. A mere gateway or teaser—like an open API that only functions in tandem with a paid backend—doesn't qualify.

2. The company must also be serious about financial sustainability. That means being committed to generating revenue, ideally turning a profit, and behaving like a business rather than a well-intentioned but economically incoherent collective.

This is an interesting framing. It doesn't romanticize open source as a utopia free from market forces, nor does it reduce it to a clever distribution channel for proprietary software. Instead, it acknowledges the tension and proposes a path through it: transparency in licensing, paired with a clear commitment to building a viable business.

In practice, this often means that while the code remains free to inspect, adapt, and redistribute, the knowledge required to scale, secure, or customize it in production settings becomes a billable service. The

---

[3] Emilie's article: https://www.emilyomier.com/blog/what-is-an-open-source-company

commons is cultivated through community contribution; value is extracted not from enclosure but from implementation. The open source project is the soil, the business is the greenhouse—what grows depends on the relationship between the two.

So the question isn't simply "how do you make money from open source?" but rather, "how do you participate in a commons-based ecosystem while sustaining the labor it requires?" The answer will vary by context, but Omier's criteria provide a useful diagnostic for distinguishing between companies that engage with open source as a foundational principle, and those that merely accessorize with it.

Yet, recognizing this balance is not intuitive within a financial culture shaped by venture capital imperatives—where growth is often pursued at the expense of long-term resilience, and value is equated with exclusivity. Open source disrupts this logic. Its abundance mindset challenges venture capital's reliance on artificial scarcity and extractive cycles of "fast innovation," much of which, as recent critiques have revealed, is neither necessary nor sustainable.

To articulate the deeper economic significance of these shifts, we can turn to the work of Elinor Ostrom, the first woman to win the Nobel Prize in Economics. Her research on commons-based governance challenged the "tragedy of the commons" myth, demonstrating that shared resources can be managed sustainably through polycentric, participatory, and transparent governance—features strikingly present in open source ecosystems. Ostrom's principles illuminate why open source can be not just technically effective but economically rational. Where traditional economics locates value in exclusion, commons-based models derive value from contribution, stewardship, and reciprocity.

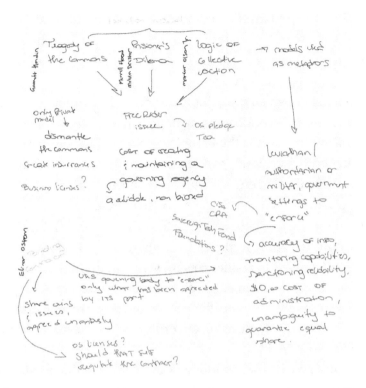

Figure 2-1. *This is a representation mind map showing different models of the commons analyzed by Ostrom in her book Governing The Commons. The figure includes some open source initiatives that I understand correlates with some of the models, which I find helpful to deepen my understanding about each proposition and maybe using the respective theories to avoid common issues it may bring.*

When we code, fund, or govern open technologies, we are not merely solving technical problems—we are engaged in world-making. The architectures we build ripple through legal, social, and economic domains. In open source, we glimpse an alternative grammar of value: one that prizes interdependence over domination, and sustainability over speculative gain.

Open source business models remain contested, especially in a landscape still governed by short-termism. But at their best, they serve as testbeds for more ethical, cooperative economic relations. They show that abundance is not a utopia—it is a design choice. And like all choices, it carries responsibility: to the community, the infrastructure, and the futures we dare to imagine.

OSPO (Open Source Program Office)

The friction between communities and business gave rise to a new institutional actor: the Open Source Program Office (OSPO). OSPOs are almost a conceptual effort to align the interests of businesses and community within corporations and, more recently, governments. This methodological bet has been instrumental in enabling those outside the traditional open source software to get involved in its sustainability. Initially conceived within corporations to manage licensing and compliance, OSPOs have evolved into strategic hubs for open source. They now serve as stewards of collaboration, internal culture change, and ecosystem engagement. In 2024, this shift was formally recognized on a global stage when a symbolic yet strategic intervention unfolded at the United Nations.

A joint initiative between the UN's Office of Information and Communications Technology, the Secretary-General's Tech Envoy, OSPO++, and Open Forum Europe convened the second OSPOs for Good event in the ECOSOC Chamber—an architectural emblem of unfinished global work. With 600+ participants, including policymakers, researchers, FOSS maintainers, and heads of state, this gathering reframed the OSPO not as a corporate tool but as a methodology of cross-sector collaboration in service of the UN's Sustainable Development Goals (SDGs).[4] These goals are designed to encourage collaboration across borders and disciplines

---

[4]UN SDGs https://sdgs.un.org/goals

and serve as an urgent reminder to care for the world that sustains us all. It offered a sharp contrast to nationalist withdrawals from international institutions, asserting instead the value of globally coordinated, open, and inclusive knowledge infrastructures.

Redefining Open Source

With all that said, this chapter has two intentions. The first is to recover a historical sense of why we share things. The second is to broaden our repertoire of how collaboration and openness can have many meanings and impacts, both personal, social and economic, beyond what we experience in our own spheres.

Compiling stories of various actors in Latin American and European contexts will give you a repertoire on how open source have changed how we produce knowledge, create a representation, understand our bodies and create public programs focused on knowledge sharing and social empowerment. In short, how the ideal of the commons, especially in the cultural field, has changed society.

Recounting these stories is a way to learn from other contexts and seek new ways of dealing with some undesired side effects.

Aware of its own issues, the increase of financial support from industry and governments, multiplication of license types aiming to bring more clarity about profits made from the projects, and the creation of open source departments within companies have tried to mitigate it. Is it working? What has changed? And most importantly, how are we researching, and critically thinking about it in ways that can indeed leverage the whole ecosystem?

While the Global South have appropriated open source as a political way to claim access, the Global North tends to circumscribe within the technical and business realm. Regardless of geolocation and despite innumerable efforts to regulate and create metrics, open source is still an open door to an exploitative and unregulated territory. I hope that, by bringing in various aspects not commonly mentioned, a space is created to seek more equitable methods, metrics, and a system that considers humans and more-than-humans by design.

This part of the book is written through, across, and within several voices and dialogues with people who have guided me, influenced my perception of the world, and whose background could not be further away from software.

This is my way to contribute, adding an indisciplary view, a personal perspective from what I have experienced with my involvement in open source in Brazil, Mexico, and Germany in the past 16 years that led me to understand it as a contradiction, just like life. I was taught that open source is a contradiction, such as life, a "possible utopia," a real possibility of changing the axis, where access, and collective and collaborative construction could change the asymmetric conditions among humans.

What is open source to you?

Open Source As Code: Software, Product, and Business

Since free software is not a matter of price, a low price doesn't make the software free, or even closer to free. So if you are redistributing copies of free software, you might as well charge a substantial fee and make some money. Redistributing free software is a good and legitimate activity; if you do it, you might as well make a profit from it.

—STALLMAN, Richard M (p.43)

Open source is commonly recognized as code that is developed collaboratively by contributors from all around the globe.
Yet, this collective creation has evolved far beyond its humble beginnings. Today, open source stands at the core of a multi-billion dollar industry, with its libraries, languages, and frameworks shaping products consumed

by billions and influencing business models across sectors. This widespread adoption underscores its significance not just as a method of developing software, but as a transformative force in the modern business landscape.

The 2025 Black Duck Open Source Security and Risk Analysis report[5] found that 97% of the codebases they scanned contained open source software, highlighting just how deeply these collaborative projects have penetrated even the most proprietary environments. This ubiquity raises crucial questions about how organizations engage with communities that exist outside traditional corporate boundaries.

Embracing open source software by consuming or relying on open projects requires a distinguished approach from traditional business models. This model fundamentally emphasizes collaboration and transparency, fostering an environment where collective input and open access prevail. Separately, it challenges conventional profit-driven approaches by enabling businesses to tap into community-driven development. This can lead to cost reductions, as companies utilize the shared expertise and efforts of a global community rather than relying solely on in-house resources. However, companies often underestimate the in-house resources required to maintain these dependencies— the time spent tracking patches, fixing bugs, and managing software operations without the safety net of vendor support that proprietary solutions typically provide.

However, this model also means that businesses do not own the projects on which they depend. Well...in theory, they lack the authority to unilaterally direct project trajectories or prioritize specific features; such decisions are typically made through consensus within the community and among various stakeholders. This can be both a limitation and a

---

[5] 2025 Black Duck Open Source Security and Risk Analysis report https://www.blackduck.com/resources/analyst-reports/open-source-security-risk-analysis.html#introMenu

strength, as it encourages broader participation and can lead to diverse, user-driven enhancements that might not emerge in a more controlled, top-down development environment. In practice, we collect several scandals among the communities. Contributor License Agreement, CLA, is a common practice among company-owned open source projects, intending to protect the project's intellectual property (IP) and avoid potential legal issues down the line. However, it goes both ways. CLA is a legal document that contributors sign before they can contribute to an open-source project. These legal agreements that contributors sign before they can contribute to an open-source project grant the company controlling the CLA specific rights to use, distribute, and relicense the contributions. In reality, CLAs have been used to allow companies to relicense open source projects, moving from open source licenses to non-open source or more restrictive licenses.[6] This often happens when projects' main contributors happen to be the employees of a single company.

This is a deeply contentious issue in the open source ecosystem, one that strikes at the heart of what we mean by "open." When companies relicense open source projects—particularly when they shift from OSI-approved licenses to so-called source-available or more restrictive licenses—they are often responding to perceived threats from cloud providers, competitors, or unsustainable contributor dynamics. However, such moves tend to reveal much about the underlying power structures at play and can erode community trust.

Those who contributed under the assumption that their work would remain part of a freely accessible and reusable commons may feel betrayed. The social contract—however implicit—is broken. This breach

---

[6] Some cases are Elastic, MongoDB, Terraform and many other. Some articles address the issue https://medium.com/@stephenrwalli/forked-communities-whose-property-is-it-anyway-2ddee71f2ef1 https://shkspr.mobi/blog/2020/09/please-stop-inventing-new-software-licences/ https://www.cockroachlabs.com/enterprise-license-update/

undermines the legitimacy of the project as a commons-oriented initiative. In some cases, it has led to forks, where communities try to preserve the project's original spirit. For example, ElasticSearch was forked into OpenSearch after Elastic re-licensed from Apache 2.0 to SSPL. Redis modules were forked into Valkey after Redis moved parts of its ecosystem to more restrictive licensing. These forks underscore how relicensing can fracture communities and dilute project momentum.

At its core, the distinction between open-source and source-available isn't just legal—it's political. Open source was designed to resist enclosure. Relicensing, especially when done unilaterally by a company, can be understood as a form of privatization of the commons. It reflects an extractive impulse: to retain control, to gatekeep monetization, and to mitigate the "free rider" problem—not by fostering reciprocity, but by rewriting the rules in one's favor. Once a project shifts away from an OSI-approved license, it no longer belongs to the open source commons—it becomes part of a private strategy wrapped in open-source aesthetics.

As Eghbal notes, much of the modern open source landscape is dominated by platforms and power asymmetries. Relicensing is one of the clearest expressions of these asymmetries. It shows that while the rhetoric of open collaboration persists, the governance structures are often centralized and brittle.

In short, and being redundant as this is really important, relicensing reveals a tension at the heart of open source-as-business: who controls the terms of collaboration? And who bears the risks when those terms change? While some companies may argue that relicensing is a survival tactic, it often alienates the very communities they depend on. Sustainable open source business models must navigate this terrain with care, transparency, and a commitment to shared stewardship—not opportunistic enclosure.

Choosing to adopt open source for business means diving deep into its ecosystem. It's not just about picking software that seems robust—it's about understanding the nuances that define its foundation. Let's walk through what you need to consider:

1. Project Maturity: Is the project in its early beta stages, or does it have stable releases? The maturity of the software can significantly affect its reliability and suitability for your business needs.

2. Community and Ownership: Is this a solo project or one backed by a vibrant community? The breadth and activity of the community can often reflect the project's resilience and potential for continued development.

3. Governance and Diversity: How is the project governed? Is there clear, equitable governance that ensures diversity and balances decision-making among stakeholders? Understanding the governance structure is crucial for assessing how decisions are made and how inclusive those processes are.

4. Stakeholders and Management: Who are the key stakeholders? Is the project managed by an individual, a community, or a foundation? The stakeholders' identities and their roles can influence the project's direction and stability.

5. Community Health: How healthy is the project's community? We'll delve deeper into community health metrics in Chapter 3, but it's important to gauge the vibrancy and activity level of the community as it significantly impacts the project's sustainability.

6. Security Practices: How does the project handle vulnerabilities? Are there regular security audits, a transparent disclosure policy, and timely

security patches? The security posture of an open source project can significantly impact your own organization's risk profile.

And, of course, maybe the first question to be asked:

7. License: What type of license is used? Is it a license under which I can use the software for profit-making business purposes? The licensing can affect everything from your ability to use, modify, or redistribute the software to how you integrate it into your own offerings.

These foundational questions are just the starting point. They're not overly technical but are a start for aligning your business with the right open source project. Is this enough? In today's complex scenario, I am afraid it is far from enough. Following this, more technical and legal considerations will provide a fuller picture and help you decide if a specific project aligns with your business objectives. Engaging with open source is not just about accessing free software—it's about participating in a broader ecosystem with its own culture, rules, and expectations. And understanding that, and adapting to it, is surely not an easy task. For those used to hierarchies, like a CEO accustomed to dictating how things are done, it may feel like an incompatible paradigm shift.

In 2024, I proposed and mediated two panel debates, one in Berlin,[7] Germany, and other in Raleigh,[8] USA, focused on open source sustainability trying to understand where do we stand today and what are we understanding as nowadays as a bothering conflict between

---

[7] The recording from FOSS Backstage can be found at https://www.youtube.com/watch?v=bsQ9-e7L5lU&list=PLq-odUc2x7i-ww77dGasjo-d54ohCAb8k&index=20
[8] Unfortunately there's no recording, the abstract can be found here https://2024.allthingsopen.org/sessions/freedom-vs-sustainable-a-candid-necessary-debate

the commons and the business. I choose people from different sides of the scales trying to gather a broad panorama of voices: from legal, the maintainer, the foundation, the civic and the business perspective. One thing that I have learned is that we need to do more of this as an exercise, to put some of those pieces together to try to understand the gaps in the longevity, ethical, and economical perspectives that is causing fissures and breaking its sustainability.

I turned to Thomas Steenberg for another perspective on how business and open source align. Thomas has been both hands-on and a strategist, bringing a practical and strategic perspective to open source initiatives for over 15 years when I interviewed him for this book. He has contributed to the Linux Foundation's Software Package Data Exchange (SPDX), an open standard for representing systems with software components as Software Bills of Materials (SBOMs), and other projects involving Artificial Intelligence (AI), data, and security. With this experience, Thomas became actively engaged in the OSS Review Toolkit (ORT) project, a FOSS policy automation and orchestration tool designed to manage open source strategically and safely.

Let's step back, because this is hard to grasp. SBOMs are critical documents that provide comprehensive details about the components used in a software product, including open source and third-party components, their licenses, versions, and patch status. It is a nested inventory, a list of ingredients that make up software components. They have become a key part of software security and supply chain risk management because they provide visibility into the software supply chain and can help organizations identify security vulnerabilities and risks. Recognizing their importance, the National Security Agency now mandates SBOMs for any software used within the US government. These are also a topic of significant discussion within the Cybersecurity and

Infrastructure Security Agency (CISA)[9] and are increasingly becoming part of regulatory requirements, particularly in the European Union's Cyber Resilience Act (CRA).[10]

SBOMs, akin to the bills of materials used in manufacturing that detail the components of a product, serve a similar purpose for software. Take, for example, the automotive industry, where a bill of materials lists all parts needed for a vehicle. However, unlike a car, software consists of dynamic, evolving parts, each dependent on others in a complex web. How can one maintain a clear, static document in such a dynamic environment? Although still confusing and challenging and not a one-size-fits-all solution, SBOMs, supported by tools like the OSS Review Toolkit (ORT),[11] offer a pragmatic way forward. These tools are increasingly crucial as software becomes an integral part of business infrastructure, striving to provide transparency and manage risks in the software supply chain.

Attempting to articulate why open source is crucial for businesses, Thomas offered an interesting analogy. He described open source as a vibrant ecosystem—a complex mesh of interactions involving various elements: people, technologies, and circumstances. Within this network, each node is interlinked and dependent, creating a dynamic that is partially unpredictable yet follows discernible patterns, much like ocean currents. This comparison highlights the contrast with traditional business models driven by venture capital investments, who tend to focus on disruptive technologies because early movers in new ecosystems can capture substantial market share and revenue, having competitive

---

[9] See documents https://www.cisa.gov/sbom https://www.whitehouse.gov/briefing-room/presidential-actions/2021/05/12/executive-order-on-improving-the-nations-cybersecurity/

[10] CRA proposal https://digital-strategy.ec.europa.eu/en/library/cyber-resilience-act

[11] ORT https://oss-review-toolkit.org/ort/

advantage by aggressively introducing innovative products or business models to gain market share before competitors can respond—an approach seen in tech startups like Uber and Airbnb.

These companies reshape entire industries, but open source, emerging predominantly from community efforts, invites us not to disrupt but to standardize, understand, and synchronize with these natural flows, creating opportunities to everyone instead, integrating them into our strategies and operations. This approach encourages a more sustainable and inclusive way of integrating technology into our lives and work.

The intersection of open source and business evolution is indeed multifaceted and complex, reflecting the ongoing transformation of various industries as they adapt to new technological paradigms.

A thermometer to understand how this has been reflected in the open source ecosystem can be found in the evolution of open source foundations, which have shifted over time to have more of a business focus. The original foundations, like the Free Software Foundation (FSF) and Apache, still exist but operate as 501(c)(3) nonprofit charitable organizations. These organizations, by IRS definition, are "organized and operated exclusively for religious, charitable, scientific, testing for public safety, literary, educational, or other specified purposes." Their focus remains primarily on public good and social benefit.

In contrast, the majority of growth has occurred in business-oriented foundations like the Linux Foundation, including the highly successful Cloud Native Computing Foundation (CNCF). These operate as 501(c)(6) organizations—business leagues or membership organizations that the IRS defines as "an association of persons having some common business interest." This fundamental difference in tax status explains their more business-centric approach, as they're explicitly designed to serve their member companies' interests rather than charitable purposes. This shift reflects open source's evolution from a primarily ideological movement toward a mainstream business strategy.

In the end of the 1990, businesses across industries began automating their processes extensively, shifting from manual systems to digital ones, and without some standards the growth of the industries would be compromised. One significant example of technology transformation enabled by open standards is the development of the World Wide Web or, the Internet as we know it. Tim Berners-Lee, a British engineer and computer scientist, invented the World Wide Web in 1989. It was his proposal to create a system for scientists around the world to share information that ultimately revolutionized how we access and interact with data globally.

The pivotal element in this transformation was Berners-Lee's decision to not patent his invention. Instead, he ensured that the web's core specifications—HTML (HyperText Markup Language), HTTP (HyperText Transfer Protocol), and URLs (Uniform Resource Locators)—were documented as open standards. These open standards were crucial because they allowed any individual or business to create web servers and browsers that could communicate across a vast and growing network. This openness is what rapidly propelled the web's widespread adoption and the digital transformation of numerous industries.

By making the web's foundational technologies freely available and governed by open standards, Berners-Lee facilitated an environment of innovation and collaboration that led to the digital economy we know today. This shift from proprietary systems to a universally accessible network exemplifies how open standards can drive the digital transformation of entire sectors. Today that standard is found under the official World Wide Web Consortium (W3C) formed by different knowledgeable and committed individuals and business.

Open source projects often serve as the "glue" that helps disparate systems and standards work together by providing flexible, adaptable frameworks that evolve over time. It is also often the only one able to solve too complex issues.

The OSI (Open Source Initiative) has recently developed a definition for open source AI, but I didn't include this in the section as it's still evolving and might not be fully stabilized by the time your book is published. The definition seeks to establish criteria for when AI systems can genuinely be considered "open source," addressing concerns around transparency, reproducibility, and meaningful access to model weights and training data.

Some key elements of OSI's developing AI definition include requirements for access to model architecture, parameters/weights, training methodologies, and inference capabilities—extending traditional open source principles to the unique challenges of AI systems. The initiative aims to prevent "openwashing" where companies claim openness while maintaining proprietary control over critical components.

This definition represents an important expansion of open source principles into new technological domains, though its practical implementation and industry adoption remain works in progress.

This continuous evolution of open source is likened to navigating ocean currents or winds; understanding these patterns can give businesses a competitive edge. Just as mariners must understand and predict ocean currents to navigate effectively, businesses must navigate the ever-changing landscape of open technology standards and ecosystem dynamics.

But, how to distinguish the good, the bad, and the ugly from inside of the ocean?

Take the Cloud Native ecosystem, of which Kubernetes is a prominent project within a broader landscape of related technologies. This substantial open source ecosystem requires businesses to discern which projects within it are viable in the long term. This discernment requires a deep understanding of the technology and the market. There's an advantage in how American companies systematically analyze ecosystem components to differentiate themselves from competitors, as betting in ecosystems that complex required some protocols and risk taking.

This analogy underscores the necessity for businesses to not only adopt open source technologies but also to deeply engage with and understand the open source communities and the evolving standards that drive these technologies forward. Such engagement is crucial for leveraging open source effectively in competitive business environments.

According to Thomas, businesses must recognize that open source is not just a tool for cutting costs but a strategic asset that requires careful management and integration. He points out that while open source can indeed save money, it does so not by avoiding costs but by providing the flexibility and adaptability needed for long-term infrastructure development. This perspective is critical for businesses aiming to leverage open source effectively and sustainably. It is about the "plumbing," good engineering and management capable of seeing the flow, and creating standards that allow for cross team collaboration and efficiency. It's all about the intricate parts that will save your business in the long run. But who has the real expertise to manage all that? Thomas points out that this is definitely not an easy task and, unfortunately, we may not yet have capable professionals with that skill, which will become essential in a few years.

Seeking to foster such professionals, Thomas is also a co-founder of the European chapter of the TODO Group, having helped in 2020 write a report called "Why open source matters to your enterprise,"[12] providing a quick overview of the pros and cons of businesses using open source software in the European context.

The group, often simply called TODO, stands for "Talk Openly, Develop Openly" and serves as a go-to resource for Open Source Program Offices (OSPOs). TODO, part of the Linux Foundation, is known for its focused approach to standardizing what they are and how OSPOs operate.

---

[12] Report can be found at https://project.linuxfoundation.org/hubfs/ Reports/Why-open-source-software-matters-to-your-enterprise_090820. pdf?hsLang=en

They create tooling, organize events, run regular meetings, and offer plenty of free courses and materials that make it easier to set up OSPOs from scratch, prove their worth, and stay on top of the ever-changing open source scene across different regions like America, Europe, and Asia. The group works as an open source project, divided into working groups, and they hold regular open and open communication channels. Members are typically those involved in company OSPOs who help each other with common issues the department often faces, such as explaining their value from a business point of view or finding tooling for compliance.

Earlier when I packed up and moved to Germany, my whole thing with open source was pretty straightforward—I was just a user and an enthusiastic supporter. My world was all about contributing to the helpful tools I consumed and connecting with other passionate individuals involved in these projects, not thinking about how these projects I was deep into might matter to some big company or the entire industry. Honestly, the thought kind of annoyed me. I wasn't punching a clock, I was pouring my heart into projects that really meant something to me, and I was genuinely irritated by the idea that someone might be profiting from my volunteer work as if it were just business to them.

But then, things shifted when I started needing something more stable, you know? Sustainability became a big deal not just for my projects but for me personally. Coming from a financially unstable background as an artist in Brazil, I needed to make a living. That's when I transitioned into becoming a developer, and, funnily enough, it all started in an OSPO that had recently been set up by Diego Molina, one of the core maintainers of Selenium, and Christian Bromann, founder and core maintainer of WebdriverIO, two important open source projects for web automation.

This work opened my eyes to the whole scene—from the nitty-gritty of maintaining a project to the business end that keeps the lights on. Seeing open source from this inside angle and understanding why the business side matters changed how I look at everything. For example, working for Sauce Labs, a company that was founded by one of the creators of the

Selenium project, which now has an OSPO, showed me how could an open source project be a profitable business model capable of supporting the life of about 500 employees around the United States and Europe and be one of the main stakeholders to keep Selenium alive. This is one possible sustainable model for a profitable business built on top of an open source project, either offering special features, for example, using a cloud data center, or offering special services, mostly related to customer services.

As for me, open source has also matured from a passionate belief into finding sustainable ways to make this passion work in the long term and benefit different stakeholders and needs. Interestingly, without expecting it, this new perspective on business ties back to the core values that brought me to open source in the first place. This shift has deepened my connection to my core values: sustainability now encompasses both the health of the ecosystem and the personal well-being of those contributing to it. This journey led me to appreciate the business side of open source, not as an exploitative profit-driven arena but as a space where sustainability supports both healthy profit and human rights. OSPOs for Good symposium, mentioned at the beginning of this chapter, reinforces that this is not a lonely view, it underscores the critical role of open source in achieving broader societal goals with the collective effort from all sectors, including the private.

OSPOs may play a big role in this alignment; at least, it is a possible framework. What is an OSPO?

In 2020, the former CEO of Bitergia, J Manrique Lopez de la Fuente, wrote an article for opensource.com entitled "A guide to setting up your Open Source Program Office (OSPO) for success."[13] In this piece, they presented OSPOs as crucial for managing a company's relationship with the open source ecosystems on which it relies. In his view at the time, OSPOs help maximize return on investment and minimize risks

---

[13] Full article is accessible at `https://opensource.com/article/20/5/open-source-program-office`

associated with using, contributing to, and releasing open source software. Furthermore, he emphasized that maintaining the health and sustainability of the open source ecosystem is integral to ensuring the company's own health, sustainable growth, and evolution. However generalistic, this view goes in line with what Thomas argues, that the true value of an OSPO lies in its ability to deeply understand the complex mesh of the open source environment, which provides stability and business advantages.

Recently updated—consider the writing of this book in 2024—by the TODO group, the current OSPO definition[14] avoids generalizations and reflects a deeper and more structured understanding. According to it, an OSPO serves as the center of competency for an organization's open source operations and structure. It is tasked with defining and implementing strategies and policies that cover a broad range of activities: from setting policies around code use, distribution, and selection to auditing and contributing. Moreover, OSPOs are responsible for providing education and training, enhancing software development efficiency through sustainable use of open source components, guiding teams in open sourcing their software, ensuring legal compliance, and promoting and building community engagement. This comprehensive view underscores the evolving recognition of the strategic significance of OSPOs in navigating the complexities of open source integration and community collaboration.

From a broadly defined role to a more detailed set of responsibilities, the evolution of the Open Source Program Office (OSPO) definition reflects a deeper recognition of its critical function in modern businesses. An OSPO is not just a mediator among technical, legal, and cultural domains; it is a hub where the integration and adoption of open source strategies are managed. This role, enriched with a clearer understanding of expectations, highlights

---

[14] OSPO definition from ospodefinition.org https://github.com/todogroup/ospodefinition.org

how central OSPOs are in aligning diverse business needs with open source values. However, this broad scope can sometimes be daunting, particularly for teams that are small or positioned outside core engineering groups without significant decision-making power. This scenario often presents challenges, as these teams need to manage extensive responsibilities without the full authority to enforce changes or direct outcomes.

Transitioning from the broader manual-like definition of OSPOs, I'd like to bring in a personal narrative that sheds light on how these concepts manifest in real-world applications, particularly through the eyes of someone I admire: Christian Bromann. I had already been deeply involved with open source in Brazil and Mexico, but not as a developer, nor from an OSPO perspective. My journey into the world of development and open source in business began in Germany under Christian's mentorship in Sauce Labs' OSPO founded by Christian.

Christian Bromann is a notable figure in the scene, advocating for open standards and involved in institutions such as the W3C (World Wide Web Consortium) and the OpenJS Foundation. The W3C manages web standards to ensure long-term growth for the web, while the OpenJS Foundation supports the healthy growth of the JavaScript ecosystem. Christian has shaped his career around this advocacy heavily contributing to several projects such as Selenium, Appium, and, of course, WebdriverIO and proposing standards changes for a better web at W3C. Christian also puts lots of his efforts in fostering communities by mentoring people, offering office hours, helping organize events, or serving in the program committees. His extensive experience in maintaining major projects and his involvement in influential tech bodies like W3C and OpenJS Foundation opened my eyes to the complexities and strategic importance of open source in a corporate setting.

I never actually asked Christian why he decided to take on the challenge of creating an OSPO. But if I had to guess, I'd say it's probably because he knows, firsthand, how hard it is to be a maintainer. He's seen how vital that code is for the company, so setting up an OSPO likely seemed to be a good way to bring in some stability and support for both the sides—the company and the community. He's not alone in this; a lot of smart people have been trying to figure out this whole sustainability thing for open source.

Josh Goldberg, maintainer of well used open source projects like mocha and typescript-eslint, author of *Learning TypeScript* published by O'Reilly, thinks a lot about how to make sure maintainers get the support they need to keep projects alive without burning out or losing motivation. One of the projects he worked on, the Open Contributions Project,[15] is around developing metrics to actually measure the impact and value that open-source contributions bring. It's this idea that, sure, companies benefit from open source, but the value often remains invisible - especially when it comes to the projects that sit deep in the dependency chain, the background patches, or the documentation work that keeps everything running smoothly. These are essential contributions, yet rarely the ones that attract attention. Josh wants to make that value visible, to translate it into terms decision-makers can recognize and support.

His approach is all about making the impact of open-source contributions visible, quantifiable, and, ideally, supported. Josh sees that if companies had a better understanding of how much their tech stacks rely on these contributions, they'd be more inclined to allocate resources back to these projects. It's a framework that's less about "doing good" for the sake of it and more about showing companies the real, practical benefit they get when they actively invest in open source ecosystems. Not that decentralized projects have not tried this crowdfunding approach, for example, `https://tidelift.com/`, `https://www.stackaid.us/`, `https://thanks.dev/home`, and fresh out of the oven at the point I am writing this book, other two projects launched by well-known open source figures `https://tea.xyz/` led by Max Howell and `https://opensourcepledge.com/` led by Chad Whitacre. Yet, what Josh is missing is the monetary value understood by decision makers to grasp this relationship.

---

[15] Project repo: `https://github.com/OpenContributionsProject`

This was probably the main challenge faced by Christian. Reflecting on his first experience creating an OSPO from the ground up, Christian expressed some frustration. Christian advocated for a more open approach, proposing that by integrating open source practices across all engineering teams, engineers would gain a broader perspective and deeper insight into how users interact with products. He envisioned tearing down the metaphorical walls that boxed engineers into narrow frameworks, thus enhancing their exposure to the broader technological and user environment.

However, this initiative hit a significant roadblock when new executive priorities led to budget cuts, with the open source initiatives among the first to be scaled back. Despite these challenges, the team managed to contribute significantly to various projects, including Puppeteer, under the leadership of Christian, Diego, and myself. But as the open source team's aspirations grew, the support from Sauce Labs waned, leading to a refocus on internal R&D that aimed at delivering platform features directly tied to immediate business outcomes.

He aimed to have more impact over the way features were developed— often dictated by product managers based on customer interactions, leaving engineers with a limited understanding of broader user needs and the external tech ecosystem. This process, he argued, was not optimal as it didn't allow engineers to grasp the full spectrum of user issues or the technological landscape they were part of.

While some successes were evident, the lack of executive buy-in, particularly around addressing noncritical but essential issues like security vulnerabilities, showcased the ongoing struggle. Christian noted that establishing an OSPO or similar structures might not be feasible for every company, especially those still trying to carve out a market niche without the robust backing of a well-established foundation. He emphasized the importance of a solid open source setup from the start, including clear governance documents, to support sustainable and effective open source engagement within a business context.

For Christian, addressing engineering culture directly was crucial not only for his personal development but also for the growth of his colleagues, which is why it was a foundational aspect of his Open Source Program Office (OSPO). Born and raised in Germany and now residing in the Bay Area in the United States, he reflects on the significant differences in regional engineering cultures and their impact on an engineer's career and business success. He observes that the Bay Area's dynamic scene, characterized by daily meetups and collaborative projects, stands in stark contrast to Germany's less frequent gatherings, such as monthly JavaScript meetups. According to Christian, these disparities influence how open source projects and engineering cultures evolve in each region. It's not that Germany lacks collaborative spaces; rather, it's the frequency and volume that differ. These regional cultural differences directly affect people's daily work lives. Open source projects are often inspired by daily challenges and needs, which means the local job culture and collaborative environment significantly shape the open source landscape.

Both Thomas and Christian tell us how fundamental open source is, from the code we produce as engineers to the businesses we work for. However, they also emphasize that industries, including software industries, struggle to incorporate the needed cultural shift required to first improve engineering itself and, secondly, to understand open source flows to benefit from strategic business advantages.

OSPOs as a framework have gained importance beyond business scopes, as we will explore in the following section.

Open Source As Infrastructure

In recent years, the European Union (EU)—a union of 27 countries with diverse cultures and varying levels of digital adoption—has increasingly seen open source as a vital framework for enhancing collaboration and accelerating digital competitiveness. This shift is essential for the EU, where diverse protective laws and slow bureaucratic processes can hinder rapid digitalization. Recognizing this, the EU has embraced open source as a necessary infrastructure to promote interoperability, which refers to the ability of different systems and organizations to work together, bypassing bureaucracy that wasn't designed for digital speed, which most of the time translates into an impediment.

Launched on December 9, 2011, the European Commission created Joinup[16] to provide a common venue that enables public administrations, businesses, and citizens to share and reuse IT solutions and good practices and facilitate communication and collaboration on IT projects across Europe. Joinup is a collaboration platform created by the European Commission and funded by the European Union via its Interoperability Solutions for Public Administrations Programme (ISA Programme). It replaces the Open Source Observatory and Repository (OSOR.eu) and the Semantic Interoperability Centre Europe (SEMIC.eu).

From 2021, Joinup is the home to Interoperable Europe, the European Commission's initiative for a reinforced interoperability policy showcasing news and events about government-related interoperability, along with initiatives and best practices that support the digitalization of EU public administrations. Joinup covers the hands-on aspects of interoperability, while Interoperable Europe covers the policy angle. These initiatives aim to promote the use of open source software in the public sector and to address issues related to cost, interoperability, and innovation. By adopting open source solutions, government agencies can reduce costs and increase collaboration while also promoting the principles of openness and transparency.

---

[16] Know more about it in their website https://joinup.ec.europa.eu/collection/joinup/about and in the Wikipedia https://en.wikipedia.org/wiki/Joinup#External_links

Let's pause to understand what "reduce costs" for a government agency means. During FOSDEM 2025, Leonhard Kugler,[17] head of openCode—Germany's nationwide open source platform for public sector software—revealed in his Government Collaboration DevRoom presentation that the German government spent over €1 billion on proprietary software licenses in 2024, underscoring the fiscal imperative driving the country's strategic pivot toward open source solutions and digital sovereignty.

During FOSS-Backstage 2023,[18] several public representatives took part in the conference, sharing several different projects in place.

Axel Thévenet, from the European Commission presented the talk "The Role of Open Source for an Interoperable Europe." During the talk, they presented the Interoperable Europe Act (IEA) proposal, led by the European Commission's Open Source Observatory (OSOR) Team. They spoke about its implications for the free and open source software

---

[17] Talk is available at https://fosdem.org/2025/schedule/event/fosdem-2025-5572-opendesk-on-opencode-developing-a-secure-office-suite-and-sdlc/

[18] To see the talks in its integrity:

1. Munich: Laura Dornheim – Cooperation and Inclusion through Open Source https://www.youtube.com/watch?v=HvHydkpuKtA&list=PLq-odUc2x7i9Zrs4oyM1I3V5xlYICEL2g&index=1
2. Berlin Victoria Boeck & Ingo Hinterding – git init Berlin https://www.youtube.com/watch?v=lb8IVGpfnAI&list=PLq-odUc2x7i9Zrs4oyM1I3V5xlYICEL2g&index=4
3. Open Source Business Alliance. - Miriam Seyffarth – Why isn't the German administration procuring more FOSS? https://www.youtube.com/watch?v=1GxPlNavFrE&list=PLq-odUc2x7i9Zrs4oyM1I3V5xlYICEL2g&index=10
4. Axel Thévenet – The Role of Open Source for an Interoperable Europe https://www.youtube.com/watch?v=VW9PoOW4m1A&list=PLq-odUc2x7i9Zrs4oyM1I3V5xlYICEL2g&index=20

ecosystem. The Act, which the European Commission adopted as a proposal for a regulation in November 2022, aims to reinforce the cross-border interoperability of the public sector in the EU. Practically, it aims to facilitate "the co-creation of an ecosystem of interoperability solutions across the EU."

In 2020, the European Parliament Research Service (EPRS) published a briefing toward a more resilient Europe with the title "Digital sovereignty for Europe."[19] The briefing is a response post COVID-19 pandemic to concerns about the influence of non-EU tech companies, particularly from the United States and China, which challenge the EU's ability to protect personal data, support its own tech companies, and enforce its laws to push the European Union (EU) to focus on becoming more self-reliant in the digital realm. To achieve the desired *digital sovereignty*, the EU has started implementing policies and financial measures aimed at closing the investment gap and boosting its industrial and technological capabilities while positioning itself as a leader in privacy and data protection.

In Germany, the term *digital sovereignty* has been used to finance several initiatives, from cultural to technical landscape. In July 2022, the "Zentrum Digitale Souveränität" (ZenDis), or Center for Digital Sovereignty, was established as a national initiative by the German government. This center is focused on promoting digital sovereignty for public administration in Germany by enhancing the technological independence of government functions. ZenDis acts as a competence and service center, aiming to guide public administrations toward technological self-determination. This funding shows the government's dedication to fostering a robust framework for open source software adoption, ensuring that public administrations can operate with greater autonomy and security in the digital domain.

---

[19] The full briefing can be read here https://www.europarl.europa.eu/RegData/etudes/BRIE/2020/651992/EPRS_BRI(2020)651992_EN.pdf

Less than one year after, in October 2023, its capital, Berlin, won The Open Source Kompetenzzentrum (OSK), part of the IT-Dienstleistungszentrum Berlin (ITDZ Berlin), which represents a significant commitment to digital sovereignty within the German administration. The newly inaugurated center was established as a part of the broader digital strategy of the Land Berlin, intending to provide a critical advisory role to the Berlin administration in the adoption and integration of open source solutions, advocating for digital sovereignty through the use of open source software and open standards. This initiative underscores a shift toward greater control over digital resources, echoing Germany's strategic move to enhance administrative autonomy and reduce dependency on proprietary software providers.

The establishment of such centers indicates a significant allocation of resources aimed at developing and sustaining open source capabilities within public administration. It only underscores the strategic importance of open source at the public level.

But why?

The mission definition of the Sovereign Tech Agency (STA) states that digital sovereignty cannot be achieved without a robust open source ecosystem. The agency started as a fund in October 2022 and was fully financed by the German Federal Ministry for Economic Affairs and Climate Action. With €11.5 million available for 2023 and another €17 million in 2024, we can verify from such numbers that they are correct in affirming this. The fund is a pioneer in supporting open digital infrastructure and foundational technologies that enable the creation of other software, such as libraries and standards. Their mission articulated well the need for and importance of such a fund: "The Sovereign Tech Fund supports the development, improvement, and maintenance of open digital infrastructure. Our goal is to sustainably strengthen the open source ecosystem. We focus on security, resilience, technological diversity, and the people behind the code." In other words, the biggest value of the STA is that they are focused on maintaining critical infrastructure while similar funding is focused on new features and new software, which are great, but the STA is really helping with the sustainability of what is already in use.

Although € 17 million per year seems like a lot, it is not nearly enough to cover all the costs, including the technical and human resource behind the code that sustains our business and digital sovereignty. But how much is needed to make open source sustainable and sustain the so-desired digital sovereignty? In February 2024, Tobie Langel reached a number: $ 1 billion per year.

At the State of Open Conference[20] in London, Tobie shared an interesting idea about how we should fund open-source projects. He thinks we need to rethink how money is spent, focusing on creating new features and maintaining what's already there. Right now, a lot of funding goes toward building new stuff, but this overwhelms the people who maintain these projects. They end up having to keep many different features running, often getting burnt out because they don't have the resources to properly take care of the essential parts that everyone relies on. Tobie is basically saying we should look at open-source projects like any other kind of project. Just like with anything else, if we want these projects to grow and last, we need to invest in their maintenance, not just their development. It's about making sure that the foundation is solid so everything doesn't fall apart down the line.

I've been following Tobie for years, actively proposing methodologies to make open source more equitable and sustainable.

In 2022, at FOSS Backstage, he gave a talk on "Does open source need its own Priority of Constituencies?"[21] in which he proposes a system, based on W3C's priority of constituencies[22] as a decision making way

---

[20] The talk called "$ 1 Billion for Open Source Maintainers" was recorded and its accessible on YouTube at https://www.youtube.com/watch?v=oB-v2_YnrHk

[21] Talk recording is accessible at https://www.youtube.com/watch?v=6YTcILOAEZY

[22] W3C Design Principles https://www.w3.org/TR/design-principles/#priority-of-constituencies

that considers different people and yet creates limits to enable conflicts resolution in an open project. As open source has permeated every corner of technology, the landscape of its constituencies has also changed: from a small community of users in a time when the lines between users and developers were blurred, because effectively utilizing software often required programming skills, to a today's ecosystem that includes a wide array of participants: from independent and corporate contributors to open source software vendors, from developers integrating open source into proprietary products to end-users who interact with software without any understanding of its origins, and also those indirectly affected by open source software without ever directly using it, cloud providers, and everything that interfaces with software.

The W3C's priority of constituencies is founded on the ethical principles[23] that recognize the web as a profound platform designed to empower an equitable, informed, and interconnected society. The web's purpose has been and should continue to be a facilitator of communication and knowledge-sharing for everyone. The order of constituencies is crucial because it provides a guideline for making necessary trade-offs during the web's development.

This guideline is about always prioritizing user needs above all others. It acts as a compass, guiding decisions when balancing the various factors that impact web development. The document acknowledges the enormous impact that any change can have, potentially affecting the lives of a vast number of users, "and may have a profound impact on any person's life."

The order of priorities is straightforward: user needs come first, followed by the needs of web page authors, then user agent implementors, specification writers, and lastly, theoretical purity. However, this principle is not absolute. User agents must prioritize their finite engineering

---

[23] Ethical Web Principles https://www.w3.org/TR/ethical-web-principles/

resources, influencing how features are developed for authors. Similarly, specification writers also face resource limitations, and theoretical concerns must consider the underlying needs of all these groups.

Considering the multifaceted ecosystem that open source is today, this priority may not be as straightforward as it is for the Internet. However, Tobie poses a critical question: when conflicts arise among these diverse groups, whose interests should take precedence, and why? He pointed out that neither the traditional Four Freedoms of free software nor the Open Source Definition (OSD) provides clear guidance on how to prioritize these competing interests. The priority of constituencies could be a framework in which the different stakeholders are prioritized in open source projects, emphasizing that while everyone's input is valuable, the project's longevity and health should guide decision-making.

What would that look like for open source then? This is how Tobie proposes it: first, we should have a look at who exactly are the main stakeholders when we think of open source software. At the heart, we have maintainers. We also have contributors to the project. Then we have app developers, who are people using the software to build applications. Next, we have cloud infrastructure, which is deploying open source software so app developers can use it. Then we have end users, people actually using the software. Finally, we have people because when we think about software, we can use a piece of software to do something for someone who isn't using that software but is impacted by it.

This is the example Tobie offers us to explain about the people impacted by the software: imagine you're walking down the street, and there is a camera filming you and using AI to identify you. You're technically not using the software, but it is being used on you, and it impacts you because maybe you didn't want people to know you were walking down that street, or you're in a surveillance state, which you're really concerned about.

This whole setup ties back to what Benjamin Bratton talks about in *The Stack*, which I explored in Chapter 1. The book maps out this idea of a layered global system where each layer affects the others in complex ways. In this world, a user isn't just a person; it's any interaction between parts of the system, human or not. So, when we think about open source in the context of *The Stack*, we start to see how everything connects. It's not just about the software or who's coding; it's about this massive, intertwined system where what happens at one level can ripple through to all the others. It's a reminder that in today's world, our actions and the technologies we develop are deeply interwoven, impacting a wide array of individuals and systems—sometimes in ways we don't even realize.

In short, the priorities of constituencies in open source could be ordered as such: people ➤ end users ➤ app developers ➤ cloud infrastructure ➤ contributors ➤ maintainers ➤ theoretical purity. That's what an open source priority of constituencies would look like.

Also, compared to the priorities of constituencies in the web context, Tobie reminds us that this framework won't solve all the open source problems. One key issue for the web is that if you want to move the work as upstream as possible toward the spec editors, you quickly realize this implies that spec editors have a lot more work to do than implementers. Implementers have a lot more work to do than authors, and authors have a lot more work to do than end users. This setup works if the economic situation of all players matches this structure. End users are just people on the web who tend to have fewer financial resources compared to a corporation. Moving to authors, which in W3C lingo means web developers, software vendors are usually small corporations and better off financially than individual end users. Implementers, such as browser makers like Microsoft, Apple, and Google, have significantly more money.

However, when we move to spec editors, although many of them work for implementers, there are also invited experts by the W3C who contribute because they care about the specs. These experts often work in their own time or as freelancers with little financial support. Additionally, some organizations could benefit from being involved in the spec editing process but lack the means to contribute.

We quickly realize there's a huge discrepancy in resources between implementers and spec editors. To address this, money needs to flow upward to help spec editors take on a larger share of the work, which benefits the whole chain and moves all the work as upstream as possible.

Moving this back to open source and thinking about money, we notice a similar problem again. This makes the priority of constituencies not only a direction for where work should move and who to prioritize when there are conflicts of interest but also highlights discrepancies in the economic situation of different stakeholders and how that impacts the overall ecosystem's health, which is at the heart of the open source's lack of sustainability all of those models are trying to address.

It is from this model of thinking where fairness is sought by considering all those involved and affected, yet with awareness of certain weights and factors that lead a project to maturity and stability, that Tobie reaches the $1 billion mark.

Tobie's calculation for allocating $1 billion annually to open source maintainers is based on the total global expenditure on software development. He references an estimated 16 million professional developers worldwide with an average annual salary of $65,000. Multiplying these figures, he arrives at a total expenditure of approximately $1 trillion per year on software development. Tobie suggests that allocating just 0.1% of this amount, which is $1 billion, could significantly support the sustainability and security of open source projects.

When we see this fraction as a block graphic, Tobie questions the audience again: is it really too much? Effectively paying the developers behind the code not as full-time but for maintenance work, $1 billion, he says, is "pocket money" when you actually see the value of open source.

The question of how to share those resources and where the money would come from still remains, but Tobie offers some practical solutions. He is proposing a structured approach to open source maintenance, where maintenance is organized as dedicated team efforts rather than ad hoc tasks managed through informal channels like Slack. He suggests creating dedicated practices for maintenance, providing proper training and management for maintainers, and establishing clear career paths. For smaller projects, he envisions fractional maintenance roles where resources can be shared across projects. The focus of this maintenance work would include security, support and training, tooling and infrastructure, bug triaging, release engineering, documentation, and compliance.

Tobie believes this approach would greatly benefit maintainers, offering part-time opportunities that are currently hard to find. In the current tech landscape, you either work for a big tech company or struggle to navigate an ad hoc gig economy style if you want to work in open source. Many people in open source face challenges because they are not well-aligned with the ethos of larger tech companies and lack other options.

The management of the funding would involve dedicated legal entities, which could include a mix of existing open source foundations, new for-profit or nonprofit organizations, and platforms like Open Collective. These entities would be responsible for hiring and supporting maintainers, organizing dedicated maintenance practices, and ensuring proper management and career development paths for maintainers. This structured approach aims to provide a sustainable and organized way to manage and allocate the funding, addressing the specific needs of different open source projects and ensuring the effective maintenance and security of the open source ecosystem.

Tobie's insights from the State of Open Conference and FOSS-Backstage, along with his ongoing work to rethink existing frameworks—such as prioritizing constituencies—highlight the importance of reevaluating the funding structure for open-source projects. He stresses the necessity of investing in the maintenance of existing software rather than focusing solely on developing new features. This approach not only alleviates the burden on maintainers but also ensures that the essential components everyone relies on are sustainably supported.

His advocacy for structured maintenance as a fundamental aspect of funding demonstrates a deep understanding of both the challenges and potential of open source to foster and strengthen digital sovereignty. Tobie sets the stage for exploring how open source can serve as a practical tool against structural inequalities. He is not alone in this mission; we will also hear from others who are deeply committed to harnessing the transformative potential of open source as a genuine solution to technological and social disparities. At its core, open source is a tool designed against asymmetry.

Open Source As a Real Possibility Against Asymmetry

2. We reaffirm our desire and commitment to build a people-centred, inclusive and development-oriented Information Society, premised on the purposes and principles of the Charter of the United Nations, international law and multilateralism, and respecting fully and upholding the Universal Declaration of Human Rights, so that people everywhere can create, access, utilize and share information and knowledge, to achieve their full potential and to attain the internationally agreed development goals and objectives, including the Millennium Development Goals.

3. We reaffirm the universality, indivisibility, interdependence and interrelation of all human rights and fundamental freedoms, including the right to development, as enshrined in the Vienna Declaration. We also reaffirm that democracy, sustainable development, and respect for human rights and fundamental freedoms as well as good governance at all levels are interdependent and mutually reinforcing.

10. We recognize that access to information and sharing and creation of knowledge contributes significantly to strengthening economic, social and cultural development, thus helping all countries to reach the internationally agreed development goals and objectives, including the Millennium Development Goals. This process can be enhanced by removing barriers to universal, ubiquitous, equitable and affordable access to information. We underline the importance of removing barriers to bridging the digital divide, particularly those that hinder the full achievement of the economic, social and cultural development of countries and the welfare of their people, in particular, in developing countries.

Resolutions adopted by The World Summit on the Information Society (WSIS), Tunis Phase,[24] at its Eighth Plenary Meeting, 18 November, 2005.

We have just read about open source as infrastructure, but I ask you, dear reader: what better represents our spinal structure as culture?

Back in the early 2000s, Brazil was a hotspot of cultural and technological revolution, with Gilberto Gil at the forefront as the Minister of Culture. During his tenure from 2003 to 2008, Gilberto Gil significantly promoted free software and digital inclusion. Picture this: Brazil, a vibrant country known for its rich music and unique cultural heritage, but also grappling with stark economic disparities. Under Gil's leadership, there was a palpable shift toward embracing open-source technology—a move that might seem technical but was deeply cultural at its core. Under his leadership, Brazil's push for open innovation and digital sovereignty became part of a broader narrative of self-determination and social justice.

Gilberto Gil wasn't just any politician. Gilberto Gil is a Brazilian singer and songwriter born in Bahia and is one of the pioneers of the Tropicália movement. Bahia, a northeastern Brazilian state that served as the primary entry point for the largest forced migration in history—enslaved Africans—bears the indelible marks of Portuguese colonization that

---

[24] The full general assembly document can be read at https://documents. un.org/doc/undoc/gen/n06/254/42/img/n0625442.pdf

established profound socioeconomic inequalities continuing to shape its cultural landscape and contemporary social challenges. Tropicália was a revolutionary cultural movement in Brazil during the late 1960s that combined traditional Brazilian music with international influences like rock and roll, psychedelia, and avant-garde art, creating a new, politically charged musical style that challenged Brazil's military dictatorship, in other words, a form of cultural resistance against the authoritarian regime in Brazil during that era. An outspoken advocate for social justice, environmental sustainability, and the promotion of Afro-Brazilian culture, Gil is a beloved figure in Brazil, and his lyrics often address issues such as racism, poverty, and political oppression.

As a pop star turned minister, as expected, he was not someone sitting in an office. He was someone with power actively involved in the communities, often seen interacting closely with local artists and technology advocates. His approach was quite unconventional. While traditional politicians might focus on regulations and policies, Gil was strumming a guitar, literally tuning into the rhythm of the Brazilian people's needs and aspirations.

The government in which Gil served as Minister of Culture was one of intense economic and social reforms. Aiming to decentralize the economic and cultural power traditionally concentrated in the capitals of the Southeast, the government sought to bring jobs, education, and culture to the most remote areas from north to south, east to west, across this vast, continental-sized country. This approach created the opportunity for the technological systems supporting this government to be more open, aligning with the principles of free software.

It was not just about saving on software costs but about fostering a breeding ground for innovation and independence from costly foreign software licenses. There's a background recounted in an article written by *Wired* magazine[25] in 2004 about Gil and his connection with the free

---

[25] Interview can be read at: https://www.wired.com/2004/11/linux-6/

software movement. The article recounts Brazil's daring approach at the end of the 1990s to afford AIDS treatment to a wider population when the country was facing a daunting challenge: an alarming rate of HIV infections and the prohibitive costs of patented drugs. Brazil's government decided to stand up to big pharma in a bold move that would redefine the global pharmaceutical landscape. Wired tells us that when drug companies refused to reduce prices, José Serra, then Health Minister, threatened to break drug patents and produce the medication locally, which led Merck and eventually Roche to cut prices dramatically. This was a pioneering step toward making essential medicines accessible to all Brazilians, not just those who could afford them.

This spirit of defiance was mirrored in the realm of digital technology under Gil's watch. The government's adoption of open-source software was not just a cost-saving measure; it was a declaration of Brazil's intent to forge its own path, free from the heavy hand of international software giants. This approach extended into the broader cultural sphere, where Gil envisioned Brazil unshackled by the restrictive norms of global intellectual property rights.

During this period, a unique "tinker" culture emerged in Brazil, closely tied to the government's push for digital inclusion. The terms "tinkers," "hackers," and "makers" fit well within the Brazilian context, largely because of the deeply ingrained culture of gambiarra[26]—sometimes translated as "cultural hotspots"—a Brazilian Portuguese word that captures the creative, informal solutions people come up with to address everyday life and infrastructure challenges. In a country mostly known and used for raw materials, research and innovation are not traditionally fomented, and economic barriers limit access to technology. Brazilians

---

[26] For a better understanding about the meaningful cultural significance of this word, read Gabriel Menotti's article "Gambiarra And The Prototyping Perspective" https://www.medialab-matadero.es/sites/default/files/import/ftp_medialab/5/5379/5379_4.pdf

have developed their own ways of adapting and repurposing technology. Reverse engineering and exploring closed systems have become both a political and economic necessity.

For this reason, "tinkers" in Brazil often carry a political significance, creating numerous hacker and maker spaces across the country. These spaces brought together individuals who, when the opportunity arose, began collaborating with the government on digital inclusion initiatives around and through the continental-sized country. This collaboration represented a unique alliance aimed at technological empowerment, where the open-source community played a significant role in shaping national policies—a rare achievement on the global stage.

In the broader picture, Brazil, under Gil's cultural stewardship, was making a bold statement for the global scenario. By advocating for open-source software and rejecting the stringent IP regimes championed by wealthier nations, Brazil was carving out a path not just for itself but as a leader for other developing nations. This wasn't just about technology; it was about asserting a national identity, one that values creativity, accessibility, and autonomy over corporate profits and rigid control. Gil's efforts were emblematic of Brazil's broader aspirations to reshape not just national but global policies on technology and intellectual property. Brazil championed a model where knowledge and technology were viewed as public goods, accessible to everyone rather than locked behind the gates of profit-driven corporations. This stance was particularly poignant in a world where access to technology increasingly dictated social and economic opportunities.

One of the key initiatives during Gil's tenure was the creation of Pontos de Cultura (Culture Points), a decentralized, Brazil-wide community center equipped with free software technology to promote cultural and digital activities. These points served as hubs of digital inclusion, providing internet access and digital tools to underserved communities. Millions of Brazilians accessed technological and cultural resources that were previously inaccessible, and workshops, from basic digitals, literally targeting the youngest and the elderly, were free and abundant, aiming to fill the knowledge gap.

The Ministry also adopted open licenses, such as Creative Commons, to facilitate the distribution and use of cultural content, promoting greater visibility and participation in global cultural circuits. International visibility was enhanced when Gilberto Gil appeared on the cover of *Wired* magazine and was present on the internet and open technology forums, highlighting Brazil as an example of governmental adoption and promotion of open technologies.

The Casa Brasil Project, launched in 2005, was another initiative aimed at promoting digital and social inclusion in low-income regions. Community centers provided access to the internet, digital training, and free software tools for content creation and sharing. In partnership with local governments and civil society organizations, these centers offered spaces for education and community development, including libraries, reading rooms, audiovisual workshops, and cultural activities. Casa Brasil integrated digital inclusion with cultural and social development, fostering citizenship and community participation.

It was through projects like these that I got to know and become involved with free software, and I met two important figures who were instrumental in promoting and implementing these projects: Angelo Pixel and Dr. Felipe Schmidt Fonseca. Recently, they joined me at the UN headquarters to participate in the OSPOs for Good event I mentioned before.

In a conversation with Angelo Pixel—with whom I have traveled across Brazil and through the Amazon region—about whether teaching audiovisual with free software or implementing open source hardware in communities to test water quality, he recounts how the government, under Lula's first presidency, adopted open source as a cost-effective, transparent, and collaborative approach to technology. He shares his personal journey of organizing events that combined open source with multimedia and art, which eventually led to his involvement with the Ministry of Culture.

Angelo Pixel points out that transitioning the government's infrastructure from proprietary to free software was challenging. He highlights issues such as resistance within and outside the government and the adaptation difficulties faced by government employees who were accustomed to proprietary systems like Windows. He also mentions the huge bureaucratic hurdles and the necessity of aligning free software initiatives with the existing legal framework for government procurements, which was not initially designed to accommodate the collaborative and decentralized nature of open source projects.

However, what remains are not the challenges but the successes of these initiatives, such as the widespread adoption of free software in various government departments and the empowerment of communities through projects like Pontos de Cultura. He emphasizes the transformative impact these projects had on millions of Brazilians, providing them with access to technology and digital tools that were previously inaccessible. Angelo Pixel also shares anecdotes about the collaborative atmosphere and the sense of validation that community members felt when their open source efforts were recognized and supported by the government.

He highlights the long-term impact of these initiatives, noting how the seeds planted during Gilberto Gil's time continue to influence cultural and technological practices in Brazil. Angelo Pixel reflects on the ongoing relevance of these projects, the continued challenges in maintaining them, and the importance of fostering a collaborative culture within both the government and the broader community. He expresses a deep sense of fulfillment in seeing the lasting positive effects of the work done during that period and the empowerment it brought to many individuals and communities.

Felipe Fonseca, who recently published his PhD thesis "Generous Cities," proposes an alternative approach to handling excess materials. He promotes the development of commons-based systems to collectively identify and realize the value of excess materials through reuse practices to benefit local communities, organizations, and businesses. Fonseca also recalls this period in Brazil.

He explains that the integration of free software into the Brazilian government was driven by a blend of expertise and serendipity, acknowledging the critical role of visionaries like Gilberto Gil, who brought contemporary issues to the forefront of cultural policies. Fonseca shares his experiences of engaging with international and local projects that promoted digital culture and open source, noting the significant influence of these initiatives on global and local scales.

Fonseca also reflects on the broader implications of open source beyond mere technology, touching on cultural, social, and economic aspects. He discusses the paradox of open source being both normalized and diluted in its revolutionary potential. His involvement in projects like MetaReciclagem and his participation in international forums illustrate the dynamic and often contentious nature of promoting open source principles within different cultural and political contexts.

Let me step back and tell you about MetaReciclagem because the project itself tells a lot about Fonseca and his ideals. MetaReciclagem is a fascinating project that emerged in Brazil in the early 2000s, blending digital inclusion, sustainability, and free software culture into a social project aimed at empowering people. It started with a simple yet powerful idea: why not take old, discarded technology—like computers, phones, and other electronic devices—and repurpose them in ways that benefit communities? Of course, this is embedded in the already mentioned gambiarra spirit, where people are known for their resourcefulness and ability to come up with creative, do-it-yourself solutions. The project is community-driven; it encourages folks to learn how to take apart and reassemble computers, experiment with open-source software, and use these skills to make a real difference in their communities. It operates as a decentralized network, with people and collectives all over Brazil sharing knowledge and resources to foster digital inclusion and sustainability. There's no top-down direction here; instead, it's all about local initiatives. The people involved decide how to use the refurbished technology to tackle the challenges they face in their own communities. This might mean setting up computer labs in underprivileged areas, using tech to support local arts and culture, or creating educational programs that teach coding and digital literacy.

Over the years, MetaReciclagem has had a significant impact. It shows how technology can be used as a tool for social change, especially in a country like Brazil, where access to technology isn't always easy. The project has inspired similar initiatives and contributed to a broader conversation about how we can use technology to build more inclusive and sustainable communities. It's a great example of how grassroots movements can reshape our thinking about technology, community, and what it means to be truly sustainable.

Ok, now back to Fonseca highlighting the blend of cultural and technological movements during Gilberto Gil's time as Minister of Culture. He describes how various groups, including those involved in electronic art, media activism, and social movements, converged to promote digital inclusion and progressive cultural policies. This integration was evident in events like Mídia Tática Brasil, which brought together hackers, artists, and activists to explore the potential of open technologies for social change.

He emphasizes the influence of key figures such as Cláudio Prado, who played a crucial role in promoting digital culture and free software within the Ministry of Culture. Prado's unconventional approach, which included organizing informal meetings and leveraging personal networks, helped to embed the principles of openness and collaboration in cultural policies. Fonseca acknowledges Prado's contribution despite his controversial nature, highlighting the importance of visionary leaders in driving change.

Felipe Fonseca's reflections from recent events in New York City further contextualize the evolving discourse around open source. He highlights the normalization of open source as an efficient and innovative development method yet notes a dilution of its revolutionary potential. Fonseca discusses the concept of "open source program offices" (OSPOs), specialized departments promoting the transition toward open source, primarily focusing on software but potentially expanding to other areas. Events like "OSPOS for Good" at the United Nations (mentioned in the beginning of this chapter) and "What's Next for Open Source?" by the Linux Foundation emphasized implementing OSPOs in government and international agencies, promoting open source as a crucial tool for addressing contemporary challenges, such as climate change and digital transformation.

Fonseca observed that while the UN events highlighted open source's potential to accelerate progress toward Sustainable Development Goals (SDGs), they also showcased structural challenges, such as formal discussions and limited interaction. Despite its venue's irony, the Microsoft event allowed for more interactive and meaningful networking. Fonseca emphasizes the importance of storytelling and community in open source, advocating for a broader understanding of open source beyond code or technology.

Many seeds were planted during Gil's administration, which is reflected in the impact and changes in the lives of all who were involved in these projects at that time—a reflection of myself, Felipe, and Angelo Pixel. However, the lack of economic and political stability in most South American countries also led to the discontinuation of such programs. What Europe is now striving to achieve under the banner of Digital Sovereignty was already accomplished 20 years ago in Brazil. Still, much of it has been lost due to a lack of support, the resurgence of closed and opaque systems in government, and a generational shift, where the new generation was neither taught nor experienced a diverse, collaborative, and collective system.

Fonseca's reflection on the OSPOs for Good event begins with a sense of frustration, noting that he's been repeating the same message for 20 years and had to travel to NYC, where there was minimal participation from the Global South—or, as one participant aptly put it, the Global Majority—as if collaboration and open source were new concepts. However, he pauses and recognizes that it's not about 20 years wasted but rather a spiral of progress and the necessity of retelling these stories. Some of those stories I am recounting and sharing with you here.

Paulo Schor: Opening Medicine and Science

If there's one thing that connects all of us—regardless of culture, geography, economic status, or any other category that separates us—it's the fact that we all inhabit bodies that, sooner or later, will fail. That's why I firmly believe that the knowledge to heal these bodies should be a cornerstone of what we must share without hesitation or restriction.

I am not alone in this conviction. I had the opportunity to learn from a very inspiring individual, Dr. Paulo Schor, whose vision about openness in healthcare and science has the potential to inspire others to rethink the way we approach these fields. Schor is the founder of MedHackers Brasil, a multidisciplinary tinkering group seeking innovation in healthcare. MedHackers uses a collaborative process to connect different sectors— academia, government, engineers, designers, and...people—and propose practical solutions for a more accessible and adaptable healthcare system, mostly considering what is relevant to local needs.

Schor's journey is rooted in his upbringing. His mother was a psychoanalyst, always reflecting on human behavior, while his father, a plastic surgeon, was focused on practical, hands-on work. This combination of thought and action became his foundation. He grew up participating in science fairs, where he explained complex ideas to others, and this experience shaped his belief that thinking must have practical utility. It's a concept that has followed him throughout his career—thinking isn't enough unless it leads to something that can be used.

Schor was never satisfied with purely theoretical academic work or research in basic sciences. He always sought ways to put ideas into action, steering away from traditional academic paths and instead focusing on combining medicine with engineering, a passion he didn't follow through to follow his family medicine footsteps.

One of the turning points in his career was finding others who were also trying out distinct collaborative and transdisciplinary strategies for healthcare. While in an exchange research time in Boston, he met David Miller, an engineer affiliated with MIT. This connection opened his eyes to the potential of merging medical practice with bioengineering. When Schor returned to Brazil, he met pioneers like Adolfo Lerner, who were already working on integrating engineering into medical fields. Together, they laid the groundwork for innovation in ophthalmology and bioengineering in Brazil.

Pioneer work comes along with frustrations, which Schor knows well, quoting a major disconnection between Brazilian healthcare and academic systems since the 1980s and 1990s. At that time, medical education was divided between research and patient care, and there was little space for innovation that could lead to scalable solutions. Schor's vision was to change that, placing the patient at the center of the innovation process. He wasn't just interested in treating individual patients or conducting research, he wanted to create technologies and processes that could make a broader impact and be accessible to many.

In 2005, MedHackers Brasil was founded, an initiative that brought together engineers, medical professionals, students, biologists, designers, makers, artists, and curious people in a collaborative space. The project was inspired by MIT's innovation workshops and adapted them to the Brazilian context. One of the core principles was co-development, where users and patients were involved from the start. The focus wasn't on who owned the idea or product but on how it could be adapted and used to benefit as many people as possible.

In order to propose something innovative, Schor compares two main models. The European model focuses on equity and accessibility, with the more commercial approach seen in the Unites States, yet neither seems ideal. For Schor, true sustainability means addressing systemic inequalities and finding collective solutions rather than focusing on expensive treatments for a few. He explained that the real challenge in healthcare isn't just developing treatments, it's making sure patients understand and follow through with them. This, for him, is where real complexity lies: not in creating the treatment itself but in ensuring that people can and will use it effectively.

Schor argues that the current system, with its heavy reliance on technology and short consultation times, undermines the most important thing: the doctor–patient relationship. According to Schor, the real strength of healthcare lies in listening to patients, ensuring they understand their treatment, and building a relationship based on mutual trust. This kind of interaction, he said, is more modern and necessary than any technological advancement.

Another key issue for Schor is the role of academia in society. He believes that universities have become disconnected from the communities they are meant to serve. For him, academia should be responsive to society's needs, producing solutions that have a real impact. He called for a shift in focus from what benefits institutions or individuals (often measured by patents or academic recognition) to what benefits the broader public. This shift, Paulo argues, is necessary for real innovation to take place. While patents are often seen as a mark of success, they can also limit the spread and development of new ideas. The current obsession with patents, particularly in Brazil, is misguided. He pointed out that countries like South Korea may produce a lot of patents, but this doesn't necessarily lead to better innovation. Instead, Schor supports a more open and collaborative approach, where ideas are shared, adapted, and built upon rather than locked away under restrictive intellectual property laws.

At the heart of Schor's vision is the idea that collective effort—bringing together different fields, communities, and voices—can drive meaningful change in healthcare. MedHackers embodies this approach. The goal isn't to claim ownership of ideas or products but to focus on how many people can benefit from them. This collaborative spirit is key to creating solutions that can scale and make a lasting impact on society.

Schor's vision for healthcare and innovation goes beyond technical achievements. He is focused on how we can transform systems to better serve society, and his work reflects that. The goal is impact over ownership—creating solutions that address real needs at a cost and scale that to make them accessible to all. This is the future of healthcare that we are striving to build together.

Pedro Medeiros: The Dualities of Open Source and Its Societal Implications

I first met Pedro Medeiros and Otto Heringer at a Campus Party in São Paulo in 2014. I was running a workshop on video mapping with open-source tools, and they were presenting Synbio Brasil and the possibilities of open science. As fellow USP students, we clicked immediately. Here we were, from different fields but sharing the same drive—to make knowledge accessible, to open up technology, and to find ways for people from all backgrounds to engage and create. It was one of those rare moments where paths crossed, and you realized that the mission to democratize knowledge can unite us across disciplines.

Pedro is an unquiet critical thinker: a biologist and bioinformatician from São Paulo's East Zone, whose journey in synthetic biology and open science has inspired me to apply open source to real social needs. For Pedro, synthetic biology is a means of questioning and shaping how technology can be more inclusive and purposeful. Like Paulo Schor's work in medicine, Pedro's path in science raises questions about who gets access to knowledge and who benefits from technological advances.

Pedro's introduction to open science didn't come from the usual technology fields. While he had some exposure to open-source tools through Linux, his first meaningful experience came through applied biology. As he recalls, access to proprietary scientific tools and resources was often limited by their cost, as dollar-based pricing placed essential resources beyond the reach of many in Brazil. "In Brazil, piracy became a tool of access," he explains. However, this approach offered only a one-sided experience: while they could use the software, they couldn't contribute back. For Pedro, open science was transformative because it offered a two-way interaction, allowing people in the Global South not just to consume but to actively shape scientific innovation.

Pedro perceived synthetic biology as a platform that embodies this philosophy. Synthetic biology, or Synbio, combines biology with engineering principles, allowing scientists to design and build new biological parts, devices, and systems. It's a relatively new field but one with massive potential across medicine, agriculture, and environmental science. When Pedro was at university, Synbio Brasil was a platform that sought to democratize access to these technologies, breaking down barriers for students, scientists, and curious minds across Brazil.

Things have changed, and Synbio Brasil is now a copyrighted brand with another purpose, but its origins trace back to the Synthetic Biology Club at the University of São Paulo (USP), founded in 2014 by biochemical engineering student André Herman. André and the club aimed to bring synthetic biology knowledge beyond the walls of the university. The club is still active in its mission as a student organization that promotes events and activities to make synthetic biology more accessible to the public. A major part of this mission involved the participation of USP students from different fields in iGEM (International Genetically Engineered Machine), an annual competition in synthetic biology in which students design, build, and test biological systems.

iGem was an excuse that allowed students to organize as a political community, gain access to university resources, and receive support from professors—a crucial advantage in Brazil, where academia and applied science often take separate paths. As Paulo Schor also observed, Brazilian academia tends to separate research from real-world application. Still, this organized club allowed students to be hands-on in labs, driven by curiosity and motivated to solve real-world problems. Through iGEM, Synbio Brasil could contribute to a global community while creating an open, impactful science experience.

However, for many participants from Brazil, the financial cost of entry is a huge challenge. The students, including Pedro, organized a few years of crowdfunding campaigns to cover the competition expenses, rallying together to create an experience that was by and for students. This effort allowed them to participate on their own terms, with their values and ideas front and center.

Otto Heringer, one of Synbio Brasil's first members, organizer, and fellow student, played a significant role in shaping the group's approach. Otto's emphasis on intellectual independence and pushing academic boundaries resonated deeply with Pedro, who shared an aversion to strict hierarchies in science. Their teaching assistant at the time, João Vitor Dutra Molino, also encouraged the group to learn through experience rather than dictating a strict path. This spirit of autonomy helped define the group's culture, where students could experiment, question, and collaborate without feeling bound by conventional academic structures.

Pedro appreciates the interdisciplinary nature of synthetic biology, especially within iGEM and Synbio Brasil. At their best, these spaces bring together students from diverse fields—biology, engineering, sociology, and the arts—to ask tough questions about the implications of their work. Reflecting on his early enthusiasm, Pedro admits that he was initially drawn to the technical aspects of synthetic biology. However, his colleagues' critiques of the broader social impacts of their work encouraged him to think more deeply. "I was captivated by the engineering magic of biology," he says, "but the tough questions raised by my peers have been crucial in shaping my thinking." For Pedro, the opportunity to engage with these questions has made him a more critical, reflective scientist.

Pedro observes that the culture around iGEM and synthetic biology in Brazil from a decade ago has shifted, increasingly driven by a commercial agenda. He questions the corporatization of open science, where large companies promote open-source projects not solely for the common good but as a business strategy to leverage unpaid contributions. This shift, he believes, undermines the initial ethos of collaborative science, turning open science into a tool for profit rather than progress.

A powerful example Pedro shares involves iFood, a prominent Brazilian food delivery company that has invested in a startup incubated at the University of São Paulo. While the startup hailed this investment as a success, Pedro saw another side. He criticizes the project's focus on business without acknowledging the labor exploitation underlying the gig economy. A BBC News Brasil[27] article clarifies this critique, "In a time of economic crisis and high unemployment, services like Uber, iFood, 99, and Rappi attract unemployed people with the promise of income...But the growth of these companies comes with criticism. Experts say these companies contribute to precarious working conditions, as they often do not follow labor laws." In other words, while such companies and their affiliated projects may appear successful from a tech perspective, Pedro sees a troubling human cost—one that is ignored in favor of profit.

In this comparison between tech "success" and social cost, Pedro emphasizes that the real impact of science and technology should be measured by the quality of life it supports, not just its profitability. He argues that open science should strive to lift the base rather than only enable the select few to "escape precarity," as he puts it. For Pedro, the goal should be to raise the standard for everyone involved, not merely to offer individual avenues out of poverty through corporate funding and limited opportunities.

---

[27] Article can be read here in Portuguese https://www.bbc.com/portuguese/brasil-48304340

This critique of synthetic biology in Brazil extends his concerns about how open science sometimes loses sight of its own ideals. While initially driven by a utopian vision of collaboration, Pedro observes how open science has, over time, adopted aspects of the very systems it once aimed to disrupt. He reflects on how the narrative of the "garage inventor"—the lone individual achieving success—reinforces a neoliberal myth that emphasizes individual triumph over collective progress. In this environment, technology, initially a collective tool, becomes a commodity for personal gain.

Pedro's perspective on equity intersects with Brazil's policy of affirmative action, which introduced racial quotas in universities to address long-standing inequalities. The policy has brought more Black and Indigenous students into higher education, creating a generation of scientists and professionals who represent Brazil's diversity. However, Pedro laments that these graduates are often recruited by international institutions, leading to a "brain drain" that prevents Brazil from reaping the full benefits of their talent. Despite this, he views affirmative action as an essential step in democratizing education and bringing new voices into spaces that have traditionally excluded them.

Even as Pedro's critical views sometimes place him at odds with mainstream academia and tech, he remains committed to advocating for change from within. He speaks of feeling like a "strange body" in these spaces—a person who belongs but still doesn't fit. There's an ongoing pressure to either assimilate or to serve as a token of diversity, which Pedro resists. "I could use my background as a badge, as a mestizo from the periphery entering the world of technology," he reflects, "but I find that disrespectful and alienating." For Pedro, the goal is not to be co-opted by these systems but to challenge and expand them.

Pedro believes that real change requires more than a few diverse faces in elite spaces. As he sees it, true progress will involve "opening fractures" within established structures, breaking down barriers to make room for voices that have long been silenced. This process won't be easy, he acknowledges. There will be conflict and discomfort as more people from diverse backgrounds enter these fields and push against the status quo.

In many ways, Pedro's vision for synthetic biology and open science parallels Paulo Schor's work in open medicine. Both seek to bridge the divide between who has access to scientific knowledge and who benefits from it. They challenge the conventional metrics of success, prioritizing collective empowerment and impact over individual gain. For Pedro, synthetic biology and open science are not just tools; they are pathways to a future where technology serves humanistic purposes grounded in equality and inclusion.

As we reflect on Pedro and Paulo's stories, we see a shared belief in the potential of open knowledge to transform not just individual lives but entire communities. Their work serves as a reminder that science, at its best, should lift the base, fostering a world where innovation isn't limited to the privileged few but shared across borders, cultures, and backgrounds.

Luciano Ramalho: Software As an Excuse for Collaboration and Solidarity

Luciano Ramalho's story brings us right back to the core of what open-source and free software stand for: autonomy, collaboration, and solidarity. For Ramalho, software isn't just about writing code; it's about creating spaces where people come together, share what they know, and build on each other's strengths. I connected with him during my master's research, where I set up an interdisciplinary lab at the USP engineering department meant for artists, engineers, biologists, and anyone curious to experiment with DIY (do-it-yourself) gadgets that explore body augmentation. Seeking support, I offered an exchange with Garoa Hacker Clube—Brazil's first hackerspace in São Paulo, of which Ramalho is one of the founders. I gave a workshop about how to make bread, and Ramalho taught us programming for microcontrollers. He embedded everyone with the spirit of open knowledge and community-driven learning that he's carried with him through decades in the field.

Ramalho got his start with software in the 1970s, but it was in the 1980s that he encountered free software. This was a turning point that reshaped his understanding of technology. Free software wasn't about transparency and remixing software code, it introduced a world where knowledge and tools could be shared openly, giving anyone who wanted it a chance to participate, a two-way, horizontal participation, as Pedro reminded. Figures like Linus Torvalds, who made the Linux kernel available for anyone to study and build on, and platforms like Wikipedia, which rely entirely on community contributions without corporate interference, are, to Ramalho, a defiance against the "neoliberal bubble" that prioritizes profit as the only motivator, revealing a model where people come together out of shared purpose, not financial gain.

Garoa Hacker Clube, founded in 2011, was Brazil's first hackerspace, and it's still active in São Paulo today. It's an open environment where people of all backgrounds gather to experiment, share skills, and learn from one another. The club's structure is built on member support, with small contributions that keep it going without corporate or government funding. This independence is strategic and crucial for its autonomous sustainability; it allows Garoa to stay true to its values and be a space where curiosity and community matter most. This self-sustaining approach has given Garoa resilience that's rare in community spaces, especially in the tech world.

Reflecting on the early days of open-source in Brazil, particularly during the first Lula administration, when the government actively supported free software, Ramalho reminds us of the flourishing of initiatives and events like the Fórum Internacional Software Livre (FISL). FISL attracted people from Brazil, Latin America, and across the globe, but it was heavily reliant on public support. After Lula's departure, the event lost its strength, and since 2018, no other major free software event has taken place in Brazilian territory. When political priorities changed, many community initiatives lost their funding and momentum. Ramalho's takeaway? Real resilience comes from within the community itself, not from the top down.

Relying on government support or large corporate sponsorships can lead to dependency, making communities vulnerable to shifts in political and economic interests. Garoa Hacker Club made a conscious choice to avoid long-term dependence on any single sponsor. Although Mozilla once offered to support a makerspace in São Paulo, Garoa declined, recognizing that sustainable community action must be self-reliant.

In the context of sustainability, Luciano contrasts the approach of Brazil's Python community with that of the United States. In the United States, the Python Software Foundation (PSF) is run as a nonprofit with a governance model that emphasizes community involvement rather than corporate control. In Brazil, the goal is to keep Python events as accessible as possible, so even speakers pay for their tickets, reinforcing the community's independence and minimizing reliance on sponsorship. For Luciano, the principles of solidarity and autonomy are essential to building resilient communities. By keeping costs low and ensuring everyone contributes equally, the community can stay focused on inclusivity rather than profit.

For Luciano, solidarity is both a deeply human impulse and a practical choice, rooted in our natural inclination to support one another. Reflecting on recent political movements in Brazil, he recalls the gatherings during Bolsonaro's presidency, when groups camped outside military barracks calling for a military intervention to overturn election results. Many of these people, especially older women, even chained themselves to tanks, pleading for a coup. This disturbing scene seemed to ignore Brazil's own painful history of military dictatorship, marked by torture and repression against democracy. Luciano views this as a misguided expression of solidarity, where people found a sense of purpose and community but at the cost of advocating against democratic values.

For many in these camps, this was the first time they experienced a "wonderful sensation of solidarity," as Luciano puts it—a shared bond of mutual support, as they shared resources and looked out for each other. While he disagrees profoundly with their cause, he recognizes that the feeling of togetherness was real and meaningful to them. He sees a similar but more vital form of solidarity in Brazil's poorer communities, such as the favelas, where people rely on one another daily for survival in ways that contrast sharply with the individualism often seen in wealthier areas. For Luciano, open-source software taps into this same quality, creating spaces where people come together, not for profit or power, but to build something greater than themselves.

Yet even with its focus on openness, Garoa faces challenges, especially when it comes to inclusivity. The club has welcomed people from many backgrounds, but Ramalho admits that they've struggled to bring in more women and maintain their participation. He's not quite sure why and believes that sometimes creating an inclusive environment requires rethinking what openness looks like—perhaps even offering separate spaces for specific groups to engage comfortably. It's a concept that can conflict with traditional open-access ideas, but Ramalho sees it as necessary if the goal is a genuinely inclusive community.

As seen, his ideas about open-source reach far beyond just the technical. Ramalho often draws on the work of thinkers like Yochai Benkler, whose book *The Wealth of Networks* explores how collaborative projects challenge the traditional economic model that revolves around competition and profit. Benkler argues that open-source projects like Linux show that success doesn't have to be about market forces; instead, it can be driven by cooperation and shared goals. For Ramalho, this way is both sustainable and liberating. It allows people to come together not because they have to but because they want to. This is powerful. And for open-source communities to truly thrive, he believes they have to avoid relying too heavily on corporate or government support, which can introduce dependencies that erode their autonomy.

Another aspect Ramalho is passionate about is user experience, and he has a great story that highlights why this matters. Back in the 1990s, while installing Debian Linux on a custom-built computer, he found himself confronted with an endless list of CD-ROM drivers but no clear way to know which one he needed. After trying unsuccessfully to figure it out on his own, he finally had to call a friend for help. This experience made him realize how often developers overlook the practical challenges that users face. Spaces like Garoa, along with interdisciplinary labs, are vital in bridging this gap. When people from various fields come together, they bring different perspectives that can expose blind spots in software design, pushing developers to consider how real users experience their creations. For Ramalho, this diversity is what makes open-source spaces so essential—they bring together people who aren't just technically skilled but who also have a sense of what it's like to navigate technology as a user.

Teaching has also been a big part of Ramalho's work. In his 40s, he returned to university to study library science, driven by a desire to understand how knowledge can be organized and made accessible. His approach to teaching programming reflects this focus on accessibility. He talks about the "gesturality of programming," a term he uses to describe the physical and mental actions involved in coding, like switching screens or typing commands. These movements become second nature to experienced programmers but can feel intimidating to beginners. Ramalho believes that teaching programming isn't just about learning syntax; it's about helping students feel comfortable with the entire process, from the gestures to the logic.

His contribution to the programming world and education includes his book, *Fluent Python*, which is known for its depth and clarity. But while it's a valuable resource for seasoned programmers, Ramalho recognizes that there's still a need for beginner-friendly materials. This drive to make programming accessible to all reflects his broader vision that technology should be open, approachable, and shared.

When asked what is "open source" about, Ramalho brought tears to my eyes, saying "is all about autonomy and solidarity." Garoa Hacker Clube, as he describes it, is a place for "autodidact anonymous"—a community where people can learn and explore on their own terms while knowing they have support when they need it. For him, autonomy isn't about isolation; it's the freedom to pursue knowledge and creation within a supportive community. Open source, in Ramalho's world, is a balance of self-reliance and collective progress, a way to empower individuals and build connections that go far beyond the code.

Intersecting Visions: The Diverse Narratives of Open Source

The mosaic of voices and narratives presented in this chapter draws significant inspiration from Lucy Delap's thorough exploration of feminisms in her book *Feminisms: A Global History*. Delap offers a panoramic view of feminist movements, underscoring their complexity and the necessity of addressing multiple narratives to fully comprehend their scope and impact. She critiques the internal exclusions within feminism based on race, class, and sexuality, and how these exclusions shape the movement. This framework of understanding feminisms through a multifaceted lens informs my approach to discussing open source.

Inspired by Delap's methodology, I've explored the realm of open source through its philosophical roots in the free software movement, including the theoretical framework from the very controversial persona of Richard M. Stallman, the free software movement founder. His insights, emphasizing freedom over cost and user control over software, resonate with the broader implications of autonomy and power that Delap discusses in the context of feminist movements. The misunderstandings around open source and free software echo the misconceptions and internal conflicts within feminism, highlighting how both movements grapple with evolving identities and ideological purity versus practical considerations.

In weaving together personal stories from individuals who have influenced my journey in open source, I aim to illuminate the rich interplay of ideologies and cultural shifts that define and sometimes challenge the open source community. Each narrative serves as a microcosm of broader debates—about freedom, ownership, and community engagement—that are pivotal to understanding open source. These stories are not merely anecdotal but are emblematic of larger societal trends and ideological battles, much like the vignettes Delap uses to highlight key issues within feminisms.

By juxtaposing narratives such as a developer from a developing country advocating for open source for technological sovereignty against a Silicon Valley executive who views open source as a strategic business tool, I draw out the economic, social, and political dimensions of open source. This mirrors Delap's examination of feminist movements, where progress often meets resistance and where ideological battles are waged over practical realities.

This chapter, therefore, is not just a recounting of the evolution of open source but a deeper reflection on its nature as a cultural and technological phenomenon. By integrating insights from Delap's examination of feminisms, I emphasize the importance of recognizing open source as a complex, contested, and continually evolving field. My analysis encourages readers to consider how the detailed stories of individuals within open source are not isolated incidents but part of a broader narrative that reflects significant societal shifts and ideological currents.

In this way, I provide you, dear reader, with theoretical tools to link seemingly unrelated stories and to appreciate the significance of the finer details within these narratives. This approach not only enriches our understanding of open source but also frames it within a larger discourse on technology, power, and society, echoing the depth and complexity that Delap brings to her study of feminisms.

Where Do We Go from Here?

Let's pause and gather what we've excavated. This chapter began with the philosophical schism between free software and open source—not just terminological quibbling, but a profound political divergence. Stallman's free software vision centered user control and technological liberation, while open source reframed these principles in language that businesses could embrace without ideological discomfort. This shift wasn't merely semantic—it reflected a fundamental tension between liberation and accommodation, between revolution and evolution. Free software demanded ethical commitment; open source offered pragmatic alliance. Both now exist in uneasy symbiosis.

From this foundational tension, we traced open source's evolution across multiple domains. Thomas Steenberg and Tobie Langel illuminated its transformation from hobbyist pursuit to essential infrastructure. Companies now maintain entire Open Source Program Offices (OSPOs), recognizing that extracting value without contributing back creates unsustainable imbalance. And, of course, we can't ignore the financial angle. Open source has created real career opportunities and wealth. Money matters and this model generates wealth, creates opportunities for developers, and strengthens the ecosystem around open-source projects. So, there's a clear, business-backed need to recognize open source as a commitment, more than a cost-saving tactic - a critical resource that keeps the wheels turning.

Christian Bromann and Josh Goldberg, speaking from maintainer experience, emphasized that sustainability demands attention to the humans behind the code. Maintaining open-source code, much of which powers critical infrastructure, isn't easy, and it doesn't happen for free.

While open source has become foundational for business, there's often a gap between corporate use and community support, leaving maintainers with significant workloads and few resources. Bromann and Goldberg speak to the importance of structuring funding, recognition, and resources for maintainers so they can continue their work without burning out, keeping the ecosystem healthy for everyone involved.

In areas outside traditional tech, we see open source take on an equally transformative role. For instance, Pedro Medeiros has been part of projects in synthetic biology that bring open principles to scientific fields, challenging who gets to participate in creating new knowledge. His work pushes back against the "garage inventor" myth, showing that innovation doesn't come from individuals working alone but from communities empowered to learn, share, and build together. It's a powerful reminder that when knowledge is accessible and openly shared, it doesn't just benefit the privileged few—it can become a source of strength for people from all backgrounds.

Paulo Schor brings a similar perspective to healthcare, where he uses open principles to develop solutions that better meet local needs. His work with MedHackers Brasil exemplifies how open knowledge can make healthcare more effective and accessible by focusing on practical solutions that communities can adapt for themselves. For Paulo, open source is about creating healthcare tools that address specific, real-world problems, which becomes especially crucial in regions where traditional, top-down systems often fail to meet people's needs. These experiences emphasize that open source isn't just a technical model; it's a way to bridge gaps in fields where access can be life-saving.

Open source has also become rooted in a cultural movement. Angelo Pixel showed us how Brazil has used open source to decentralize power structures and reclaim technology adapted to regional needs in the farthest landscapes. MetaReciclagem is the perfect example, made for communities to repurpose discarded technologies, representing Brazil's "gambiarra" spirit—creative problem-solving with whatever's available. For many, open source is about making technology work for people in personal, meaningful ways.

Felipe Fonseca expands on this by noting that while open source is celebrated worldwide, we need to be mindful of who's included in that celebration. At a recent "OSPOs for Good" event, Fonseca saw how open source is often praised for addressing global issues, yet voices from the Global South were largely absent. This exclusion yields a crucial tension: open source can't be inclusive if it doesn't integrate values and participation from all regions and cultures, not just those of wealthier nations.

Open source thus becomes, as I've come to define it, "a real possibility to shift the power axis from a narrow group of homogeneous leaders to a diverse and multicultural one." This isn't mere idealism, it is a practical recognition that genuine diversity—structural, not cosmetic—transforms both process and outcome, generating solutions attuned to broader human needs.

This chapter has illustrated that open source is, as I like to define it, *a real possibility to shift the power axis from a narrow group of homogeneous leaders to a diverse and multicultural one*—it took me a minute to come up with that. Still, I love it, don't you? It's about giving voice and agency to communities previously excluded from the tech landscape, creating an ecosystem that values autonomy, accessibility, and solidarity, as Luciano Ramalho reminds us. But it's also clear that to succeed, open source needs to confront its own limitations, acknowledging and dismantling structures that replicate the very power imbalances it set out to change.

This chapter was based on interviews with people who have shaped my journey in open source, showing me its many faces and teaching me what it means to build something bigger than ourselves. I finish it by enormously thanking them: Angelo Pixel, Christian Bromann, Felipe Fonseca, Josh Goldberg, Luciano Ramalho, Paulo Schor, Pedro Medeiros, Thomas Steenberg, and Tobie Langel for showing me how powerful and transformative open source can be.

CHAPTER 3

Unraveling Diversity and Labor Issues

I won't sugarcoat it—this is a heavy chapter. You can skip it if you wish, but I encourage you to embrace this challenge and dive deep into the following pages as they offer a succinct summary of a decade's worth of research into the complexities behind social movements' demands. As a result, the next chapter, a very practical and applicable one, will serve instead of another template you copy and paste blindly and will serve you as an effective, valuable guide, helping you to easily and consciously implement all the essential elements to increase diversity on your open source project.

Writing it made me feel like I am being punched in the stomach almost every line as, one way or another, we are together, both being harmed from and causing the same harm I am here unveiling. But oh well, better understand it and be able to address it, than keep it under the rug. So take a deep breath, make yourself a nice, cozy cup of tea, and let yourself be immersed in this heap of academic discussions. After this chapter, I hope, you will be deeply transformed and will be able to address issues around you—the ones that quite often come as something antsy but you can't quite grasp—with some good basic tools. Ready? Let's do this.

Yes, open source can be great, but it has also failed. While we are not able to unveil underlying issues, we will keep piling up at a point of no return. As it has grown significantly, as we have discussed extensively, we

P. Oliveira, *Diversifying Open Source*, https://doi.org/10.1007/979-8-8688-0769-5_3

need first to understand that scale is essential—not just the scale but the system underneath it, as Georgina Voss shows in her book *Systems Ultra*.

There's a bitter irony at the heart of open source: a movement born to liberate users has itself become a vehicle for new forms of exploitation. While promising freedom and collaboration, the scaling of open source into a trillion-dollar industry has exposed fundamental contradictions. The very openness that enables innovation also facilitates extraction— corporations harvest immense value from community labor while contributing minimally to sustainability. Meanwhile, the movement's democratic rhetoric masks deeply entrenched power structures that systematically exclude marginalized voices. This isn't an oversight; it's the predictable outcome of a system that adopted revolutionary language while preserving the underlying power relations it claimed to challenge.

While the open source ecosystem is widely perceived as a large, unified front, it is, in reality, a patchwork of diverse project types. In *Working in Public*, Nadia Eghbal categorizes open source projects into distinct classes: Federations, Clubs, Stadiums, and Toys. She creates a matrix matching high or low growth of users versus contributors. This framework dissects the diverse ecosystem, demonstrating variations in operations and governance models. It provides a structured approach to systematically compare and address specific issues rather than becoming overwhelmed by the range of differences.

Toys are small projects with low contributor and user growth. These personal-end projects embody individual GitHub repositories started for development or exploration. Initially not intended for broad use, they can evolve into something significant if they gain community traction. This includes the one-off projects you put on GitHub and never expect anyone else to use.

Clubs are projects with low user growth and high contributor growth. They are the community manager's dream and how we usually think open source is: cozy collaborations of passionate participants. In reality, clubs cater to more niche interests, such as those of a specific scientific community such as SciPy, which operates on a smaller scale, maintained by a tight-knit group of experts deeply familiar with each other's work and the project's core elements. These projects thrive on close relationships and a deep mutual understanding that enhances collaborative efficiency.

Stadiums are projects with high user growth and low contributor growth. Their rapidly expanding user base typically depends on few maintainers. Due to low contributor growth, these projects tend toward centralized social structures, with maintainer availability becoming the primary bottleneck.

Finally, at the further end of the scale spectrum are the Federations, which have high user and contributor growth. In Eghbal's own words, federation type projects are *"more complex to manage from a governance standpoint, so they tend to develop processes—voting, leadership positions, foundations, working groups, and technical councils—that address coordination issues within their contributor community. These contributors, in turn, make decisions for a broader constituency of passive users."*

Eghbal's classification helps us better understand open source complexities, which depend not just on quantified scale but significantly on relational ties and community quality.

This framework contextualizes discussions of equity and exploitation. A small, volunteer-run library faces vastly different power dynamics than a corporate-backed platform with millions of users. Yet across all categories, patterns of exclusion and extraction mirror broader societal inequities. As scale increases, so does the urgency of addressing who benefits from these community-created resources.

It is critical to understand the significance of scale in this matter, as Voss will shortly describe: scale is political; it is social and cultural. Scale profoundly influences our perceptions and imaginations. Small things evoke affection and endearment, seeming lovable and approachable. Conversely, immense entities engender intimidation and oppression, appearing tyrannical and overwhelming. This dichotomy shapes our emotional responses and alters how we interact with the world. Open source embodies both, creating a paradoxical landscape: formed by small, lovable projects people join out of care, while simultaneously existing as a huge, often tyrannical structure embedded in and reproducing existing power imbalances through its systemic invisibility.

It is not uncommon to hear the colloquial term "benevolent dictatorship" to address the style of some open source governance models. This is a controversial model in the context of open source's democratic ethos, and the term itself is an oxymoron, juxtaposing the notion of kindness with authoritarian rule. While efficient for decision-making, this model frequently contradicts the principles of open collaboration and transparency, as it centralizes power with individuals or small groups, creating strange power dynamics in itself. When, on top of that, the governance type is not communicated ahead, this opaque centralization can obscure the assumed collaborative nature of the "open," masking how decisions are made and who gets to make them.

The concept of rupture is often associated with decentralized technologies, a metaphor for transformative change; however, open source, as the heart and driver of our technology, may require instead continuous, thoughtful reevaluation of how communities govern themselves and share power, as its own system.

The Invisible Architecture That Shapes Us

But what do we mean by "system"? Clifford Siskin (2016) argues that "system" emerged as a powerful conceptual tool that fundamentally reshaped how we organize knowledge and understand the world. For Siskin, systems are "genre machines" that actively produce and constrain what we can know and how we can know it. A system doesn't describe reality, it shapes how we perceive it, what questions we can ask, and what solutions seem possible. In open source, the systemic frameworks we adopt—from governance models to contribution metrics—are not plainly organizational work; they determine whose contributions count, whose voices matter, and ultimately, who belongs.

The understanding of "system" as both a knowledge form and a power structure helps us see why the seemingly neutral technical and organizational choices have profounder implications. When we examine the historical development of system as a concept, we can better understand its influence on contemporary open source dynamics.

According to Voss, the idea of a "system" is inherently tied to the Enlightenment, a period marked by an intense pursuit of knowledge, reason, and scientific inquiry. Thinkers and scientists began to see the world as a complex but decipherable system governed by natural laws that could be understood and manipulated through reason and scientific methods. This shifted from viewing the world as a mystery controlled by divine forces to a framework where everything was interconnected and could be explained through cause and effect.

System as a concept took on a new dimension as the world entered the Industrial Age, beginning to encompass natural phenomena and human-created entities like factories and, later, computer networks. The systematization of production processes maximized efficiency, predictability, and scalability. This mechanistic systems view primarily concerned outputs, efficiency, and control, mirroring the factory model in societal and economic structures.

Cybernetics, founded by Norbert Wiener in the mid-20th century, advanced the systems concept by focusing on understanding and managing complex systems through feedback loops and self-regulating mechanisms. It aimed to create a universally applicable theoretical framework.

Cybernetics reinterpreted "system," drawing from the Enlightenment philosophy's tendency to abstract concepts. Early biologists recognized living forms exhibited distinct behaviors compared to mechanical structures, yet cyberneticists repurposed their insights. Biological systems' diversity was simplified into cybernetic language of feedback, control, and homeostasis. Everything, assumedly, integrated into the cybernetic framework—emerging redefined, understood, and manageable.

Promoted as a "universal language," cybernetics captivated government and military organizations by promising integration of biological principles, autonomous machines, and computational languages. This predictably designable and controllable ideology resonated globally, influencing military strategies, economic frameworks, and political structures. Cybernetics provided the foundation for Cold War control technologies, offering a structured lens through which the world was increasingly viewed—a system amenable to technological management.

The US military, in particular, recognized the significant value in this synthesis, envisioning a more effective war machine. Over two decades, substantial funding supported cybernetic research; however, the transition from theory to practical application revealed severe limitations. Grounded in abstract mathematical and informational theories, cybernetics struggled when faced with the unpredictable complexities of human behavior and culture, ultimately leading to its decline.

Outside the United States, cybernetics raised different questions. Chile's Project Cybersyn, initiated under President Salvador Allende in the early 1970s, applied cybernetic principles to national economy management using telex machines interconnected with Cyberstride software. This system enabled real-time data collection and processing for efficient resource allocation while respecting worker autonomy and minimizing bureaucratic control.

However, the project faced multiple challenges that led to its eventual downfall. The implementation hurdles included technological limitations of the era, resistance from factory managers and workers who feared increased government control and surveillance, and a lack of widespread understanding of its complex cybernetic principles. Additionally, the political landscape of Chile was highly volatile, with increasing opposition to Allende's government. The 1973 military coup, led by General Augusto Pinochet, abruptly ended not only Allende's presidency but also Project Cybersyn itself. The new regime dismantled the project, viewing it as a tool of socialist management incompatible with their market-oriented economic policies. The theory was seductive but flawed, marked by a blindness to its inherent biases and a detachment from human agency.

Historian Paul Edwards,[1] quoted by Voss, noted how different metaphors drawn from cybernetic ideology sustained various belief systems, contributing to the metaphorical and practical construction of a world seen through the prism of systems theory.

Imagine living inside a metaphor you never chose—where your mind functions as a "processor," your memories exist as "storage," and your relationships operate as "feedback loops." Edwards will call that "cognitive colonization" to explain how the language of cybernetics infiltrated our collective consciousness through Cold War military projects that crafted entire epistemologies—fundamental ways of knowing and being.

These computational metaphors migrated from SAGE defense systems and Pentagon war rooms into everyday understanding, reshaping institutional functions and self-conception alike. When therapists today inquire about your "coping mechanisms" or managers evaluate your "performance metrics," you experience the lingering aftereffects of this metaphorical architecture.

These cybernetic constructs serve as constitutive metaphors—they structure reality itself rather than simply describing it. The massive SAGE air defense system, with its glowing screens tracking potential Soviet bombers, embodied a worldview where phenomena could be contained, calculated, and controlled. This "closed-world discourse" permeated psychology (brain as information processor), education (learning as data acquisition), and intimacy (relationships as transactional systems).

---

[1] Paul N. Edwards, *The Closed World: Computers and the Politics of Discourse in Cold War America* (Cambridge, MA: MIT Press, 1996).

We continue living within this inherited cognitive framework. Dating apps algorithmically match "compatible" partners; workplace surveillance software monitors "productivity"; social media platforms optimize for "engagement"—each instance reflects belief systems reducing human complexity to computable variables. Edwards helps us recognize that technologies wield their greatest power not through visible machines but through invisible metaphors embedded in our imagination. These metaphors determine which questions we ask, which problems appear solvable, and ultimately, which futures we can envision.

In this context, the concept of a feedback loop emerges as particularly insidious, mainly when applied to the regulation of biological systems that are constantly evolving and in flux. This dynamic creates a sort of entrapment, aptly illustrated by Voss (p.64) through the history of queer activists in the United States: *"bound by structures that seemed immutable; and in doing so, reproducing and enforcing existing power structures into the future...Rather than truly making things otherwise, the System abided."* Their experiences reveal a pattern that resonates across numerous narratives in human history: individuals and groups can become ensnared by structures that appear unchangeable, inadvertently perpetuating and reinforcing existing power dynamics for future generations. Instead of fostering genuine transformation, the system tends to endure. In other words, the system's dominance is rooted not in power but in its ability to perpetually rely on articulated and assertive methods of control.

In cybernetics, which encompasses partially applied control theories in political frameworks, "system" isn't a singular, cohesive entity. Its complexity lies in multiple subsystems operating at varying timescales and rhythms rather than perfect harmony, resembling an intricate old watch mechanism.

From a cybernetic perspective, time passage within a system is defined by checks and controls maintaining persistent behaviors. This cybernetic legacy envisions a system existing beyond linear time constraints, harboring inherent capacity to learn and adapt for equilibrium. However, feedback delays complicate matters—by the time a problem is recognized, addressing it becomes significantly more challenging, yet established control mechanisms remain firmly in place.

This implies the system inherently anticipates "anomalies." Rather than facilitating organic change, it embraces disruptions to force adaptation, ultimately incorporating them into normalcy. Thus, the system transforms variations not as catalysts for genuine evolution but as elements co-opted into its ongoing narrative.

Cybernetics, seeking to unify control across various systems, ultimately couldn't fully transform into an applicable biological system. Its foundational assumptions of control and predictability clash with biological systems' inherent complexity and unpredictability. Nevertheless, cybernetic thought's pervasive control ethos continues influencing technological systems, which frequently attempt to delineate their impacts on biological systems, perpetuating a problematic separation overlooking the intertwined nature of technology and biology.

"You can't beat The System, not because it's more powerful than you, but because it contains within it the means to persistently revert to its mode of an articulated and assertive dominance."

—Georgina Voss, *Systems Ultra* (p.63)

Open source exists within this broader systemic context—not as a revolutionary alternative but as another territory where cybernetic rationality plays out. The meritocratic ideals and governance models of many open source projects reflect the same control-oriented paradigms Voss critiques. While communities often speak of empowerment and democratization, their organizational structures frequently reproduce hierarchical patterns that privilege certain bodies, languages, and forms of contribution while rendering others invisible. Contributors from the Global South, women, and other marginalized groups often find themselves caught in these systemic feedback loops—technically "welcome" yet structurally excluded.

It's critical to emphasize the significant role of military funding and interests in the development of cybernetics and systems theory. This military embedding steered cybernetics toward applications enhancing surveillance, control, and warfare capabilities rather than humanitarian or ecological betterment. This historical context reveals how systems thinking, particularly in cybernetic form, has been influenced by and contributed to military objectives, embedding these technologies within specific power structures and ideologies.

These ideas found fertile ground in California's Silicon Valley, where technology and ideology entanglement birthed entities more powerful than nations. In the Californian Ideology's shadow, narratives around technology and its world-order role became entrenched in industry, politics, and culture. Stories spun around these technological constructs carried implied neutrality, suggesting a natural order preordained by technological inevitability.

The cybernetic dream, infused with the conviction that the proper technological setup could solve anything, overlooked the complex realities outside its controlled systems. It demonstrated not just a technological ambition but a broader cultural ethos, profoundly shaping our interaction with the world and with each other, under the guise of neutrality and control.

By the late 20th century, as tech firms grew in influence, a blend of countercultural ideals and free-market capitalism emerged. Systems thinking centered this ideology, emphasizing networked systems as models for social and organizational structure. This ideology advocated for a society model mirroring decentralized, networked, and feedback-driven technology systems, positing that economic and social systems could operate efficiently under minimal government oversight like self-regulating technology systems.

Today, a strong technocratic belief that leads to whatever is being produced *"is not engineering expertise being carefully applied to solve urgent problems, but the imagining of a problem whose existence and solutions is couched in the language of engineering expertise"* (Voss, p.20). The implications deserve a separate book, but we'll explore how this lack of responsibility and consciousness about production profoundly impacts marginalized, invisibilized, and excluded people in decision-making spaces.

The technology field became a magnet for some of the world's brightest engineers and thinkers. However, as Voss points out, these individuals were often recruited not just to solve needed existing problems but to create new markets and needs—essentially manufacturing problems to provide profitable solutions.

Let's acknowledge other consequences of this disruptive industry not mentioned in her book. Technological innovation in this profitable industry supports liberal economic policies favoring deregulation and market freedom at job security and workers' rights expense. The innovation and disruption ethos frequently couples with pushing to dismantle government regulations seen as barriers to technological and economic growth. This deregulatory impulse has often increased work precarity and deteriorated basic human conditions.

Cities known as tech hubs, emblematic of wealth and technological advancement, starkly illustrate vast disparities in wealth and living conditions. High living costs, gentrification, and erosion of stable, well-paying jobs for lower- and middle-class workers are critical issues we face today.

These phenomena underscore a troubling trend where large tech companies, driven by profit motives, contribute to and exacerbate social inequalities. Remember that open source sits at the core of this enormous "innovation" growth and therefore contributes to this picture.

While open source is celebrated for its collaborative nature and technological advancement role, it also plays into the broader narrative of systems prioritizing rapid development and disruption at the cost of more sustainable and equitable growth practices. Open source projects can contribute to labor precarity, often relying on unpaid or underpaid work from global contributors who may not receive fair compensation or recognition for their contributions...yet this system uses the romantic collaboration ideology as if by rule it serves the commonwealth. Are we sustaining another belief system that maintains the same people in power and profits a growing few?

I've identified some underlying socio-political issues that plague open source, drawing from theories designed to remove the blinders from our collective vision. We'll explore working conditions and exploitation, the myth of meritocracy that pretends we all stand on level ground, how "normal" becomes invisible, and why we need an intersectional lens to see the full picture.

To help you navigate this journey—and to kindle your righteous rage while preserving your hope—I'll structure each section in two parts: "The System" will dissect the problematic structures, while "The Uprising" will showcase how communities are challenging these structures, patching the cracks in open source, and creating pathways to something better. You'll see both the wounds and the healing already underway.

Working Rights, Affective Labor, and Free Time

Putting it in a nutshell: In this section, we will analyze how unpaid, often voluntary labor in open source can become exploitative, drawing from theories of affective labor, economic disparities, and cultural perceptions of labor. In this section, we will create a dialogue among a few authors to enrich our understanding of how systemic inequalities are perpetuated. Kathleen Gerson offers insights into the socio-economic implications of unpaid labor, which we will juxtapose with Michael Hardt and Antonio Negri's theories on affective labor and a sip of Ruha Benjamin on free time. These theories stress the emotional and intangible aspects of labor that directly affect human interactions and social relationships.

Reckoning Open Source As Affective Labor

Affective labor is a concept used by Michael Hardt and Antonio Negri to describe a form of labor that goes beyond the traditional physical or cognitive tasks and dives into the emotional and relational aspects of work. It has its roots in feminist critiques of unpaid labor, particularly the work of sociologists and feminist theorists who have explored the importance of emotional labor and care work, tasks that have historically been undervalued and often performed by women.

But let's step back. In 1983, the sociology professor Arlie Hochschild wrote *The Managed Heart: Commercialization of Human Feeling*, in which she offers a foundational framework for understanding how emotions are shaped, regulated, and commodified within the capitalist labor system. In the book, Hochschild challenges the assumption that emotions exist purely in the private sphere, arguing instead that they are deeply structured by social norms and economic demands. Her analysis of emotional labor lays the groundwork for examining how feelings become not just expressions of personal subjectivity but integral components of labor power, rendering them a crucial site of both exploitation and resistance in modern economies.

She defines the concept of emotional labor as the management of emotions to produce a particular emotional state in others. This form of labor, distinct from physical or intellectual work, requires individuals to align their feelings with the expectations of their roles, often dictated by employers. Hochschild explores this process through the lens of service-oriented professions, where the emotional expressions of workers are treated as part of the commodity being sold. In these contexts, emotions are no longer private experiences but are instead subjected to external control and transformed into tools for profit generation.

Is that restricted to service workers? Of course not. In the tech workers speech, and mostly required in open source environment, words like "passion," "love," and "excitement" are often used as a necessary expression to engage and affirm the commitment of one in the space.

Emotional labor involves the regulation of both outward expressions and internal states, often taking the form of *surface acting* or *deep acting*. In surface acting, individuals perform emotions they do not genuinely feel, such as a forced smile or feigned enthusiasm. Deep acting, by contrast, involves actively reshaping one's internal emotional state to match the required outward expression. With this definition, Hochschild stresses the dual nature of emotional labor: it is both a performance and a form of internal work, blending the boundaries between the public and private self. This dynamic underscores the profound ways in which capitalism extends its reach into the personal realm, turning even the most intimate aspects of human experience into sites of economic production.

Hochschild illustrates the operation of emotional labor in two different archetypal occupations, flight attendants and bill collectors. Flight attendants are required to maintain a cheerful and accommodating demeanor, even in the face of stress or hostility, as their emotional expressions are integral to creating a positive experience for passengers. Their emotional labor becomes a commodity, marketed by airlines as part of the service they provide. Conversely, bill collectors must project authority and intimidation to ensure compliance from debtors, demonstrating how emotional labor can be used to elicit not only positive feelings but also fear and submission. In both cases, workers' emotional expressions are meticulously calibrated to align with organizational goals, underscoring the extent to which emotions are shaped by institutional forces.

Hochschild's work also brings attention to the alienation that results from the commercialization of emotions. When workers are required to suppress their authentic feelings and adopt emotional states dictated by their employers, they often experience a disconnection from their own emotions and a sense of estrangement from their true selves. This emotional alienation mirrors the Marxist concept of alienation in physical labor, where workers are estranged from the products of their work and the process of production itself. In other words, workers become alienated from various aspects of their labor and, by extension, from their humanity. Emotional labor, as Hochschild shows, extends this alienation to the realm of feeling, as workers struggle to reconcile their authentic emotions with the demands of their roles. This alienation is further exacerbated by the power dynamics of the workplace, where employees have little control over the emotional expectations imposed upon them.

She adds a gender perspective to it, observing that emotional labor is disproportionately performed by women, reflecting societal norms that associate caregiving and emotional management with femininity. Women are more likely to be employed in service-oriented roles that require extensive emotional labor, such as nursing, teaching, and customer service. This unequal distribution of emotional labor reinforces traditional gender roles while contributing to the economic exploitation of women. Hochschild's insights reveal how the undervaluation of emotional labor, both in the workplace and in the home, perpetuates gender inequality and obscures the economic and social significance of this form of work.

When framing emotions as both personal and public, Hochschild demonstrates ways in which emotional labor is shaped by broader social structures and cultural norms. She talks about the concept of *feeling rules*, which dictate how individuals should feel and express emotions in specific contexts. These rules are not simply internalized expectations but are actively enforced in the workplace as part of organizational policies and training programs. The imposition of feeling rules serves to align workers' emotional expressions with the goals of the organization, ensuring that their emotional labor contributes to the production of value.

By commodifying emotions, capitalism extends its logic of exchange and exploitation into the most intimate aspects of human life, reshaping the ways in which individuals relate to themselves and others.

Hardt and Negri expanded on this idea in their book *Empire*, where they discuss *immaterial labor*. They identify *affective labor* as a specific type of immaterial labor that produces or manipulates emotions such as ease, well-being, satisfaction, excitement, and passion. They argue that this form of labor is essential to the information economy and emphasize its crucial role in the modern capitalist system. It's about the management and production of emotions and social relationships, which have become increasingly recognized as central to the functioning of contemporary political and economic systems.

At its core, affective labor involves tasks that require emotional engagement from the worker. Think of service industry jobs, health care, or education, where success depends not just on performing a service but on how emotionally engaged the worker is with their audience or clients. This engagement can influence, for example, customer satisfaction, educational outcomes, and patient recovery rates. It's the human touch in a digital world, the smile of a caregiver, the empathy of a teacher, or the supportiveness of a customer service agent.

Moreover, affective labor has significant implications for political and economic systems. In an economy where services play an important role in market interactions, affective labor becomes a commodity—something that can be bought and sold. This commodification significantly impacts workers, as it requires them to continuously perform emotionally under the guise of professionalism, often without proper recognition or compensation. Additionally, in a political landscape increasingly influenced by digital platforms, affective labor shapes public opinion, influences political debates, and can even affect election outcomes through social media campaigns where emotional appeals to voters are as strategically important as policy proposals.

But why is this important? In our digital age, where technology is present in nearly every aspect of life—ubiquitous technology that tracks, anticipates, and often influences our interactions—affective labor has infiltrated areas we wouldn't typically consider. It's no longer just about face-to-face interactions.

Why does this matter for open source? Open source is much more than just transparent lines of code; it embodies collaboration and the collective efforts of its communities. Contributors do more than just write code—they also provide support, mentorship, and documentation, promote events, manage disputes, and, most importantly, cultivate a community that is vital for the project's sustainability. The emotional investment involved in managing community dynamics often goes unrecognized and uncompensated, yet it plays a crucial role in the project's success.

The challenge lies in how these emotional efforts are valued. In traditional economic models, labor is valued based on its output and time spent. But how do you quantify empathy, care, or community building? This is a significant issue in industries like tech, where the rapid pace of "innovation" and the impersonal nature of digital interactions can overshadow the human element that affective labor brings. The risk is that as technology becomes more ubiquitous, the emotional work that supports the digital infrastructure is rendered invisible, treated as a byproduct rather than as an integral component of the labor ecosystem.

In the grand scheme, recognizing and adequately valuing affective labor is crucial for creating more equitable workplaces and a more humane society. Going forward in this complex interplay of technology, labor, and emotion, understanding affective labor offers a lens through which to view our current economic and political dynamics, urging us to reconsider what we value in our digital age and why. It draws our attention to the need for a shift in how we conceptualize work, compensating not just for the end product but also for the emotional and relational labor that sustains our interconnected world.

Somehow, open source communities have been pushing for more consideration of the importance of their communities and the ones fostering those communities. However, we—all of us as a collective group—are still incapable of getting out of this technocratic feedback loop, which is sustained and dragged back by the technology system itself, as Voss educates us in *System Ultra*.

Having volunteered and worked as a developer advocate and community organizer, I have observed how this type of emotional labor extends beyond regular working hours. It is now widely recognized in marketing that branding is closely tied to the individuals behind it; people, particularly on social media, are often hesitant to trust companies' opinions. To personalize their messaging and increase profits and trust, companies are leveraging individuals' presence on social media as an extension of their interests. There is a certain pressure and sometimes a bonus connected to this presence, which creates a problematic boundary between work and personal time and space.

This dynamic mirrors the approach taken by many open-source projects, where the credibility of a few core maintainers is paramount. This situation presents a double-edged sword for maintainers. On one hand, their identities become deeply intertwined with their projects, causing them to exceed healthy boundaries, which can lead to mental health issues. On the other hand, this close connection can create a power structure that is difficult to challenge or change.

This passionate commitment of contributors often requires them to invest immense personal time and energy into widely used projects that may not provide financial or other remuneration. While this labor is foundational to the collaborative nature of open source, it raises critical questions about the sustainability and fairness of such labor practices.

Working Rights and Free Time As Societal Health

In *The Unfinished Revolution: Coming of Age in a New Era of Gender, Work, and Family*, Kathleen Gerson explores dynamic shifts in family structures, gender roles, and work-life balance in the United States from the late 20th to the early 21st century. However, we should take this work with a grain of salt. Published in 2010, in an optimistic era, her analysis does not follow the past decade's backs on equity brought by political shifts and conflicts worldwide. To mention a US example, legislative attacks on gender rights, for instance, the rollback of gender-affirming care and the overturning of Roe v. Wade, which directly affects women in the workspace. That alone, paired with conflict in several regions around the globe, led to the increasing number of rape as a tool of power, according to the United Nations (UN) report on gender equity. Such violence and the lack of ability to rule over women's own bodies reveal a very far possibility of equity.

For a broader perspective in time and space, Silvia Federici in *Caliban and the Witch* explores how the transition to capitalism involved significant changes to women's roles and the division of labor, marking periods where women had different kinds of agency or oppression in relation to work. Lucy Delap's *Feminisms: A Global History*, as mentioned in Chapter 2, will bring feminist struggles examples and other demands from around the globe and time, reflecting different cultural needs.

Although Gerson offers a simplified study in terms of time and geography, she takes a very interesting approach to grasp that what we might understand as small victories for gender equality are interwoven in the social and legislative complex of work. For these changes to be effective, it is necessary to reassess and rethink the context surrounding them.

She frames the contemporary era as a time of significant but incomplete transformation, where the potential for gender equality in work and family life has not been fully realized. Her optimism is cautious; she acknowledges progress in gender roles and family dynamics but also points out the ongoing struggles and systemic barriers that prevent these changes from benefiting everyone equally.

Gerson's analysis is rooted in the understanding that historical progress toward gender equality is not linear and that each advance often brings new challenges or reveals deeper systemic issues that need to be addressed.

The transformation in family structures, moving away from traditional models toward more complex and varied forms such as dual-career families, single-parent households, and blended families, impacts the socialization of children, the expectations of adults entering the workforce, and family life. It also affects the ongoing transformation of gender roles. Societal expectations and workplace demands often still adhere to outdated norms. Women, in particular, face the "second shift"—managing household duties and caregiving after their formal workday ends. Men, on the other hand, while increasingly involved in family life, often struggle with the expectations of being both a provider and an active parent.

The Gender Equity Policy Institute published a report[2] in October 2024 about the free-time gender gap. The report shows, in numbers, how unpaid care and household labor continue to reinforce women's inequality. On average, the report shows that women have 13% less free time than men, which varies on ethnicity.

FIGURE 1: WEEKLY HOURS SPENT ON CHILDCARE AND HOUSEHOLD WORK BY GENDER AND RACE/ETHNICITY, 2022
Men
Women
Childcare
Household work
Hours per week
0
5
10
15
20
25
7.5hrs
16.6hrs
10.3hrs
14.8hrs
6.5hrs
12.5hrs
6.8hrs
21.6hrs
7.7hrs
16.1hrs
All
Asian American
Black
Latino
White
Note: Labels represent weekly hours spent on combined childcare and household work, by gender and race/ethnicity. Estimates for certain race/ethnicity groups are not included due to small sample sizes. See appendix for a comprehensive description of the tasks included.
Source: Gender Equity Policy Institute Analysis of ATUS 2022.

Figure 3-1.

[2] The full report can be red on the institute's website at `https://thegepi.org/the-free-time-gender-gap/`

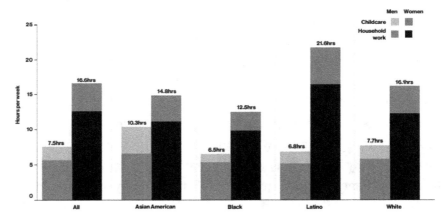

In addition to the numbers, sum up the mental and organizational work, the "beauty time," and the resources dedicated to meeting social expectations. These expectations directly affect how we trust and perceive our co-workers and leaders. CNN senior political commentator Van Jones precisely defines this reality about social expectations when analyzing the 2024 presidential race, comparing Donald Trump and Kamala Harris candidates and examining how they were held to different standards.

"He gets to be lawless, she has to be flawless."

—Van Jones[3]

Yet tech workers, particularly young adults, felt that the workforce could significantly change to achieve work-life balance, a theme Gerson discusses extensively in her book. During the pandemic between 2020 and 2022, the forced need to transform office jobs into remote jobs has shown itself to be a real hope for concrete and lasting change.

Remote work is an employment model that offers significant benefits, particularly to historically marginalized or geographically isolated groups. These include black women, people with disabilities, rural residents, and parents, each facing distinct challenges that remote work can help alleviate. The flexibility offered by remote roles can be particularly beneficial for people who often juggle multiple responsibilities, including caregiving and community involvement.

For people living in places where jobs are scarce and without economic opportunities, accessing broader job options beyond their local geographic constraints may be a way to decentralize wealth, which could directly impact social imbalances and migrations across the globe.

---

[3] The comment can be watched on CNN YouTube channel at https://youtu.be/mz_cPUwD2MU?si=RTMdq3nb8GccCdif

In rural areas, remote work serves as a bridge to economic activities concentrated in more developed regions without the necessity of relocation, which can be both costly and disruptive. It helps prevent the talent drain often seen in rural communities and from the Global South, where individuals move away in search of better opportunities. The demand for better internet connectivity, driven by remote work needs, also promotes infrastructure improvements, further integrating these areas into the broader economic landscape. Furthermore, the lack of employability in rural areas and the Global South leads to massive population migrations and recurring stories of the precarious lives of people who leave their land in search of "opportunity" in the big city or in the Global North. In the rural areas context, lands end up being bought by large monoculture or agricultural companies, causing a climate problem due to the impoverishment of the soil and commonly related to water pollution.

For black women, remote work provides opportunities where discrimination in the workplace is more prevalent. The virtual nature of remote work can help reduce racial bias and microaggressions, focusing more on the quality of work rather than physical appearance or unconscious biases.

The availability of remote jobs can increase employment opportunities for people with disabilities, who have historically faced higher unemployment rates. Remote work benefits people with disabilities immensely as it allows them to create a work environment tailored to their specific needs, circumventing the potential accessibility issues of many physical workplaces. The removal of the need to commute, which can be physically demanding, logistically complex, and implicate higher expenses, enhances physical and economic safety and comfort.

Lastly, parenthood is one of the primary beneficiaries of remote work, as it offers the flexibility needed to balance professional responsibilities with childcare. Remote work can also significantly reduce childcare and commuting costs, making it financially beneficial. For mothers, in particular, it provides viable opportunities to remain in or re-enter the workforce after childbirth, aiding in narrowing the gender gap in career progression.

Gerson already made this call before COVID challenging time, calling for a rethinking of workplace policies, including the implementation of flexible work hours, remote work options, and robust parental leave policies. She points out that such changes benefit individuals and are crucial for fostering productive and loyal workforces.

However, the rigid structures of most workplaces do not support such aspirations. In this post-pandemic period, we are experiencing a rollback of these rights and accommodations led by big tech companies like Amazon. By 2023, even open source teams within major corporations found themselves subject to return-to-office mandates that contradict the distributed nature of their work. Despite building and maintaining globally collaborative projects, these teams face geographical constraints that undermine the very philosophy underpinning their technical practice. This regression disproportionately affects those who benefited most from workplace flexibility—parents (particularly mothers), people with disabilities, and residents of economically disadvantaged regions—revealing how technological capability alone cannot guarantee equitable working conditions without corresponding institutional commitment.

Amazon appears in several other resources as an example of a critique of work precarization, as it maintains labor practices that often compromise the safety, security, and dignity of its workforce. Ruha Benjamin, in her book *Viral Justice: How We Grow the World We Want*, discusses the paradox of workers being deemed essential but treated as disposable, emphasizing how the relentless pursuit of efficiency and profit by companies like Amazon can lead to a devaluation of human labor. This devaluation is particularly evident in the lack of sufficient rest and leisure time for workers, which is crucial not only for their physical health but also for their mental well-being and social engagement.

Benjamin argues that free time is not merely a luxury but a fundamental right that is essential for fostering creativity, dissent, and community engagement—all of which are necessary for a thriving democratic society. By denying workers adequate free time, corporations limit their ability to engage in civic life and pursue personal and collective growth.

Free time is integral to the labor rights movement, it encapsulates a profound dialogue on individual well-being and societal health. In the contexts of Europe and South America, it is deeply enmeshed with the legacies of colonialism and slavery, reflecting the historical struggles of indigenous and black populations, encapsulating a history that has not faded into the past, but lingers in the present.

In Europe, the burgeoning labor movement of the Industrial Revolution, which was marked by severe exploitation, catalyzed the demand for balanced lives. Notably, the Factory Act of 1847 in the United Kingdom, a legislative milestone, inaugurated the eight-hour workday initially for women and children, setting a precedent that gradually extended across the labor market. The European struggle for labor rights did not occur in isolation but rather in a complex overlay with colonial endeavors that exploited both the resources and peoples of subjugated territories, often under conditions of brutal enslavement.

Conversely, in South America, the labor rights movement has carved a distinct narrative, shaped indelibly by the continent's colonial past and the enduring influence of its indigenous and African-descended demography. In comparison with the United Kingdom, Brazil abolished slavery on May 13, 1888, being the last country in the Americas to do so. The last country in the world to officially abolish slavery was Mauritania, in 1981. But it wasn't until 2007 that the government passed a law that allowed slavers to be criminally prosecuted.

The legal prohibition of slavery does not mean that slavery has ended in current times around the world. As of 2023, an estimated 50 million people[4] are living in modern slavery globally. Modern slavery

---

[4] For full report, check the global slavery index 2023 https://www.walkfree.org/

encompasses a range of exploitative practices, including forced labor, human trafficking, servitude, and forced marriage, and is exacerbated by various global crises such as conflicts, economic instability, environmental degradation, and the rollback of critical human rights protections. Notably, almost two-thirds of all forced labor incidents are linked to the operations of global supply chains, emphasizing the role of economic demand and consumer behavior in perpetuating these inhumane conditions.

In regions like Brazil and Colombia, the labor movements have transcended mere calls for fair working conditions; they have challenged the pervasive social inequalities that trace back to colonial and enslavement epochs. The Brazilian context is particularly poignant, being the country where the largest number of enslaved Africans were brought to the Americas, the labor movement has interwoven with the country's racial dynamics, addressing the systemic relegation of Afro-descendant populations to precarious labor conditions.

The linkage between labor rights and the historical exploitation of Indigenous and black communities under colonial and slave systems is a stark reminder of the economic frameworks that historically devalued human dignity in favor of profit. This historical exploitation has set a somber precedent for labor practices, influencing contemporary labor rights discourses that seek to rectify these deep-seated injustices.

For these communities, the fight for labor rights transcends economic concerns, touching on cultural survival and autonomy. In South America, for instance, indigenous activism against multinational encroachments—often in mining and agriculture—highlights a broader struggle for land rights and cultural recognition, which is closely tied to labor practices.

The discourse on free time within this context emerges not merely as a labor rights issue but as an essential facet of social justice, empowering marginalized communities through opportunities for cultural expression, community engagement, and political activism. Legislative advancements like France's laws protecting the right to disconnect illustrate a growing acknowledgment of the need to reformulate labor rights for the digital age, ensuring these rights reflect both contemporary challenges and historical contexts.

This holistic approach serves as a critical lens through which we can understand and address the lingering socio-economic structures that perpetuate inequality and exploitation. Thus, the conversation on free time and labor rights is not only about enhancing personal well-being but about fostering a more equitable, just, and humane global society.

I hope, dear reader, that the next time you see a talk about burnout at an open source conference, again, you'll be able to understand all the nuances of what it entails. That working long hours and weekends doesn't make you or your colleague heroes, and that your right to use your time for what gives you pleasure and makes you human is a responsibility to yourself and to the collective.

Within the framework offered by Gerson and the critiques brought by Benjamin, we should note that employers alone should not drive effective change, as societal and economic barriers remain formidable. The impact of financial insecurity, exacerbated by a lack of supportive public policies, highlights the crucial role of governmental and organizational policies in either supporting or hindering progress toward race and gender equality, accessibility, and family well-being. It is a call to reimagine labor practices that prioritize human well-being and justice, suggesting that changes in corporate practices, sustained by government regulation, can lead to broader societal transformations.

Parallel to Hardt and Negri's discourse, Gerson's research on socio-economic disparities sheds light on who can participate in open-source, mostly labor-intensive projects. Not all individuals have the luxury of contributing without compensation, which points to a significant equity issue within the open-source ecosystem. The concept of "free time" as a resource that is not equally available to all underscores the systemic inequities that can make open source less accessible and equitable.

The intersection of the ideas brought by Hardt, Negri, and Gerson provides us with a framework for understanding the complexities of labor in the open source sphere, mainly through the lenses of affective labor, race, and gender dynamics.

Hardt and Negri's exploration of immaterial and affective labor reveals how these forms of labor are central to the functioning of the global economy, especially within the technology and service sectors. Open source communities exemplify a shift toward collaborative and non-commodified forms of production and represent a form of resistance against traditional capitalist structures while being absorbed by them. In open source environments, contributors engage not only in technical tasks but also in emotional and relational labor that are crucial for the sustainability of these projects.

Conversely, Gerson's insights challenge us to consider how these evolving work forms intersect with persistent societal norms and structures, especially concerning gender roles and work-life balance. There's a need for substantial changes in how labor is organized, recognized, and rewarded to ensure equitable participation and support for all, regardless of their body, their language, their religion, or their gender. While open source projects may offer new avenues for collaborative work, they must also address how they perpetuate or challenge existing disparities, particularly in how they manage and value the often-invisible labor that keeps these communities thriving. Open source communities must critically evaluate how they incorporate principles of equity, fairness, and support for diverse life circumstances.

Open source can be a model for future democratic and inclusive work structures. To start, it is and has always been remote. However, for it to be revolutionary, it must integrate nuanced understandings of gender and equity into its core practices to avoid reproducing the inequalities found in the broader society. This means structuring communities and developing policies and practices that not only encourage participation but also actively support contributors, including recognizing and compensating the affective labor involved.

And if you have a narrow view of labor, economics, and democracies, Benjamin mentions two examples that, for me, are closely related to what a diverse and equitable open source could aim for: participatory budgeting and a universal wage system.

Participatory Budgeting (PB) in Brazil is a democratic process that allows residents to decide directly how to spend part of a public budget. It was first implemented in 1989 in Porto Alegre, the capital city of the Brazilian state of Rio Grande do Sul, as part of an effort to tackle deep-rooted issues of inequality and promote social justice. The process involves community members at multiple stages, from the discussion of budget priorities to the decision-making on specific projects. Citizens participate in regular meetings to identify, discuss, and prioritize public spending projects and then vote on which projects should receive funding. The scope of these projects can range from infrastructure improvements, like roads and sanitation, to community services, such as health and education facilities. Participatory Budgeting has been praised for enhancing transparency, increasing public participation in the democratic process, and improving trust between citizens and government entities. It has also been seen as a tool for empowering traditionally marginalized communities, giving them a voice in government decisions that directly affect their lives. The success of PB in Porto Alegre has inspired numerous other cities in Brazil and around the world to adopt similar initiatives. This model of budgeting is recognized for its potential to make local governments more responsive and accountable while addressing the specific needs of the community through a more equitable distribution of public resources.

One example of a universal wage system is the Tunnel Vision, founded by Madeline Pendleton Hansen. She has implemented a unique profit-sharing model at her Los Angeles-based clothing store. She pays herself and her employees—seven full-time and four part-time—the same salary of $70,200 annually. This approach is quite distinct from typical corporate pay structures, where CEO compensation vastly exceeds that of other employees. In her model, when the business generates extra profits, these are redistributed among the staff based on their needs, such as for new cars or paying off car loans, rather than accumulating as additional income for Pendleton herself. Pendleton engages in a universal wage system, where all full-time employees, including herself, earn the same amount, which she believes fosters a more equitable and cooperative work environment. This practice stands in stark contrast to the norm in many businesses where the distribution of profits and wages heavily favors top executives. By adopting this model, Pendleton aims to demonstrate a viable alternative to traditional capitalist business practices, which she discusses openly in her advocacy against labor exploitation.

Both Participatory Budgeting and the universal wage system are loose examples, offering glimpses into alternative ways of organizing labor and resources that challenge traditional business and governance models. They are not definitive solutions but prompts to think beyond conventional frameworks, urging us to collectively envision and create approaches that address systemic historical inequalities. For open source to embody its potential as a model for equity and inclusivity, we must strive to leave no one behind. This requires not only validating and recognizing those already contributing but actively identifying and incorporating those who have been marginalized or excluded. Additionally, we must shed the technocratic weight that idolizes those with burnout and measures value solely by metrics like the number of lines of code written. Instead, the focus must shift to valuing the ecosystem as a whole, recognizing and making space for other bodies, perspectives, and contributions that are essential to a thriving and equitable open source community.

Exploitation in the Guise of Volunteering?

Open source projects, particularly those with large-scale impact and visibility, attract a diverse range of contributors. However, the lack of structured compensation and the often informal nature of these contributions can lead to exploitation, particularly, under neoliberal systems. Some contributors, driven by a passion for technology and community, may find themselves giving more than they receive, not just in terms of code but in community management, documentation, and support. This disparity becomes particularly pronounced when commercial entities enter the open source arena, leveraging the freely available resources without adequate reinvestment into the community—either financially or through other forms of support.

This issue is further complicated by the legal structure of open source. Under intellectual property laws, software is protected as a form of creative expression. Open licenses, designed to foster sharing and innovation, can sometimes inadvertently undermine the rights of creators by allowing others to profit from their work without appropriate compensation or acknowledgment, challenging traditional notions of ownership and control.

The theoretical frameworks provided by Gerson, Hardt, and Negri offer a lens through which to view these complex issues. By juxtaposing Gerson's analysis of socio-economic implications with Hardt and Negri's concepts of affective labor, we gain a deeper understanding of how systemic inequalities are perpetuated in the tech industry, particularly in open source communities. These dialogues highlight the need for a more equitable approach to managing labor in technology development, suggesting that the ethos of open source could evolve to more consciously address these disparities.

There is this bitter and ill-defined feeling in the open source ecosystem, which has partly opened up possibilities for the invention and sustainability of a trillion-dollar technology industry due to its legal freedom of reappropriation. On the other hand, the frequent discussions about the lack of sustainability, which, in some well-known cases, led to the tragedy of the commons, show us that something is wrong.

Eleonor Ostrom analyzes various successful and unsuccessful cases from the economics and governance perspectives, examining how communities can organize themselves independently, whether through an external institution or internal self-regulation by their members.

I argue that there is an unease about how to deal with this ecosystem, which depends mainly on voluntary work, in a global and neoliberal setting. I complicate the question and the unease by asking who the people behind the projects and the ecosystem are who have enough free time to devote to them.

I also wonder about the role that such projects play in promoting more equitable forms of work since what we often call contribution and volunteering are also work.

You see, dear reader, the force that sustains this trillion-dollar industry can be the force that maintains a controlling and normative system, sustains a false belief in meritocracy, and invisibilizes the biological and human complexities of the system and its impacts. Or it can be a force for transformation, equity, and historical reparation. It's up to us.

It is essential for each contributor to take a moment to reflect on the impact of their efforts. They should ask themselves who truly benefits from their contributions. Is their most precious resource—their free time—being utilized in a manner that genuinely supports the common good and enhances the well-being of the community? Or is it being exploited merely to line the pockets of a select few, while the needs of the larger population go unmet? Such contemplation can guide individuals toward making more meaningful and impactful choices in how they dedicate their time and energy.

Establishing the necessary conditions falls upon regulatory bodies— such as the foundations that frequently oversee these initiatives—and a diverse range of stakeholders, including state governments. By doing so, they can help turn the persistent tragedy of the commons into a sustainable and equitable landscape, ensuring that shared resources are managed wisely and benefit everyone involved.

The Uprising: Three Active Interventions into the Problems of Open Source Work

The persistent extraction of affective labor within open source ecosystems has catalyzed emergence of interventionist frameworks that fundamentally reconfigure relationships between contribution, compensation, and community sustenance. These initiatives move beyond ameliorative gestures toward structural transformation, recognizing that technological sustainability requires attending to the full spectrum of labor—emotional, organizational, and relational—that maintains digital infrastructure.

The Outreachy[5] program exemplifies this systematic reorientation through its explicit focus on historically marginalized contributors entering free and open source software communities. The program distinguishes itself through its recognition that diversity requires infrastructural support rather than rhetorical commitment. Outreachy provides stipends, mentorship structures, and institutional scaffolding that acknowledge the economic barriers preventing many from participating in "volunteer" technological labor. Outreachy's model makes visible the privilege inherent in unpaid contribution, creating pathways that compensate participants while building sustainable mentorship networks. This represents a direct challenge to the assumption that passionate commitment should suffice as reward for essential technological work.

Jorge Benet's cooperative research,[6] detailed in his comprehensive analysis of twelve technology cooperatives managing digital infrastructure,

---

[5] https://www.outreachy.org/
[6] https://infraestructura.digital/index-en.html

offers perhaps the most systematic alternative to extractive open source models. His findings demonstrate how cooperative structures address precisely the deficits identified in Nadia Eghbal's foundational work: lack of planning, insufficient diversity of skills, and inadequate democratic participation in project governance. The cooperatives studied integrate roles ranging from traditional development to project management, communications, and business development—explicitly valuing what Benet terms the *"diverse skills that support and complement technical programming tasks."* Through democratic ownership structures, these organizations create accountability mechanisms that prevent the concentration of decision-making power while ensuring sustainable compensation for all forms of labor, including the affective and organizational work typically rendered invisible.

The Open Technology Fund's (OTF)[7] approach further extends this recognition through its Free and Open Source Software Sustainability Fund, which explicitly supports maintenance activities, operational infrastructure, and community development alongside technical development. OTF's framework acknowledges that sustainable technology requires investment in *"the human elements necessary for project health and longevity."* Their funding model encompasses both feature development and ongoing relational work of community coordination, documentation, and user support—activities that traditional funding mechanisms systematically undervalue despite their critical importance for project viability.

These three initiatives share a fundamental insight: technological sustainability emerges through recognizing and compensating the full ecosystem of labor required to maintain digital infrastructure. Each model develops distinct mechanisms for making visible and valuable the emotional, organizational, and community-building work that sustains

---

[7] https://www.opentech.fund/

technological projects. They represent movement beyond charity-based approaches toward systematic restructuring of how technological labor is organized, valued, and compensated.

The significance of these approaches extends beyond their immediate contexts. They demonstrate possibilities for technological development that centers equity and sustainability rather than treating them as secondary considerations. Through institutional innovation—whether mentorship programs, cooperative ownership structures, or comprehensive funding frameworks—these models create conditions where diverse forms of contribution become systematically valued rather than extracted through appeals to passion or community service.

Their collective impact suggests pathways toward technological futures grounded in justice rather than exploitation, where the labor sustaining our digital infrastructure receives recognition commensurate with its essential role in contemporary life.

The Myth of Meritocracy

Putting it in a nutshell: In this section, we will examine the paradox of pursuing diversity in open source while often reinforcing existing power structures through the flawed notion of meritocracy. We will draw on critiques by Jo Littler and Daniel Markovits to explore how this ideal obscures deep-rooted power imbalances and structural barriers. These power structures, supported by the systemic biases discussed by Voss, reinforce existing hierarchies and limit the potential for diverse contributions in the open source context.

The term "meritocracy" became more well-known after Michael Young's satirical essay "The Rise of the Meritocracy," published in 1958. In this essay, Young imagined a future where social class hierarchies would be replaced by hierarchies based on intelligence and effort. Ironically, what he intended as a critique of the overemphasis on standardized testing and IQ as measures of worth became a widely accepted concept, symbolizing fairness and the promise of upward mobility based on merit.

In *Against Meritocracy: Culture, Power, and Myths of Mobility*, Jo Littler argues that meritocracy has two forms: a social system and an ideological discourse. She makes this distinction to underscore how the concept functions as both a practical organizational framework and a set of beliefs that justify and perpetuate certain social norms and values.

Meritocracy, as a social system, is context-specific and revolves around the idea that individuals can activate their talents through hard work. In this system, the majority of people should ideally attain social positions that suit their abilities and are appropriately rewarded. Social mobility and equality of opportunity are at the core of its expectation, which differentiate it from social systems focused on economic and cultural redistribution.

However, as Daniel Markovits in *The Meritocracy Trap: How America's Foundational Myth Feeds Inequality, Dismantles the Middle Class, and Devours the Elite* shows, the promise of social mobility has become more unlikely; instead, class disparity has increased while the middle class is becoming dismantled. On top of that, there's an uncomfortable reality, that individuals who achieve the dreamed success often transmit their advantages, such as wealth, educational opportunities, and social connections, to their children, creating a new form of aristocracy. This practice reinforces a cycle of privilege and continues to contribute to unequal starting conditions for different individuals. As a result, children of successful parents may benefit from resources and opportunities that are unavailable to those from less advantaged backgrounds, perpetuating disparities in social mobility and access to essential services.

Meritocracy isn't one-size-fits-all; it changes depending on the specific context or situation. This means it's crucial to take a closer look at how meritocracy works in different settings and how it impacts different groups of people. A meritocratic social system is not about one's individual talent or effort; it has to be considered alongside how wealth and opportunities are distributed and recognized in the culture it's embedded. This means, for instance, considering how things like the body one lives, their physical ability, gender, or caste, and how this body is affected and the roles they are given and their chances of thriving.

We need to consider what society defines as "success" and how it is defined. These definitions can change depending on cultural and economic factors, and they impact the rewards people receive—whether that's money, status, or acknowledgment from others. All these aspects work together to either support or challenge the existing power structures in society, so it's essential to connect the dots between them.

Meritocracy is also a set of beliefs that shapes how we see the world and influences the way power is structured within society. Littler points out that it ties back to the discussions from the 1970s about ideology and power dynamics, showing that meritocracy is not a neutral idea—it actively supports certain social hierarchies.

In the 1970s, intellectual circles were abuzz with debates on ideology and hegemony, concepts that sought to unravel the subtle mechanisms through which societies maintain and legitimize power structures. These debates were not confined to repressive or ideological State apparatus; scholars within the emerging field of cultural studies examined how media and popular culture serve as vehicles for ideological dissemination. They analyzed how cultural products—from films to literature—reinforce societal norms and power relations, subtly shaping public consciousness and perpetuating hegemonic ideologies.

The 1970s also witnessed a critical examination of the concept of ideology itself. Scholars questioned the extent to which individuals are aware of the ideologies they internalize and the possibility of achieving genuine class consciousness. This period marked a shift from viewing ideology as false consciousness imposed from above to understanding it as a complex, pervasive force embedded within everyday practices and institutions.

In other words, they were digging into how societies quietly maintain power through ideas and culture. They looked at how media—television, music, radio, movies and books—subtly reinforce the status quo, shaping how people see the world without them even realizing it. At the same time, they started questioning whether people truly understand the beliefs they've absorbed and if it's even possible to fully wake up to how the system works. Instead of seeing ideology as something forced on people, they began to see it as something woven into everyday life.

These debates have had a lasting impact on contemporary social theory, influencing disciplines ranging from sociology to media studies. They have provided tools to critically analyze how power operates not just through over political and economic means but through the subtle shaping of beliefs, values, and norms that constitute the fabric of society.

This is why Markovits calls meritocracy a trap, like *The Stuff*, the horror movie from Larry Cohen from 1985; its this mysterious substance disguised as wonderful and advertised as the trendy, but in reality it turns its consumers into zombies who begin to infest the world.

Political Rhetoric and Institution Validation

The idea of neoliberal meritocracy started taking shape as neoliberalism grew into a powerful way of organizing politics and economics, becoming a lens through which success and worth were increasingly measured.

Meritocracy, originally introduced as a critique of inflexible class hierarchies, gradually evolved into a tool for promoting competitive individualism. What began as a call for equal opportunities to rise based on talent and effort was reframed to justify a system that rewards individual achievement while downplaying the structural barriers that limit access to those opportunities. Neoliberalism, with its focus on free markets, privatization, and minimal government intervention, embraced this reimagined meritocracy as an ideological partner. Together, they reinforced the narrative that success is earned solely through personal effort and ability, effectively diverting attention away from the deep systemic inequalities that continue to shape outcomes and limit fairness.

Littler is brave in exploring how the social movements of the 1960s focused on civil rights, feminism, LGBT, anti-colonialism, anti-racist, and for the rights of people with disabilities, while pushing back against traditional power structures, have also helped shape the rise of neoliberal meritocracy. These movements advocate for equality and recognition and have indeed brought changes in the legal system as much as in cultural acceptance. However, I can't take the silent written voice of Voss here saying: "*Rather than truly making things otherwise, the System abided.*" Littler argues that neoliberalism selectively co-opted their language and ideas. By reframing the call for equality in terms of individual achievement and opportunity, neoliberalism sidestepped the deeper structural changes these movements had demanded, using their rhetoric to reinforce its own agenda.

Littler describes these shifts as mutations, where the original promise of meritocracy was re-engineered to align with neoliberal imperatives. Instead of dismantling hierarchies, meritocracy was used to reinforce them, presenting privilege as the natural outcome of talent and effort. The language of opportunity and fairness was weaponized to downplay systemic barriers, creating what Littler calls a "cruel optimism" that binds individuals to the idea of meritocracy even as it perpetuates their struggles.

Neoliberal meritocracy adopted the language of opportunity and inclusion to present itself as a system that values fairness and progress. It embraced the idea of "equality of opportunity" to translate collective demands for justice into individualized pursuits of success instead of tackling the deeper structural issues these movements are still asking for, neoliberalism reduced their critiques to a focus on personal empowerment within the same unequal frameworks. For example, the feminist fight for workplace gender equality was reinterpreted through a meritocratic lens as a push for women to "lean in." This means encouraging women to assert themselves, take on leadership roles, and strive for success through individual effort. While it can feel empowering for some, "leaning in" frames workplace inequality as a problem that women themselves can solve by working harder or changing their behavior, rather than addressing systemic barriers like wage gaps, lack of affordable childcare, or discriminatory policies. This reframing shifted attention away from the need for collective and structural changes, placing the burden on individual women to succeed within an inequitable system. By doing so, it made systemic inequalities invisible while promoting the idea that progress could be achieved through personal strategies alone.

Meritocracy as a rhetorical device has been employed across the political discourse, adapted to various contexts. When operating as a mobilizing rhetoric in political discourse, meritocracy serves as a tool to legitimize neoliberal ideologies. Meritocratic language has become a key component in shaping public perceptions of fairness and opportunity while simultaneously reinforcing structures of inequality.

Littler brings a few examples on how it has been applied in the UK political context in different time frames. She mentions how figures such as Margaret Thatcher and Tony Blair embraced meritocratic language, albeit with different emphases. Thatcher framed meritocracy as a tool for individual empowerment, aligning it with her market-driven policies, while Blair sought to position it within a framework of "New Labour" modernization, emphasizing equality of opportunity as a cornerstone of progressive governance.

This rhetorical deployment is not confined to Britain. Globally, meritocracy serves as a persuasive narrative, promising that talent and hard work will be justly rewarded, regardless of one's starting point. However, Littler critiques this narrative as deeply intertwined with neoliberalism, where the emphasis on individual competition overshadows systemic barriers and structural inequalities. She draws attention to how meritocracy's promise of social mobility becomes a way to justify economic stratification, suggesting that those who do not succeed simply lack effort or ability.

Littler also examines how this rhetoric creates what she terms "meritocratic feeling," a structure of emotional resonance that encourages individuals to internalize meritocracy's values as moral obligations. For example, citizens are compelled to view their success or failure as a reflection of their personal worth, ignoring the broader socio-economic forces at play. This emotional engagement makes meritocracy particularly effective as an ideological tool, reinforcing its dominance in political and cultural narratives.

Jo Littler uses political examples from both the United Kingdom and the United States, like Boris Johnson, Nigel Farage, and Donald Trump, to unpack how meritocracy intersects with populism and elite identity. She describes this as the "tragicomedy" of meritocratic rhetoric, showing how these leaders manipulate narratives of "hard work" and bootstrap success to their advantage. By framing themselves as champions of the everyday person, they destabilize traditional ideas of merit while ultimately propping up the same hierarchies they claim to challenge.

Boris Johnson's public persona is an example of how elite privilege can be reframed through meritocratic narratives. Johnson's career, marked by access to elite educational institutions like Eton and Oxford, is emblematic of inherited privilege. Yet, he often presents himself as a figure of "hard work," someone who has achieved his status through talent and effort. Johnson's performative bumbling and self-deprecating humor serve to mask his elite background, making him appear more relatable to the public. This comedic veneer, Littler argues, distracts from the serious structural inequalities he represents and perpetuates. It creates a narrative where privilege is reframed as personality, and systemic advantages are downplayed in favor of an individualized story of effort and success.

To be fair to Boris Johnson, we cannot deny he may indeed think he is a hard worker. Markovits reveals the impacts of meritocracy on both the elite class and the broader society. He argues that the relentless pursuit of success based on merit results in a labor market that is not only exclusionary but also unforgiving and punishing. For those at the pinnacle—the elite—this translates into a life characterized by fierce competition and a continuous cycle of overwork. This ongoing battle often comes with considerable personal and social repercussions, which are commonly overlooked in traditional economic analyses.

Conversely, the working and middle classes find themselves in profound difficulties trying to achieve social mobility. As the costs associated with higher education continue to rise steeply, alongside increasing living expenses, these individuals are often burdened with financial pressures that undermine their ability to compete effectively in a system that claims to offer equal opportunities for all.

The growing obstacles to advancement are not merely financial; they also include systemic issues such as inadequate access to quality education, networking opportunities, and resources that are often available to wealthier individuals. As a result, the dream of success becomes increasingly elusive for many. The notion that anyone can rise through sheer merit becomes far less realistic when faced with the sophisticated challenges that hinder their progress.

As Markovitz points out, the "new aristocracy," unlike the old one, cannot simply rely on inherited privilege but must indeed work absurdly long hours to maintain their elite status. However, this should not be conflated with the struggles of lower classes, who often face the same grueling work hours but under conditions of precarity and systemic disadvantage that are worlds apart from the stability and resources enjoyed by the elite.

Littler extends her critique to figures like Nigel Farage and Donald Trump, who she identifies as "blue-collar billionaires"—elite individuals who position themselves as champions of the working class. They blur the lines between merit and privilege, presenting themselves as champions of the people while reinforcing elite dominance. Both Farage and Trump have adopted populist rhetoric to align themselves with ordinary people, often emphasizing their supposed hard work and disdain for traditional political elites. However, Littler notes the deep contradictions in their self-presentation.

Trump, for instance, frequently touts his wealth as a symbol of success while simultaneously claiming to be an outsider who understands and represents the struggles of the average American. Similarly, Farage, a former stockbroker educated at private schools, uses anti-establishment rhetoric to distance himself from the very elite circles he inhabits. These figures destabilize traditional meritocratic notions by rejecting the idea that expertise or formal qualifications are necessary for leadership, yet they do so in ways that ultimately reinforce elite power structures.

Littler argues that figures like Johnson, Farage, and Trump destabilize meritocratic ideals not by challenging inequality but by shifting the focus of merit. They replace traditional markers of merit, such as education or professional achievements, with populist appeals to authenticity, charisma, or supposed alignment with "ordinary" values. This shift undermines trust in expertise and institutional pathways to success, contributing to the erosion of traditional systems.

Yet, Littler points out that this destabilization is not emancipatory. Instead of dismantling hierarchies, these figures create new forms of elitism, where power is concentrated not through demonstrated merit but through the manipulation of public sentiment and cultural narratives.

Adding to Littler's examples, in Brazil, Jair Bolsonaro's rise to power has been associated with populist rhetoric that challenges traditional political elites and institutions. While not explicitly framed in terms of meritocracy, Bolsonaro's discourse emphasizes anti-establishment sentiments and appeals to "common sense" over expert knowledge, which parallels the destabilization of traditional meritocratic values observed in other populist movements.

Applying Littler's analysis, one might examine how Bolsonaro's rhetoric interacts with concepts of merit and elitism in Brazil. For instance, his emphasis on military values and discipline could be seen as promoting a particular vision of merit based on order and authority, contrasting with more egalitarian or democratic notions. Additionally, his critiques of intellectuals and the media may serve to undermine traditional meritocratic institutions, similar to the patterns Littler identifies in other populist leaders.

But wait before you lose hope.

In the section "Aspiration for All," Littler examines how political narratives have appropriated the concept of aspiration to reshape it according to different ideological agendas. This appropriation is particularly evident in the contrasting approaches of figures like Jeremy Corbyn and David Cameron, reflecting broader struggles over the meaning and implementation of meritocratic ideals.

Jeremy Corbyn's former leadership of the UK Labour Party marked a significant shift in how aspiration was framed within political rhetoric. His slogan "Aspiration for All" sought to reorient the term away from neoliberal connotations of individual success toward collective progress and equitable redistribution. Corbyn argued that aspiration must be realized through secure jobs, affordable housing, reliable healthcare, and fair pensions—achievable not through individual competition but through collective action and systemic change. His vision directly challenged the Blairite and Conservative appropriation of aspiration, which had often linked the concept to emulating the wealthy and pursuing materialistic goals.

In contrast, David Cameron and other Conservatives wielded aspiration as part of their justification for neoliberal reforms, such as privatizing education through the promotion of private academies. For Cameron, "raising aspiration" was aligned with fostering individual success and increasing private sector involvement, effectively sidelining the collective dimensions of social improvement. Littler highlights that this divergence reflects deeper ideological rifts: where Corbyn's rhetoric emphasized redistribution and solidarity, Cameron's connected aspiration to market-driven competitiveness and the dismantling of public institutions.

Littler also explores how Corbyn's alternative vision resonated with those disillusioned by the narrow neoliberal framing of aspiration. His rise to leadership was met with widespread enthusiasm, as many saw his approach as a challenge to the political and economic status quo. Nevertheless, she acknowledges the challenges he faced, including resistance from within his own party, hostile media coverage, and a broader political landscape shaped by decades of neoliberal dominance.

The term "Aspiration for All" encapsulates these broader tensions between individualism and collectivism, between neoliberalism and more egalitarian alternatives. Littler's analysis underscores how the language of aspiration, like meritocracy itself, is deeply contested, with its meaning and implications shaped by the political forces that seek to wield it. This struggle over the narrative of aspiration reveals the ongoing conflict between competing visions of society and the ways in which meritocratic rhetoric is used to justify or challenge existing power structures.

In Brazil, Luis Inácio Lula da Silva, known as Lula, can be seen as a similar counterpart from the Labour Party. His political discourse is rooted in the fight for social inclusion and economic equality. Coming from a working-class background, Lula's policies focused on poverty reduction through affirmative actions initiatives like Bolsa Família, which provided direct financial assistance to low-income families, and policies aimed at expanding access to education, healthcare, and housing. Lula's approach has been deeply informed by Brazil's profound social and economic divides, as well as its history of systemic inequality and racial exclusion.

While both leaders have framed their visions as being about fairness and equality, their political environments reveal key contrasts. Corbyn operated within an advanced capitalist society where the focus was on reversing austerity and curbing the excesses of neoliberalism. His rhetoric appealed to working-class voters but struggled to overcome accusations of being overly idealistic or impractical, particularly within a divided Labour Party and a media landscape often hostile to his vision.

Lula, on the other hand, has navigated the complexities of a developing country with stark inequalities and a history of colonialism and dictatorship. His ability to implement social programs during a period of economic growth allowed him to significantly reduce poverty and hunger, earning widespread popular support. However, Lula's legacy has also been shaped by political polarization and challenges such as corruption scandals, which have complicated his broader narrative of governance for all.

Both Corbyn and Lula represent a politics of aspiration, focusing on inclusion and equity. However, Corbyn's vision often centered on resisting the neoliberal dismantling of social safety nets, while Lula's was about building those systems from the ground up in a country where millions lacked basic rights and services. Despite their differences, they share alternative visions that challenge these meritocratic narratives by emphasizing structural reforms over individual achievement.

Corbyn explicitly rejected the neoliberal framing of meritocracy, which he saw as exacerbating inequality by placing undue emphasis on individual effort while ignoring systemic barriers. His policies, such as free higher education, universal healthcare expansion, and public ownership of key industries, sought to redistribute wealth and opportunity across society. Corbyn's rhetoric often targeted the "rigged system," arguing that the current structures privileged a wealthy elite while leaving working people behind. His vision aligns with Littler's critique of meritocracy as a system that props up inequality by diverting attention from the need for systemic change.

Lula, on the other hand, operates in a context where the idea of meritocracy is even more starkly at odds with reality. Brazil's deep social and economic divides, rooted in its colonial history, make the promise of "equal opportunity" under meritocracy particularly hollow.

These examples illustrate just how deeply meritocracy is woven into political rhetoric, often serving to obscure the systemic inequalities it perpetuates. By framing success as the result of individual effort, meritocratic narratives shift attention away from the structural barriers that prevent true equality. However, by critically examining these frameworks—through the lens of thinkers like Littler and Markovitz, and the practices of leaders like Lula and Corbyn—we can begin to unravel meritocracy's hold on our collective imagination. Dismantling this rhetoric requires rethinking how we define success, fairness, and opportunity, and focusing instead on systemic reforms that prioritize collective well-being over individual competition. Only by doing so can we work toward a society that is truly equitable for all.

Skilled Workers and the New Aristocracy

The transformation of work in the late 20th and early 21st centuries further shaped the discourse of neoliberal meritocracy. Littler explores how the shift from industrial to post-industrial economies, characterized by the rise of service sectors, gig work, and knowledge economies, altered perceptions of merit and labor. In these new economies, the qualities associated with success—flexibility, creativity, and entrepreneurialism—were increasingly tied to the individual rather than collective efforts.

This shift redefined meritocratic ideals, emphasizing personal branding, self-optimization, and perpetual learning as hallmarks of success. Workers were encouraged to view themselves as individual enterprises, responsible for their own advancement and security, even as structural protections like unions and stable employment eroded. Meritocratic discourse, Littler argues, served to obscure these structural changes, framing precarious labor conditions as opportunities for self-actualization and upward mobility.

In *The Meritocracy Trap*, Daniel Markovits argues that meritocracy, rather than leveling the playing field, has entrenched inequality and reshaped both education and work in ways that perpetuate elite dominance.

Firstly, meritocracy has transformed education into a rigorous and intense contest aimed at securing elite status. From an early age, students are subjected to relentless academic pressures, with the ultimate goal of gaining admission to prestigious universities. These institutions serve as gatekeepers to the upper echelons of society, ensuring that only those who excel in this competitive environment can access the privileges of the elite.

Secondly, meritocracy has redefined work by creating immensely demanding and highly lucrative jobs that sustain the elite class. The labor market now fetishizes specialized skills, centering industries and compensation around a narrow cadre of superordinate workers. This shift has been facilitated by technological advancements—such as computers and automation—that have restructured production processes. These innovations, often developed by individuals who have benefited from meritocratic education, are tailored to the skills of the elite, further displacing middle-class workers and rendering their skills obsolete.

This dynamic creates a feedback loop: elite students secure the best jobs, develop new technologies that favor super-skilled labor, and thereby reinforce their own economic indispensability. As a result, meritocracy not only perpetuates inequality but also confines social mobility, making it increasingly difficult for individuals from lower socioeconomic backgrounds to ascend the social ladder.

Moreover, meritocracy disguises its external effects through its institutions and rituals—such as universities and graduation ceremonies— which project meritocratic ideals onto everyday life. These practices embed meritocratic values deeply into societal norms, capturing the imaginations and critical faculties of those within the system. Consequently, meritocratic ideology and inequality rise in tandem, each driving the other forward.

In essence, Markovits contends that meritocracy has become a modern-day aristocracy, perpetuating a cycle of exclusion and inequality under the guise of fairness and efficiency. By transforming education and work, it consolidates elite status and limits opportunities for the broader population, challenging the foundational myths of social mobility and equal opportunity.

In *Viral Justice*, Ruha Benjamin critiques the hustle economy, particularly as it manifests in entrepreneurial activities and gig work. The hustle economy, much like meritocracy, is framed as an empowering system that offers flexibility, autonomy, and financial independence. It thrives on narratives of resilience and self-discipline, encouraging individuals to "bet on themselves" and pursue opportunities on their own terms. However, Benjamin exposes a distrust on this system as it transfers economic risk from institutions to individuals, creating a precarious environment where workers bear the brunt of instability.

The hustle economy operates as a pressure valve for traditional economies, offloading responsibility for stability and security onto individuals and communities. Platforms like ride-sharing apps or content creation spaces promise democratized opportunities but are ultimately controlled by corporations that extract value from the labor of gig workers and creators. This dynamic reproduces existing inequalities, as those with resources—whether financial, educational, or social—are better positioned to succeed in these precarious systems.

In both systems, inequality is naturalized. Meritocracy justifies disparities as the logical outcome of fair competition, while the hustle economy portrays precarity as the price of independence. These narratives are deeply embedded in cultural and institutional practices, shaping how individuals perceive their roles within these systems. The result is a pervasive ideology that not only sustains but amplifies existing power dynamics.

Markovits and Benjamin both highlight the emotional toll these systems exact on individuals. Meritocratic elites, while ostensibly at the top, face relentless pressure to maintain their status, often at the expense of their well-being. Those excluded from the elite feel demoralized, trapped in a system that offers little hope of advancement. In the hustle economy, workers endure constant pressure to "stay relevant" and "keep grinding," as their livelihoods depend on their ability to navigate unstable and exploitative environments. This emotional burden compounds the economic precarity faced by gig workers and entrepreneurs.

A key feature of both systems is the feedback loop that reinforces inequality. In meritocracy, elite workers innovate technologies that prioritize super-skilled labor, displacing middle-class jobs and consolidating their own dominance. In the hustle economy, platforms and systems designed by those with power further entrench their control, extracting value from the labor of others while offering minimal support. These feedback loops not only sustain inequality but also make it increasingly difficult for individuals to break free from these systems.

Both Markovits and Benjamin call for a critical reassessment of these systems. They argue that true empowerment and equality cannot be achieved within frameworks that prioritize individual achievement over collective well-being. In meritocracy, this means dismantling the structures that concentrate privilege among the elite and addressing the systemic barriers that limit social mobility. In the hustle economy, it requires questioning the narratives of autonomy and resilience that mask exploitation, and creating systems that prioritize stability, security, and shared prosperity.

The critiques offered by Markovits and Benjamin converge on a fundamental truth: systems that claim to democratize opportunity often do the opposite. Whether through the relentless competition of meritocracy or the precarious independence of the hustle economy, these frameworks shift the burden of inequality onto individuals while maintaining the structures that perpetuate it. To move toward a more equitable future, we must challenge the narratives that sustain these systems and reimagine the possibilities of collective action and systemic change.

In their respective critiques, both authors highlight the urgent need to pull back the curtain on these systems—to reveal who is truly running the show and who is bearing the cost. Only by addressing these underlying dynamics can we create systems that genuinely prioritize fairness, opportunity, and justice.

How Is Open Source Part of It?

Open source software development is often heralded as a meritocratic arena where contributions are evaluated based on quality and innovation, ostensibly providing equal opportunities for all participants. However, when examined through the critical lenses of scholars like Jo Littler and Daniel Markovits, this perception becomes more complex.

Factors such as access to technology, free time, and existing technical knowledge can privilege certain groups over others, leading to the reproduction of social hierarchies within these communities. Thus, the open source model, while promoting inclusivity, may inadvertently reinforce the very inequalities it seeks to dismantle.

Individuals from affluent backgrounds, who have the means to contribute significant time and resources without immediate financial compensation, dominate the field. Consequently, the open source ecosystem may become an arena where existing elites consolidate their status, rather than a platform for broad-based social mobility.

The critiques offered by Littler and Markovits suggest that open source communities need to be cognizant of the potential for meritocratic ideals to perpetuate inequality. To counteract these tendencies, it is essential to implement inclusive practices that actively lower barriers to participation. This includes providing mentorship programs, ensuring diverse representation in leadership roles, and creating supportive environments that recognize a range of contributions beyond just code.

The Uprising: Coraline Ada Ehmke's Post-Meritocracy Manifesto

The most explicit and theoretically coherent challenge to meritocratic structures within open source communities emerges through Coraline

Ada Ehmke's Post-Meritocracy Manifesto,[8] which directly declares that *"meritocracy is a founding principle of the open source movement"* while arguing that *"it is time that we as an industry abandon the notion that merit is something that can be measured, can be pursued on equal terms by every individual, and can ever be distributed fairly."*

Ehmke's intervention operates precisely within the theoretical framework above—recognizing meritocracy not merely as flawed implementation but as a fundamental mechanism for perpetuating existing power relations. Her analysis reveals how *"the idea of merit is in fact never clearly defined; rather, it seems to be a form of recognition, an acknowledgement that 'this person is valuable insofar as they are like me'"*— directly echoing Littler's critique of meritocracy as ideological discourse that naturalizes inequality through claims of objective assessment.

The 2018 manifesto's structural approach dismantles rather than reforms meritocratic evaluation. Ehmke demonstrates how *"meritocracy is a system of power, and like all systems of power, that power is not evenly distributed,"* where *"a queer Black woman is at a distinct disadvantage in a system governed by straight white men."* This analysis moves beyond individual bias toward systemic critique, recognizing how meritocratic structures create what she terms "gatekeepers" who determine participation through evaluative mechanisms that privilege existing cultural norms.

Ehmke's theoretical sophistication becomes evident through her connection of technological meritocracy to utilitarian philosophy. She argues that *"meritocracy draws on many of the principles of the utilitarian philosophy"* where *"actions which benefit the majority of people are deemed to be moral actions,"* creating *"moral calculus that benefits the majority at the expense of the minority."* This philosophical grounding positions open source meritocracy within broader systems of exclusion that sacrifice marginalized communities for purported collective benefit.

---

[8] https://postmeritocracy.org/

The manifesto's transformative potential lies in its systematic replacement of competitive evaluation with values-based governance. Rather than arguing for more equitable application of merit-based assessment, Ehmke constructs alternative organizational principles that center collective well-being over individual advancement. This approach directly challenges what Markovits identifies as meritocracy's tendency to create feedback loops that consolidate elite dominance.

Ehmke's broader work includes the Contributor Covenant, a code of conduct used in over 40,000 open source projects including all such projects from Google, Microsoft, and Apple, demonstrating how theoretical critique translates into widespread institutional transformation. The Covenant's adoption across major technological institutions suggests possibilities for structural change that extends beyond individual projects toward ecosystem-wide transformation.

The manifesto has generated significant engagement within open source communities, with some observers noting "a trend in open source development culture over the past ten years or so" characterized by "the rejection of 'meritocracy." This cultural shift indicates broader recognition that technological communities require fundamental reorganization rather than incremental diversity initiatives.

Ehmke's approach exemplifies what might be termed "infrastructural abolition"—dismantling evaluative mechanisms that perpetuate exclusion while constructing alternative systems of recognition and participation. Her work demonstrates how challenging meritocracy requires simultaneous theoretical sophistication and practical intervention, creating conditions where different forms of technological collaboration become possible through values-based rather than competition-based organization.

There Is No Normal Nor Neutral. Diversity As a Foundational Imperative in Tech and Open Source

Putting it in a nutshell: This section challenges the idea that technology, including open source, is neutral, arguing instead that diversity must be built into systems intentionally, not treated as an afterthought. Drawing on the work of Safiya Umoja Noble, Ruha Benjamin, Kimberlé Crenshaw, and Caroline Criado Perez, it highlights how biases in algorithms and system design reflect broader historical and structural inequalities. Noble's examples of algorithmic bias reveal how these issues manifest in everyday technology, while Benjamin situates them within systemic and institutional frameworks. Crenshaw's concept of intersectionality sheds light on how overlapping forms of discrimination affect marginalized groups in these systems, and Criado Perez demonstrates how data gaps in design disproportionately harm women. Together, their insights underline the urgent need for intentional diversity to combat these embedded biases and build truly equitable systems.

Diversity in tech and open source is too often framed as a charitable effort, centered around beginner-only programs that perpetuate the harmful notion of underrepresented groups as less knowledgeable or capable. Shall we start to refer as underestimated people? The fact is that such programs unintentionally reinforce the idea that participants and their contributions are secondary, relegating them to the margins of innovation and influence. To truly address diversity as a foundational principle, we must reject this perspective and embed inclusion into the very fabric of how technology and open source communities operate.

Diversity is not optional or supplementary; it is a strategic necessity. It is not about helping those who "lack knowledge" but about recognizing the immense value of varied perspectives in solving complex problems and fostering equitable systems. When diversity is treated as foundational,

157

it moves from being a moral obligation to a critical element of robust and innovative design. Research consistently shows that diverse teams outperform homogeneous ones because they bring broader insights and challenge entrenched assumptions. In open source, this means shifting from the rhetoric of meritocracy—which obscures the systemic barriers that privilege some while excluding others—to a culture where everyone has equitable access to contribute and lead.

The current emphasis on diversity initiatives for beginners reflects a deeper problem: these programs often focus on participation rather than impact, limiting the opportunities for underrepresented groups to advance into leadership or governance roles. To change this, diversity efforts must include all levels of expertise, creating pathways for mid-career and senior individuals to thrive. This requires shifting from tokenistic representation to structural inclusion, ensuring that diverse contributors have the tools, mentorship, and recognition needed to shape the direction of communities and projects meaningfully.

Moreover, the focus on gender diversity, often narrowly supporting white women, neglects the broader dimensions of inclusion. Intersectionality must guide diversity efforts, addressing the overlapping systems of privilege and oppression that affect individuals differently. Implementing affirmative actions, and expanding representation to prioritize Black, Indigenous, and People of Color (BIPOC), LGBTQ+ individuals, people with disabilities, and those from underrepresented socioeconomic backgrounds is essential. This is not only a matter of equity but also a means of fostering richer, more inclusive systems that reflect the diversity of their users.

Central to this transformation is the recognition that technology and open source projects are not neutral. The pervasive belief that technology is neutral—that it operates free of human bias and functions as an impartial mediator—has long been a comforting myth, particularly in the fields of open source software and technology development. However, as scholars like Safiya Umoja Noble and Ruha Benjamin have shown, technology is anything but neutral. Embedded within algorithms, systems, and platforms are deeply entrenched biases that reflect the inequities of the societies in which they are created. This section unpacks the myth of neutrality, arguing that diversity cannot be an afterthought or a mere supplement to innovation but must serve as the foundational ethos of any technological system. Without this intentionality, technology will continue to reinforce systemic inequalities rather than dismantle them.

In open source, this shift also means challenging traditional power structures, and noninclusive governance model, which centralizes authority in ways that limit diverse voices. Democratizing decision-making processes and creating inclusive environments where all contributors can participate meaningfully are necessary steps to dismantle systemic inequities. Additionally, normalizing diverse expertise by elevating underrepresented voices as thought leaders and decision-makers can help erode the perception of diversity as secondary.

This elevation requires intentional sponsorship—established community members actively creating pathways to leadership roles rather than offering entry-level participation. Unlike mentorship, which focuses on skill development, sponsorship involves public endorsement, deliberately sharing power and visibility, and advocating for professional and paid opportunities. The CHAOSS community defines sponsorship as *"actively providing opportunities and attribution, recognition, or endorsement for other people with less privilege,"*[9] recognizing it as a crucial metric for evaluating community health.

Concrete implementations of these principles demonstrate their transformative potential. The Cloud Native Computing Foundation's Deaf and Hard of Hearing Working Group[10] exemplifies how structural accommodation creates pathways to contribution. Rather than treating

---

[9] https://chaoss.community/kb/metric-sponsorship/
[10] https://github.com/cncf/tag-contributor-strategy/tree/main/deaf-and-hard-of-hearing

accessibility as an afterthought, this initiative embedded captioning, sign language interpretation, and visual communication tools into its foundational infrastructure. The result transcends symbolic inclusion— deaf and hard of hearing contributors have shaped technical decisions, documentation standards, and community practices within the CNCF ecosystem. Their leadership has influenced how technical discussions occur across the broader Kubernetes community, demonstrating how addressing specific barriers for one group often improves participation for all.

Accountability is key to this transformation. Communities and organizations must set clear goals for diversity, track progress, and actively address barriers reported by participants. Systems should be regularly audited for bias, and feedback mechanisms must be established to ensure that diversity initiatives are not tokenistic but impactful. Only through intentional, systemic efforts can tech and open source truly move beyond the outdated frameworks of charity and tokenism to create spaces where diversity is recognized as the foundation of innovation, equity, and sustainability.

Deconstructing the Myth of Neutrality: Noble and Benjamin

Safiya Umoja Noble's *Algorithms of Oppression: How Search Engines Reinforce Racism* has become a seminal text in understanding how algorithmic systems perpetuate systemic biases and inequalities. Published in 2018, this work provides a critical analysis of how seemingly neutral technologies—specifically search engines like Google—replicate and amplify societal prejudices, particularly around race, gender, and class. Noble's insights have had profound implications for the fields of technology, data ethics, social justice, and policy, catalyzing conversations and initiatives aimed at addressing algorithmic bias.

At its core, *Algorithms of Oppression* argues that algorithms are not neutral tools but reflect the biases, priorities, and power dynamics of the societies that create them. Noble demonstrates how search engines, which many people perceive as objective and reliable sources of information, can produce results that reinforce harmful stereotypes. For instance, she reveals that searches for terms like "Black girls" often return hypersexualized or derogatory content, a stark example of how algorithms perpetuate societal biases.

Noble connects these outcomes to the profit-driven motives of tech companies, which prioritize advertising revenue and click-through rates over equitable and accurate representation. By doing so, she situates algorithmic bias within broader structures of capitalism, illustrating how economic incentives intersect with existing social inequalities to produce discriminatory technological systems.

Beyond search engines, Noble critiques the broader implications of algorithmic bias in areas such as education, healthcare, and criminal justice. She highlights how these biases disproportionately harm marginalized communities, reinforcing existing hierarchies and limiting opportunities for equity and inclusion.

Since its publication, the book has been highly influential in shaping academic, industry, and public discourse around technology and ethics. It has become a foundational text in data ethics and critical technology studies, frequently cited in scholarly work and adopted in university curricula worldwide. Noble's analysis has helped frame algorithmic bias not as a technical flaw but as a systemic issue requiring interdisciplinary approaches to address.

The book has also informed policy discussions and advocacy efforts. Noble's work has been cited in debates around technology regulation, including calls for greater transparency and accountability in algorithmic systems. Her insights have influenced initiatives to address algorithmic discrimination, such as efforts to de-bias datasets, improve diversity in tech workforces, and develop ethical frameworks for AI and machine learning.

In industry, Noble's critiques have spurred some companies to take a closer look at the ethical implications of their technologies. While progress has been uneven, her work has contributed to the growing recognition that addressing bias requires systemic change rather than superficial fixes.

Noble's work lays the groundwork by exposing how search engines and other algorithmic systems, far from being neutral, amplify societal biases rooted in capitalism and systemic inequities. Ruha Benjamin's *Race After Technology: Abolitionist Tools for the New Jim Code* expands this critique, placing these algorithmic biases within a broader historical and structural framework that connects contemporary technologies to centuries of racial oppression. While Noble highlights specific examples, such as how Google search results reinforce stereotypes, Benjamin takes this further by introducing the concept of the *New Jim Code*, showing how technologies are not just reflecting societal biases but actively re-inscribing and evolving them into new forms of exclusion and control. Together, their works dismantle the myth of technological neutrality and call for systemic reimagining, with Benjamin advancing the conversation through her abolitionist framework that emphasizes the necessity of building equitable alternatives.

Published in 2019, *Race After Technology* offers a powerful critique of how algorithms, data systems, and technological infrastructures encode and enforce social hierarchies, particularly racial ones. Benjamin's work has significantly influenced conversations around race, technology, and justice, inspiring both critical academic inquiry and real-world efforts to address systemic inequities in tech.

Benjamin's concept of the New Jim Code draws a direct line between historical systems of racial oppression and contemporary technologies that appear progressive but operate as tools of social control. The *Jim Crow* system refers to the era of systemic racial segregation and discrimination in the United States that lasted from the late 19th century until the mid-20th century. Named after a derogatory caricature of African Americans from 19th-century minstrel shows, Jim Crow laws and practices institutionalized racial inequality and reinforced white supremacy, primarily but not exclusively in the southern states. This connection between past and present makes her analysis particularly impactful, as it situates modern technological inequities within a continuum of systemic injustice.

Benjamin critiques the idea of technological neutrality, arguing that technologies are never created in isolation from the societal contexts in which they emerge. Benjamin's work is transformative not only because it exposes the harms caused by biased technologies but also because it challenges the ideological narratives that sustain these systems. She critiques the tech industry's tendency to appropriate the language of equity and innovation while perpetuating exclusionary practices that maintain power imbalances. Her insights are particularly relevant in areas like predictive policing, facial recognition, and healthcare algorithms, where the impacts of technological bias disproportionately harm marginalized communities. These systems, designed and deployed without sufficient oversight or diversity in their development teams, embed discriminatory practices into the fabric of everyday life, reinforcing hierarchies that they purport to disrupt.

Her analysis also explores how technological systems not only enforce existing inequalities but also create new forms of exclusion and marginalization. For example, she discusses how workplace algorithms can disadvantage candidates based on historical hiring data or how credit-scoring systems penalize individuals from marginalized communities. By framing these issues within a historical and systemic context, Benjamin underscores the importance of understanding technology as a social and political construct rather than a purely technical one.

What sets Benjamin's work apart is her abolitionist framework, which pushes beyond incremental reforms to advocate for systemic transformation. She argues that simply fixing biased algorithms is insufficient; instead, we must dismantle oppressive systems and rebuild technologies with justice and equity at their core. Her call to action resonates deeply in today's world, where the rapid proliferation of AI and algorithmic decision-making has outpaced the ethical frameworks needed to guide their use. Benjamin's emphasis on community-driven resistance and grassroots innovation adds a hopeful dimension to her critique, highlighting the agency of those most affected by technological inequities to shape alternatives that serve their needs.

While both works have catalyzed important conversations, the years since its publication have revealed both progress and persistent challenges. On the one hand, there has been increased awareness of algorithmic bias and its impacts, with a growing number of initiatives aimed at promoting ethical technology development. Regulatory discussions have intensified, particularly in regions like the European Union, where frameworks like the AI Act seek to address bias and discrimination in algorithmic systems.

Public discourse has also evolved. Issues of bias in algorithms, once confined to academic and advocacy circles, are now part of mainstream conversations about technology. High-profile cases of algorithmic discrimination—such as biased facial recognition systems and unfair AI-driven hiring practices—have underscored the urgency of these issues and brought them to broader public attention. This increased awareness has led to some positive developments, such as the suspension or banning of facial recognition technologies by major cities like San Francisco and the reevaluation of predictive policing programs. In addition, advocacy organizations and grassroots movements have pushed for greater accountability and transparency in tech, often citing Benjamin's work as a critical resource.

However, significant challenges remain. Many tech companies have been slow to implement meaningful changes, often opting for performative diversity initiatives rather than addressing systemic issues. It is disheartening to see how the industry often adopts these concepts either performatively or superficially without committing to meaningful systemic change. In her book *So You Want to Talk About Race*, Ijeoma Oluo highlights one of the book's central themes: the importance of valuing and fairly compensating the work of people of color. She reflects on the frequent invitations she receives to speak on race-related topics without being offered compensation, exposing a troubling pattern where the labor and expertise of people of color are undervalued, even as their insights are actively sought. This disconnect underscores a broader issue: the eagerness to engage in conversations about race often exists alongside an unwillingness to fully recognize or pay for the contributions of those leading these essential discussions.

The profit-driven motives Noble critiques continue to shape the development and deployment of technologies, perpetuating the very biases her work highlights. Furthermore, the global spread of surveillance technologies—often marketed as tools for public safety—has reinforced the racial and social inequities Benjamin critiques. Additionally, marginalized communities, who bear the brunt of these biases, often remain excluded from decision-making processes in technology development.

Does it make more sense now when I say that diversity isn't supplementary, it is foundational and must be intentional? Or do you need more data?

The Data Behind Systemic Inequities

The intersection of diversity, labor rights, and systemic inequities presents a multifaceted challenge that is frequently examined through abstract theoretical perspectives. However, the integration of empirical data into this discussion provides a significantly clearer and more compelling lens for understanding these complex issues. A pivotal work in this regard is Caroline Criado Perez's *Invisible Women: Exposing Data Bias in a World Designed for Men*, which serves as a foundational text for exploring the critical role of data—or, in many cases, the lack thereof— in shaping and perpetuating social and economic inequality.

Criado Perez's research meticulously uncovers how systemic inequities embedded in various sectors—such as labor, technology, and the broader social structure—are often deeply influenced by data collection practices that inadequately represent women and other marginalized groups.

One of the book's most impactful insights is the identification of the male default in data collection. Criado Perez argues that data collection often defaults to male perspectives, rendering women's experiences invisible. This bias results in products, services, and policies that fail to meet women's needs. For instance, urban planning frequently overlooks women's travel patterns, which are typically more complex due to caregiving responsibilities, leading to inadequate public transport systems.

In healthcare, the book highlights significant gaps in medical research, where male bodies are often considered the standard. This oversight leads to misdiagnoses and ineffective treatments for women. For example, women experiencing heart attacks may exhibit different symptoms than men, yet medical training and research have traditionally focused on male symptoms, increasing the risk of misdiagnosis in women.

The book examines how public spaces and infrastructure are often designed without considering women's safety and accessibility needs. For instance, the allocation of equal floor space for men's and women's restrooms fails to account for the longer time women require, leading to longer queues and inadequate facilities for women. I will extend this subject, as it is very infrequently touched upon. Women often require more time in restrooms than men due to a combination of biological, physiological, and practical factors. One significant reason is menstruation; managing menstrual hygiene necessitates additional time for changing sanitary products and ensuring cleanliness. This process can be intricate and time-consuming, especially in confined public restroom spaces.

Anatomical differences also play a role. Women typically need to use enclosed stalls for all restroom activities, which involves additional steps such as opening and closing doors, adjusting clothing, and sometimes cleaning the toilet seat. These actions inherently take longer compared to men's use of urinals, which are more straightforward and quicker to access.

Clothing design can further extend the time women spend in restrooms. Garments like jumpsuits, tights, or those with intricate fastenings require more effort and time to remove and readjust, adding to the overall duration of restroom use.

Women are more likely to be accompanied by children or elderly family members who require assistance, further increasing the time spent in restrooms. This caregiving role often falls to women, necessitating longer use of facilities to accommodate the needs of dependents.

The design and allocation of restroom facilities also contribute to longer wait times for women. Men's restrooms often have more fixtures due to the inclusion of urinals, which occupy less space than stalls. In contrast, women's restrooms, limited to stalls, may have fewer available fixtures within the same area, leading to longer queues and extended waiting periods.

These factors collectively result in women spending more time in restrooms, which is further exacerbated by longer queues and inadequate facilities, which shows us the need to think holistically about circumstances that involve other bodies.

Criado Perez also explores how data invisibility in technological developments, including algorithms and artificial intelligence, can perpetuate existing gender biases when they are trained on male-centric data. This perpetuation can result in products and services that do not adequately serve or even harm women. For example, voice recognition systems may be less accurate for female voices if they are primarily trained on male data sets.

Workplace inequities are also discussed, with Criado Perez illustrating how workplace policies frequently disregard the realities of women's lives, particularly concerning unpaid domestic labor. This oversight perpetuates gender inequality, as women's contributions are undervalued, and their opportunities for advancement are limited. The lack of consideration for caregiving responsibilities in workplace structures often forces women to choose between career progression and family obligations. Her analysis highlights instances where data used to inform public policy or workplace practices may overlook women's specific needs and contributions, leading to skewed outcomes that favor more privileged demographics.

By scrutinizing the biases inherent in data collection methodologies and their subsequent applications, we gain a more profound understanding of how systems that proclaim neutrality can, in fact, reinforce existing power dynamics. This is particularly evident in the realms of employment and meritocracy, where the criteria for success and evaluation may be based on data that fails to account for diverse experiences and perspectives. Ultimately, Criado Perez's work emphasizes the urgent need for more inclusive data practices that acknowledge and account for the complexities of all individuals, thereby fostering equitable systems that genuinely serve the interests of all members of society.

Criado Perez's analysis begins with a simple but profound observation: much of the data used to design policies, products, and technologies is collected with the assumption of a "default male." This data gap leads to decisions that exclude or disadvantage women and other marginalized groups in areas ranging from healthcare and urban planning to technology and the workplace. In the context of labor, this omission becomes particularly glaring. Women's unpaid labor—caregiving, domestic work, and emotional support—remains largely invisible in economic analyses despite being critical to the functioning of societies and economies. Ignoring these contributions leads to a distorted view of value and productivity, reinforcing existing hierarchies.

One of the central arguments in *Invisible Women* is that the data gaps surrounding women's experiences and contributions lead to policies and systems that disproportionately harm them. In the workplace, for example, data often fails to account for the specific challenges women face, such as the lack of maternity support, inflexible work hours, or harassment.

The systemic biases embedded within many technological systems are not incidental oversights but deliberate choices that prioritize the perspectives of dominant social groups, thereby marginalizing others. This issue is particularly evident in the technology sector, where data-driven systems—such as recruitment algorithms and performance evaluation tools—often unintentionally perpetuate existing prejudices. These algorithms are typically trained on historical data that may reflect previous discriminatory practices, leading to outcomes that disadvantage women, people of color, and other underrepresented groups.

For example, Criado Perez highlights how car safety standards are based on crash-test dummies modeled on male bodies, resulting in women being 47% more likely to be seriously injured in car accidents. Similarly, in medicine, women's symptoms of heart attacks are often misdiagnosed because research has historically focused on male presentations of the condition. These examples illustrate how the absence of women's perspectives in data collection and analysis leads to systems and policies that fail to serve half the population effectively.

In the healthcare sector, algorithmic biases have led to disparities in patient care.[11] A study revealed that an algorithm widely used to allocate health resources favored White patients over Black patients, resulting in Black patients receiving less adequate care. The algorithm predicted healthcare needs based on past healthcare expenditures, which are generally lower for Black patients due to systemic barriers to access, thus perpetuating existing health disparities.

Another well-known example of technology data bias is Amazon's AI recruitment tool,[12] which was found to be biased against women. The system, trained on resumes submitted over a decade, favored male

---

[11] Read the full World Economic Forum article about it https://www.weforum.org/stories/2024/09/racial-bias-healthcare-data-equity/?utm_source=chatgpt.com

[12] See Vice article about it when the company have claimed stopped using the tool at https://www.vice.com/en/article/amazon-ai-recruitment-hiring-tool-gender-bias/

candidates by penalizing resumes that included the word "women's," as in "women's chess club captain," and downgraded graduates of all women's colleges. This bias arose because the historical data predominantly reflected male applicants, leading the AI to replicate existing gender disparities.

Similarly, facial recognition technologies have demonstrated significant racial biases. Studies have shown that these systems misidentify individuals with darker skin tones at higher rates than those with lighter skin. For instance, a study by the National Institute of Standards and Technology found that facial recognition algorithms falsely identified African-American and Asian faces 10 to 100 times more than Caucasian faces.[13] Such biases have serious implications, especially when these technologies are used in law enforcement and surveillance, potentially leading to wrongful accusations and privacy violations.

Criado Perez's critique aligns with broader discussions on meritocracy, as seen in the works of Jo Littler and Daniel Markovits. The so-called meritocratic systems in the workplace often rely on metrics and benchmarks that are themselves products of biased data. For instance, performance evaluations that prioritize presenteeism—being physically present at work—disadvantage women who may have caregiving responsibilities. Similarly, algorithms used in hiring often favor candidates whose profiles align with historical data, perpetuating a cycle of exclusion.

Unpaid labor is another critical area where data gaps reinforce inequities. Women perform the majority of unpaid labor globally, including caregiving, domestic work, and community support, yet these contributions are largely invisible in economic metrics like GDP. This invisibility has profound implications for labor rights and workplace

---

[13] See Amnesty International article related to their campaign against the use of such technologies https://www.amnesty.ca/features/racial-bias-in-facial-recognition-algorithms/

policies. If unpaid labor is not recognized as valuable, the systems that depend on it are unlikely to provide the support necessary to balance these responsibilities with paid work.

Criado Perez emphasizes that neglecting unpaid labor creates systemic obstacles for women in the workforce. Policies lacking adequate parental leave or affordable childcare disproportionately impact women, who are often expected to shoulder these responsibilities. Cultural norms that undervalue caregiving roles compound these barriers, reinforcing the perception that such work is less important or less skilled than paid labor.

Supporting this perspective, the International Labour Organization (ILO) reports that in 2023, 708 million women were not participating in the global labor force due to unpaid care responsibilities, compared to 40 million men. This stark disparity highlights how societal expectations place a disproportionate burden on women, limiting their employment opportunities and economic independence.

Additionally, the International Monetary Fund (IMF) notes that women globally perform an average of 4.4 hours of unpaid work daily, while men contribute only 1.7 hours. This imbalance affects women's participation in the labor market and perpetuates economic inequalities, as unpaid labor is not accounted for in traditional economic metrics like GDP.

Furthermore, entrenched gender norms contribute to this disparity. The White Swan Foundation observes that stereotypes casting men as breadwinners and women as homemakers persist, leading to women spending up to ten times more time on unpaid care work than men. These societal expectations confine women to caregiving roles, limiting their opportunities for education, employment, and personal fulfillment.

Addressing these systemic barriers requires comprehensive policy interventions that recognize and value unpaid labor. Implementing supportive measures such as paid family leave, affordable childcare services, and flexible work arrangements can alleviate the disproportionate burden on women. Challenging and changing cultural norms that undervalue caregiving roles is equally essential to promoting gender equality in both the unpaid and paid labor sectors.

Women bring unique insights and perspectives that challenge existing power structures and expand the scope of what is considered a policy issue. Tina Tchen, a prominent advocate for gender equity and women's rights, exemplifies the transformative potential of women in leadership. As Chief of Staff to First Lady Michelle Obama and Executive Director of the White House Council on Women and Girls, Tchen spearheaded initiatives to address systemic barriers faced by women in the workforce. One of her most significant contributions was organizing the first-ever White House Summit on Working Families, which focused on issues such as paid family leave, affordable childcare, and workplace flexibility. These policies reflect a recognition of the interconnectedness of professional and domestic spheres.

Tchen's advocacy for paid family leave challenges the traditional separation of work and home life, acknowledging that caregiving responsibilities are integral to the well-being of families and societies. By advocating for workplace flexibility, Tchen addresses the systemic barriers that limit women's participation in the labor force, promoting policies that enable all workers to balance professional and personal responsibilities.

The struggle for gender equity in policymaking, labor rights, and broader societal systems has long been fraught with challenges. Women's contributions, whether in domestic work, caregiving, or professional spaces, have often been undervalued, marginalized, or rendered invisible. The story of *Salt of the Earth* serves as a profound example of how these dynamics play out and how transformative it can be when women take leadership roles in addressing systemic inequities. The film's narrative aligns closely with Caroline Criado Perez's *Invisible Women*, which exposes the biases ingrained in data, systems, and policies that consistently prioritize the male experience as the default. Together, these stories reveal a pressing need to center women's voices and experiences in policymaking and to address the structural barriers that perpetuate inequality.

Released in 1954, *Salt of the Earth* tells the story of a zinc miners' strike in New Mexico, based on real events. The film offers a unique perspective on labor rights by highlighting the role of women, who step into leadership positions when the male miners are barred from picketing. While the men initially dismiss the women's grievances—such as the lack of hot water for washing clothes, inadequate housing, and the burdens of domestic labor—they are forced to confront these issues when the women take over the picket lines, leaving the men to manage household responsibilities. This role reversal starkly illustrates how men, for the first time, begin to understand the weight of women's labor and the systemic inequities they face daily.

What makes *Salt of the Earth* revolutionary is its acknowledgment that labor rights cannot be fully achieved without addressing the intersection of work and domestic life. The men's epiphany—that the fight for labor rights must also include the fight for women's rights—underscores the interconnectedness of these struggles. The film challenges the traditional separation of public and private spheres, demonstrating that caregiving and domestic work are not peripheral concerns but central to the functioning of society.

Just as the men in *Salt of the Earth* only recognized the significance of domestic work when they had to perform it themselves, policymakers often fail to account for the economic and social value of caregiving roles. This oversight perpetuates a cycle of inequality, where women are disproportionately burdened with unpaid labor, limiting their opportunities for paid work and professional advancement.

Both *Salt of the Earth* and *Invisible Women* highlight the importance of lived experience in shaping policies and systems. In the movie, the women's firsthand knowledge of domestic struggles brings a new dimension to the labor movement, challenging the men to expand their understanding of what constitutes a "working rights" issue. The book similarly emphasizes that data cannot be truly objective unless it reflects the diverse experiences of the population it aims to serve.

This intersection of data and lived experience is critical for addressing systemic inequities. Without incorporating women's perspectives, systems and policies will continue to reinforce the status quo, privileging dominant groups while marginalizing others. As Criado Perez argues, the invisibility of women's experiences in data is not a neutral oversight but a systemic bias that perpetuates inequality.

In the realm of technology, the data gaps identified by Criado Perez have direct implications for diversity in open source communities. Open source projects, often heralded as meritocratic and inclusive, rely heavily on metrics to evaluate contributions, such as the number of commits or lines of code. However, these metrics fail to capture the full spectrum of work that sustains these communities, such as documentation, community management, or mentorship—roles that are disproportionately filled by women and other marginalized groups.

This data bias mirrors the broader systemic issues Criado Perez critiques. By valuing only certain types of labor, open source communities perpetuate a hierarchy that privileges technical contributions over relational or administrative work. This not only excludes many potential contributors but also reinforces the power imbalances that these communities claim to oppose. To address these issues, open source projects must adopt more holistic metrics that recognize and value diverse contributions.

The insights from *Invisible Women* extend beyond specific industries or communities to challenge the broader systems that govern labor and meritocracy. Criado Perez's work demonstrates that data is not neutral; it reflects the biases and assumptions of the people and systems that collect and interpret it. This has profound implications for how we understand and address issues of diversity and equity. If we are to create systems that are truly inclusive, we must first acknowledge and address the biases embedded in our data practices.

This requires not only collecting better data but also fundamentally rethinking what we consider valuable. For example, integrating metrics for unpaid labor into economic analyses would provide a more accurate picture of societal productivity and help justify policies that support work-life balance, such as universal childcare or paid family leave. Similarly, in the tech industry, adopting inclusive design principles that account for diverse user experiences would lead to products and systems that serve a broader range of needs.

The book's lessons underscore the need for intentionality in addressing data gaps and their implications. This means going beyond surface-level fixes to tackle the structural issues perpetuating inequality. For example, in the workplace, this could involve redesigning performance metrics to account for diverse contributions or implementing policies that support work-life balance. In open source communities, it could mean expanding the definition of merit to include non-technical contributions and creating governance structures that reflect the diversity of their contributors.

Addressing the biases in our data practices can begin to dismantle the structures that uphold systemic inequities and build systems that recognize and value the contributions of all individuals, regardless of gender or background. This is not only a moral imperative but also a practical one; diverse and inclusive systems are more resilient, innovative, and effective in meeting the complex challenges of the modern world.

Intersectionality and Structural Power

Kimberlé Crenshaw is known for having coined the today widely used term intersectionality. Her foundational work (Crenshaw, 1989; 1991) helps us see how social identities—such as race, gender, and class—overlap, creating compounded forms of disadvantage. The metaphor of a traffic intersection that she introduces so vividly shows how individuals who stand at the crossroads of multiple systems of oppression can face discrimination that cannot be understood by looking at race or gender alone. Crenshaw's analogy reveals that these intersecting forces are systemic rather than merely the product of individual prejudices. When legal or social frameworks focus on only one category (for instance, gender or race), they often fail to capture the reality of individuals who occupy both. Consequently, these people become invisible to policies and practices meant to address oppression.

This concept of invisible "intersections" is central to Critical Race Theory (CRT), of which Crenshaw is a founding figure (Crenshaw, Thomas, Gotanda, and Peller, 1995). CRT challenges the idea that the law and society are "neutral" and free of racial bias. Instead, it posits that racism is deeply woven into institutions—including education, healthcare, and the criminal justice system. Critics of CRT often claim it encourages guilt or division, but these objections typically conflate CRT with any discussion of systemic racial inequality. Despite the backlash, intersectionality remains essential for activists, scholars, and policymakers who hope to address structural inequities through more holistic approaches.

The anthology Cuerpo, Diferencias y Desigualdades/*Bodies, Differences, and Inequalities* exemplifies intersectionality in a diverse of lived experiences focusing on how marginalized bodies—whether Indigenous peoples, sex workers, domestic laborers, people with disabilities, or members of LGBTQ+ communities—navigate systems that seek to silence or exploit them. Although these groups differ in the specific forms of oppression they experience, their struggles share a common thread: they are shaped by overlapping social, political, and economic forces that often render them invisible.

For instance, Indigenous communities featured in the anthology frequently confront both colonialism's historical legacy and contemporary sociopolitical exclusion. Their forms of resistance are not confined to legal battles or protests; they extend to cultural revival, language preservation, and environmental defense. Standing firmly against harmful practices like the commodification of natural resources, these communities are bravely defending their land against industries that seek to exploit it. Their struggle is a heartfelt challenge to the wider global systems that profit from their marginalization. It's painful to witness how these communities are often overlooked, even as they fight to protect and preserve the environment and ensure a sustainable future, not just for themselves but for generations to come.

Sex workers, similarly, are stigmatized through policies and social norms that deprive them of labor rights and legal protection. Yet, many of them organize, advocate for decriminalization, and form mutual aid networks to support each other. Through these collective efforts, sex workers resist moralizing narratives that dismiss their work as immoral or marginal and expose broader labor injustices that remain unaddressed in mainstream discussions.

Domestic laborers, often women of color, occupy another intersection of race, gender, and class, making their contributions both indispensable and undervalued. Their experiences speak to the larger phenomenon in which caregiving roles are feminized and thus relegated to the periphery of economic importance. Through the formation of unions and dedicated advocacy for improved wages and enhanced workplace protections, domestic workers actively challenge the prevalent belief that care work is merely unskilled or insignificant. They emphasize the essential nature of their roles, showcasing how their labor is integral not only to the functioning of individual households but also to the broader economy. They raise awareness of the complexities and challenges of their work, bringing out the vital contributions they make to community well-being and economic stability, thus advocating for the recognition and respect that their profession deserves.

In the same vein, people with disabilities face pervasive bias that reduces their identities to medical diagnoses rather than recognizing their full personhood. Many of the essays illustrate that the fight for accessibility and disability justice is not about adding ramps or specialized technologies; it is about transforming public consciousness and institutional norms that label disabled bodies as burdens rather than contributors. Their activism ranges from grassroots advocacy for inclusive policies to broader efforts that reframe disability as a natural part of human diversity.

LGBTQ+ people, too, wrestle with intersecting stigmas of heteronormativity, cisnormativity, and transphobia. Acts of resistance and visibility—through Pride marches, art, community organizing, or legal battles—reveal how these communities persistently demand recognition. Their struggles emphasize a central principle of intersectionality: each identity category overlaps with others, complicating the ways people experience discrimination. A trans woman of color, for example, faces a constellation of biases far more complex than those encountered by a white woman or a cisgender person of color alone.

The anthology moves the discussions of power to a nuanced view of how race, class, gender, and other factors shape each other. Ultimately it challenges readers to understand that these bodies—and the communities they represent—are neither mere victims nor monolithic groups. Rather, they are active participants in public life, using resistance and mutual support as strategies for redefining societal norms.

Building on these ideas, intersectionality also plays a key role in debates around technology and data ethics, as scholars like Noble and Benjamin argue (Noble, 2018; Benjamin, 2019). They show that algorithms and digital systems can replicate and even intensify racial and gender biases when not critically examined. Marginalized communities, already at a disadvantage due to entrenched social inequities, often suffer the greatest harm from opaque technologies such as facial recognition, automated hiring software, and predictive policing systems.

Despite these challenges, there are growing efforts to bridge the gap between marginalized groups and the technological spheres that influence their lives. One illustrative example is the collaborative project between Brazilian anthropologist Laymert Garcia dos Santos and the German cultural organization ZKM. In the multimedia opera *Amazonas—Music Theatre in Three Parts*, Garcia dos Santos worked closely with the Yanomami people, integrating their cosmological worldviews into a contemporary technoscientific framework. This effort highlights an important reality: marginalized communities should not be pushed into the "past" or seen merely as folklore. They are part of our present, possessing knowledge systems that are equally modern and just as valid as those of anyone else.

Such collaborations remind us that respect for other cultures is the first requirement for any genuine dialogue. Recognizing these groups solely as "interesting" cultural subjects, without acknowledging their agency and intellectual contributions, is a form of tokenism. Instead, if we see them as co-creators of knowledge, we can reimagine the future of technology and society. Whether it involves Indigenous cosmology in environmental advocacy or the lived experiences of sex workers and people with disabilities shaping policy around data privacy and user interfaces, intersectional perspectives help us build a fairer world.

Intersectionality is much more than a theoretical buzzword. It demands that we examine how different layers of identity converge to shape experiences of discrimination and privilege. In practice, this means designing policies, technologies, and movements that address these overlapping factors head-on rather than tackling them in isolation.

From *Cuerpo, diferencias y desigualdades* to *Amazonas—Music Theatre in Three Parts*, the core message is that marginalized groups are not waiting passively to be "saved" by external forces; they already possess their own strategies, cultural insights, and leadership. Embracing intersectionality, therefore, requires humility and an openness to perspectives that challenge mainstream views. It is a call to action for scholars, activists, technologists, and everyday citizens alike, urging each of us to examine how power operates where identities intersect—and to ensure that those intersections remain visible, valued, and fully included in conversations about justice, equity, and the future of our shared world.

Or, as Crenshaw herself says at the beginning of her podcast, *Intersectionality Matters!* [14]

> *The podcast that brings intersectionality to life by exploring the hidden dimensions of today's most pressing issues—from Say Her Name to the war on "woke," DEI and CRT and the global rise of fascism. This idea travelogue lifts up on the work of activists, artists, and scholars, and helps listeners understand politics, law, social movements, and even their own lives in deeper, more nuanced ways.*

—Kimberlé Crenshaw

Paraphrasing the podcast's name, this is exactly why Intersectionality Matters. The framework offers deeper, more nuanced understandings than any single viewpoint can achieve alone, allowing us to address the complex issues we face by considering the diverse perspectives of different bodies. This is particularly critical for policymakers, who, in creating standards, risk perpetuating harmful practices if they rely on narrow or universalizing assumptions. Too often, those attempts at universality render a majority of people invisible, ignoring the intricacies of their lived realities. Intersectionality compels us to recognize these overlooked nuances, ensuring that our policies and standards are shaped by and responsive to the full range of human experiences.

The Foundations of Diversity: Intentionality As a Requirement

To tackle long-standing biases in technology, we must treat diversity not as an afterthought but as the bedrock of our communities. Benjamin calls for "structural inclusion" rather than "add-on diversity," urging us

---

[14] The podcast is available in several podcasts https://www.aapf.org/intersectionality-matters

to design every layer of our systems—be they algorithms or governance models—with equity in mind. This means asking, right from the start: Whose voices are represented, whose needs are centered, and whose work is properly valued?

Noble's findings on algorithmic bias highlight the power of a diverse development team. When people from a range of racial, gender, and socioeconomic backgrounds collaborate, they challenge assumptions that might otherwise go unnoticed. In open source projects, similar intentional efforts can include structured mentorship for underrepresented contributors, comprehensive codes of conduct, and documentation that welcomes newcomers—especially those who may lack the free time or financial resources to code around the clock.

Strategies for Inclusion in Open Source may include the following:

1. Mentorship and Pairing: Offer formal programs that match newcomers with experienced contributors. This not only boosts skill development but also builds personal connections across cultural or linguistic barriers.

2. Broadening the Definition of Contribution: Recognize community building, design, documentation, and project coordination as essential forms of labor—on par with writing code. The CHAOSS project (Community Health Analytics Open Source Software) offers useful metrics for validating these varied contributions, but more human-centered feedback mechanisms are equally important.

3. Inclusive Governance: Encourage rotating leadership roles and transparent decision-making. Smaller, community-driven projects may be more

flexible in experimenting with these approaches, while larger, corporate-sponsored initiatives can leverage greater resources to formalize inclusive practices and compensation structures. Both models influence how newcomers experience and navigate open source spaces.

4. Affirmative Action and Reparative Measures: Adopt targeted initiatives to redress historical inequities. This can range from scholarships or stipends for contributors from marginalized backgrounds to deliberate outreach in underrepresented communities. Such measures begin to bridge class divides and counteract the generational impact of exclusion, ensuring that a broader range of people can fully participate.

Not all open source projects are alike. Smaller, volunteer-driven communities may be more nimble and welcoming but often rely heavily on unpaid labor. Larger projects with corporate backing can have more formal rules, yet risk skewing priorities toward commercial goals. Understanding these diverse models helps us see how different contributors encounter different kinds of barriers, depending on a project's scale, governance, and funding.

The open source ecosystem offers critical insights for broader debates about labor and equity in tech. Practices that value relational work, cultural knowledge, and continuous learning can inform how we shape policies, workplaces, and legal frameworks. As Laymert Garcia dos Santos demonstrates through collaboration with Indigenous communities, we must treat all knowledge systems—whether digital or ancestral—as equally contemporary and valid. This approach ensures that historically marginalized voices can shape open source and the future of technology.

Yet we face a core obstacle: operating within what Benjamin calls a "blind system," one that privileges quantifiable outputs over human relationships. This technocratic mindset often overlooks contributions like community-building, mentoring, or cultural translation. Reimagining metrics to value such work is essential for genuine inclusivity.

As Verna Myers famously says

"Diversity is being invited to the party; inclusion is being asked to dance."

In practice, this means ensuring people from all backgrounds have a seat at the table—and then actively encouraging them to shape the conversation. Whether in open source or the wider tech industry, the goal is to make diverse voices integral at every level, rather than relegating them to peripheral "diversity" roles. Embracing intentionality, including affirmative action where needed, and recognizing the breadth of ways people contribute, we can build communities—and a tech sector—that serve everyone in equitable, sustainable ways.

What Happens When We Unravel Issues Around Open Source?

This chapter can be summarized with a simple question: If open source has become such an essential cornerstone for many, as illustrated by the popular *XKCD* comic, every time open source is discussed, what occurs when we allow it to be governed by a homogeneous group of individuals who look the same, speak the same, and think alike, often blindly following the influential positions and privileges they hold?

Drop the mic.

This chapter is aimed to challenge readers to consider how systemic awareness, combined with intentional diversity and equity practices, can transform open source into a more inclusive and equitable movement.

This call to action encourages awareness and active participation in reshaping open source communities.

As we saw in the previous chapter, open source is a term that encompasses a huge difference of understandings, which, rather than being divergent, are often complementary. In the book *Empire*, by Negri and Hardt, we find some clues as to why open source has become ubiquitous in our lives.

According to the hypotheses raised in the book, with the change in the nature of work from industry to information, work has become immaterial, because no matter what work is done today, it is, in one way or another, mediated by a computer or software.

This immateriality makes cooperation an immanent part of the work itself.

If we acknowledge that any technology is integrated—both physically and socially—and leads to changes in individual and societal behavior, we can recognize that software development is an intrinsic part of a system that contains inherent biases. This system often goes unnoticed by those who belong to the dominant class, resulting in the marginalization of individuals outside this group and causing their experiences and the consequences they face to become invisible.

It is increasingly clear that, although collaborative in its immanence, this immaterial work has created a more extreme separation of classes, in a globalized, neoliberal world, and without any traditional basis for the protection of social welfare dismantled by the dissipation of nation-states.

My hope in writing this book is that open source will become the power of the multitude against the Empire described by Negri and Hardt. But until we can recognize and consciously change the systemic problems that this beast carries in its belly, open source will be just another tool of oppression, exclusion, and exhaustion of a world in tatters.

CHAPTER 4

Making It a Standard

Shall we put all of this knowledge we have read so far in practice? Too often, the conversation around open source focuses on code commits, pull requests, and licenses, leaving behind crucial, people-oriented labor. This hidden, or "invisible," labor ensures that a project's ecosystem remains sustainable, equitable, and productive over time. The overarching goal of this chapter is to present a framework that combines practical, file-level guidelines—like those recommended by well know open source best practices—with a deeper application of ethics, inclusion, and governance. By integrating these elements, we can transform a basic set of best practices into a holistic blueprint for democracy-anchored open source standards, centering on historical reparation, conscious technology production, and tangible pathways to equity.

I am betting on standards as a transcendent checklist of guidelines that can catalyze radical cultural shifts. Standards are invisible forces that guide the mechanical way you do things, an enforced gentle mechanism. I am betting on this power to guide us all toward an equitable world, at least considering technological production and its effects on society.

As you read, imagine how each file-level rule or governance document clarifies your project's mission and shapes societal norms. Standards, which we are making here, are a democratizing force, a moral compass, and a practical tool all at once.

The immediate purpose of this chapter is to demonstrate how the micro-level details of open source practice—file structures, rule sets, and recommended checklists—can fuse with macro-level governance

P. Oliveira, *Diversifying Open Source*, https://doi.org/10.1007/979-8-8688-0769-5_4

structures. Such a fusion ensures that every form of contribution, from bug fixes to community stewardship, is recognized and honored. It offers a tangible response to a common open source dilemma: even if your project is fully compliant with typical best practices (for example, it has a LICENSE file, a well-written README, a Code of Conduct, and so on), how do you ensure the project also fosters equity and does not exclude historically marginalized voices? Merely passing an automated tool's checks does not guarantee social justice, balanced leadership, or community well-being.

At a granular level, we will explore how certain files—for instance, the Code of Conduct or the Ownership file—communicate shared values and priorities. If a Code of Conduct is missing, contributors have no formal recourse when they face hostility or harassment, which disproportionately affects underrepresented individuals. If the Ownership file is absent, nobody truly "holds" responsibility for the project's future direction, leading to stagnation or confusion. These files, though seemingly mundane, are signposts that can invite more conscious, inclusive behaviors—if and only if the project's broader governance model supports them. Hence, the subsequent sections in this chapter will walk through strategies to embed these smaller best practices in a larger ethical and democratic structure, ensuring that essential but intangible tasks—from translation to mentorship—also gain recognition and resources.

The broader aim is, therefore, to anchor open source in a moral and societal framework. Instead of existing as a purely technical domain, the open source world must recognize that technology is always political— shaped by its makers' intentions, biases, and power relations. This chapter stands at the intersection of these realities, hoping to sketch a blueprint that fosters genuine inclusivity, better communication, and the extension of open source's influence as an engine for social good.

Ethics and Inclusion at the Forefront

No discussion of open source standards would be complete without addressing their ethical dimension. Ethics in open source does not simply mean abiding by the letter of a license. It involves ongoing attention to how the software (and its associated communities) impacts real human lives. Are prospective contributors from different backgrounds able to participate on equal terms? Are you protecting vulnerable users who rely on your software for daily activities, from activism to personal data management? And, crucially, are maintainers and contributors able to articulate their rights, responsibilities, and boundaries without fear of retribution or marginalization?

In practice, placing ethics and inclusion at the forefront means several things. First, it involves recognizing "invisible labor"—the intangible, relational tasks that keep a project healthy but do not typically show up in commit logs. Community moderators field questions at all hours, bridging time zones and cultural contexts; documentation writers translate or clarify technical jargon for novices; designers refine user flows to accommodate individuals with disabilities; product managers help prioritize features and represent the needs of the end users within the project. All these tasks, if unacknowledged, may fall disproportionately on individuals who are already marginalized in tech spaces. Placing ethics at the center ensures these tasks are built into the project's governance, with explicit roles, resources, and acknowledgments.

Second, an ethics-forward approach calls for "restorative justice" measures in the Code of Conduct. Rather than punishing "violators," the project can set up processes for mediation and conversation, focusing on harm reduction and trust rebuilding. This restorative lens contrasts with a purely "enforcement-based" approach that might alienate or intimidate community members, discouraging the very contributions that open source so desperately needs. Finally, this perspective opens the door to a new kind of accountability: project maintainers become stewards of technical decisions and are held accountable for implications of the powerful tools they build.

Adding those principles into the tools and files that shape day-to-day workflows, this new standard this chapter proposes sets open source to its best: to be a fundamental building block for sustainable technology and a tool against asymmetry.

Why Standards Matter

In most technical circles, "standards" evoke the idea of protocols, specifications, or compliance checks that allow diverse software to interoperate. While interoperability is indeed one dimension of why standards matter, the term encompasses far more than that. A standard can serve as a social contract—an artifact that, once collectively recognized, shapes behaviors and expectations across entire ecosystems.

For example, you might initially adopt the widely used MIT License not merely because it is legally effective but because you wish to align your project's ethos with the values of openness and low restriction. Similarly, the existence of a "Contributor Covenant" Code of Conduct in thousands of repositories signals that the open source community holds certain behaviors as baseline norms, such as mutual respect and the condemnation of harassment.

From this perspective, standards function as a cultural roadmap: they define the permissible, the encouraged, and the disallowed. They provide a shared language that helps large groups of diverse people collaborate without constantly revisiting first principles. Integrating ethical principles such as inclusivity, equity, and historical awareness into these standards allows us to transform the solely technocratic aspect of open source into a movement focused on addressing societal imbalances.

Standards encourage a replicable blueprint for new and existing projects alike. When a standard is well-documented, new maintainers can quickly adapt it for their own contexts, ensuring that local variations (such as language or region) are respected while the broader principles remain intact. This fluidity prevents knowledge silos and fosters consistent improvement. Once a robust standard is established, it becomes easier to onboard newcomers, guide them through recognized practices, and let them see how the project's governance structures have been built over time. In short, a standard can be a living document that evolves in response to new contributors and new social or technological developments, ensuring that the community remains agile yet anchored to its core ethical commitments.

To help you with that, this book is accompanied by an open-source tool that shapes this blueprint into a custom project for your context.

The Nature of Standards in the Context of Democracy

Standards and democracy share a deeper relationship than one might initially suspect. At the heart of democracy lies the principle that all stakeholders—citizens, in a civic sense—should have a say in the decisions that affect them. In the technology zone, especially within open source, "stakeholders" include maintainers, casual contributors, advanced users, occasional bug reporters, and even passersby who have not yet discovered the project but may in the future. A democratic standard attempts to grant each of these groups a voice in shaping how the project's processes and values are codified. Far from being authoritarian, a democratic standard emerges from collective deliberation, feedback loops, and iterative refinements.

In an ideal scenario, open source democracy mirrors the checks and balances seen in civic governance. For instance, crucial changes to a governance document might require a supermajority among maintainers or a public comment period during which anyone can raise questions or suggest amendments. The standard then acts as a constitution of sorts: it is the stable reference that prevents any one individual or faction from accumulating outsized power. This ties deeply into the concept of "invisible labor," since it is precisely that behind-the-scenes and often volunteer-driven work—such as updating documentation, resolving interpersonal conflict, or steering the design process—that keeps democracy functioning. When the standard explicitly addresses these roles, democracy gains structure and transparency, validating that historically sidelined voices have institutional channels through which to influence the project's direction.

Democracy in open source calls for accountability. If you state that your project is "open to everyone," do your standards reflect that? Is there a well-known feedback mechanism for someone who identifies systemic bias? Does the standard define procedures for conflict resolution that avoid retaliation against vulnerable members? These are not idle questions, for when democracy is invoked as a guiding principle, it must be practiced in tangible ways. Otherwise, it risks devolving into a hollow slogan. Thus, a standard that arises in the context of democracy must ensure procedural clarity (who votes, how they vote, and under what conditions changes are accepted) and must embed equity checks into every major decision-making step.

Conscious Technology Production and Historical Reparations

At first glance, it might seem like a leap to connect file-level rules and open source governance to historical reparations. Yet technology, specifically open source, has the power to be a tool of liberation or oppression, depending on whose hands shape it. Historical injustices—colonialism, systemic racism, patriarchy, and ableism—often manifest in technology through the exclusion of certain communities and the prioritization of certain languages, geographies, or cultural norms over others. When we speak of conscious technology production, we are calling for an intentional reevaluation of how, why, and for whom we build software. Are the defaults in your system truly inclusive? Do we consult the communities most impacted by the technology before finalizing features or deciding on resource allocations?

Historical reparation in tech can be understood as a commitment to restore or offset the cumulative disadvantages that historically underrepresented groups face. In an open source context, it can look like actively recruiting maintainers from underrepresented backgrounds and vouching for them to have leadership influence or funneling project funds to training programs that uplift marginalized developers. It might also involve adopting more inclusive language throughout your documentation (e.g., avoiding ableist terms or archaic references), or partnering with organizations that center on bridging the digital divide. This is not superficial virtue signaling: it is a continuous effort to rectify systemic imbalances.

The impetus for such reparations arises naturally once we acknowledge that technology is not neutral. For instance, consider how certain open source communities developed their norms in predominantly Western, English-speaking contexts. Even well-intentioned maintainers may overlook the linguistic or cultural barriers that deter non-Western contributors. A conscious approach would incorporate multilingual support, flexible meeting times, and rotating roles so that no single group or time zone dominates the discussion. Integrating these commitments into the standard—declaring them as integral to the project's identity— establishes a "conscious technology contract." This approach postulates that every participant, whether new or veteran, recognizes historical equity as a core value rather than an optional add-on.

The Hypothesis Behind Betting in Standards

The central hypothesis tying these ideas together is that a project's success, sustainability, and fairness grow exponentially when the granular best practices are harmonized with a broader, democracy-based governance model that actively addresses ethical obligations, invisible labor, and historical reparation. In other words, it is not enough to check the boxes for the presence of essential files like a README, License, Code of Conduct, or Ownership. These files must be embedded in a governance environment that fosters participatory decision-making, recognizes the entire spectrum of contributions, and invests in rebalancing historical and structural inequities.

I hypothesize further that projects following this new standard will find the "holy grail" of sustainability, as it will develop resilience, attracting and retaining contributors from a wide variety of backgrounds who, feeling genuinely valued, will willingly pour their energy and creativity into it. This positive feedback loop is well documented in many civic contexts (communities that show respect to all members typically garner more robust engagement), and the same logic applies to code communities. When building a standard that is explicit about who gets credit, how conflicts are resolved, and which ethical lines must not be crossed, you create an environment where trust can flourish, forging a healthy cycle of mutual support and accountability.

Once these structures and rules are set up, they do not remain static. Instead, they evolve in parallel with the community's growth, challenges, and aspirations. Over time, you might see new roles emerging—like "Accessibility Lead" or "Resource Allocation Advisor"—because the standard has made space for new definitions of contribution. In a sense, the standard becomes the foundation for an organic, living organism of civic-tech symbiosis rather than a rigid bureaucratic overlay.

A Blueprint for Becoming a Standard

With the above themes in mind—why standards matter, democracy, ethics, inclusivity, and historical reparation—this chapter provides a blueprint for how your project can elevate its local guidelines and best practices into a widely adopted standard. The essence of a standard, after all, is that it transcends individual or idiosyncratic preferences, gaining acceptance or at least recognition across broad communities. To become a standard, a project must meticulously articulate not only the "what" of its policies but also the "why." This involves the following:

1. **Documenting Clear Rules:** Whether it is a Code of Conduct, license statements, or an Ownership file, each artifact should explain how it serves the community and respects ethical principles. Resist the urge to keep them purely technical. Instead, weave in short statements or references about how, for instance, the Code of Conduct aims to protect historically marginalized members, or how the Ownership file ties into the project's democratic ethos by specifying accountability roles.

2. **Facilitating Participatory Governance:** Open channels—forums, mailing lists, messaging groups—where the community can collectively refine and update these rules. The project's maintainers play a curatorial role, facilitating that proposed changes align with the core mission of equity and inclusion and remain receptive to novel perspectives. In effect, governance is an iterative dance: the standard guides decisions, while decisions also shape the standard.

3. **Credit and Recognition:** Detail how to track all types of labor. Are you using "All Contributors"— style readouts that highlight non-code tasks? Are you awarding badges for event organizers or translators? Are you regularly acknowledging community leaders who sustain healthy discourse? The standard becomes truly robust when it institutionalizes these forms of recognition, making them as visible as commit counts. Over time, these acknowledgment practices can become a norm that other projects replicate.

4. **Codifying Restorative Justice Mechanisms:** Conflicts and misunderstandings are inevitable. By setting a precedent for how they are resolved through empathy, conversation, and restitution, you embed the notion that open source communities can be safer, more humane places for everyone. This fosters a sense of collective responsibility: upholding the standard is not about punishing rule-breakers; it is about ensuring that the community heals and learns so that no one is implicitly pushed out.

5. **Scaling It:** If your blueprint is effective, people beyond your immediate circle will adopt it. That might mean forging partnerships with related projects, inviting them to pilot the rules, or adapting them to local contexts. Over time, standards flourish through references and cross-pollination, not by top-down decree. The more you can illustrate how these governance strategies solve real-world problems— like high turnover or interpersonal friction—the more likely they will be embraced widely.

The end goal is for open source communities to consciously align their practices with democratic values, ethical obligations, and the need to address historical inequalities. A single project that sets high standards but fails to share them widely will remain an isolated case. Conversely, a single project that tries to enforce a standard without community buy-in risks pushing out the very contributors it aims to protect. Thus, the notion of a "blueprint" emphasizes that these steps should be aspirational yet flexible, guiding but not micromanaging.

Every open source repository is, in miniature, a micro-society. Its day-to-day processes reveal or obscure certain labor, empower or silence certain voices, and cultivate either an atmosphere of belonging or of deterrence. Technology's imprint on society has never been more pronounced than in our time, and open source stands at a crossroads of possibility. If we treat standards as purely technical guidelines, we risk leaving behind those who have historically been excluded, creating an even wider societal gap. If we treat them as inclusive social contracts, we unlock the potential for open source to become a model of equitable, participatory development—one that produces software that in itself fosters a more just, collaborative world.

My hope is that, by choosing to use this practical standard, you will appreciate how to audit your repository's best practices and be prepared to elevate those practices into a robust, democracy-infused project—one that acknowledges its historical responsibilities and consciously steers the future toward genuine inclusivity.

Open Source Best Practices: Document Templates

Open source is more than just lines of code. It's a living ecosystem of contributors, maintainers, designers, testers, documenters, translators, and community organizers. When most people think of open source, their attention goes to commit counts, pull requests, or licenses; however, sustainable projects hinge on equitable governance, transparent communication, and recognition of all sorts of labor. This section offers a detailed template for the documents that underpin a healthy open source project—ranging from security rules (like excluding binaries) to practical guidelines (like SUPPORT.md and Code of Conduct) to forward-thinking best practices inspired by the Open Source Complex Ecosystems and Networks (OCEAN) research for Attributing Contributor Roles in Open Source Software (ACROSS) and Open Design strategies that are reshaping open source projects.

The ACROSS labeling was developed by the OCEAN project in the Vermont Complex Systems Center at the University of Vermont, supported by the Google Open Source Program Office. It was created to address the lack of standardized contribution acknowledgment in open source, particularly for non-code contributions such as documentation, moderation, found-raising, security triage, and community organization. Inspired by frameworks like CRediT, which has been widely adopted in academic research, ACROSS labeling provides a structured taxonomy for contributor roles in an effort to find equitable credit distribution and surfacing often invisible labor.

Each subsection is a document in itself, and it will follow this structure:

1. **Why it's important** – A brief rationale for the document's existence.

2. **History behind it** – Tracing its roots in open source or software development.

3. **Risks of not having it** – Consequences or missed opportunities when it's absent.

4. **Labeling and ethics behind it** – Based on OCEAN's research, propose some labeling approaches to include non-code contributions in the loop of certain tasks and recognize such efforts

5. **Checklist** – Concrete items with optional fill-in lines that can be immediately added to your own document.

Because every project is unique, each template should be adapted to your community's needs. Where relevant, we'll note ideas for labeling tasks (e.g., "translation," "design," "event organizing," etc.) and open design suggestions (like user-centered PR templates) that help bridge the gap between code-centric and people-centric work.

1. README

2. Binaries (Security Rule)

3. Code of Conduct

4. License

    4.1. License on Headers

    4.2. License Mention on README

5. Changelog and Semver

6. Contributing Guidelines

7. Ownership File or MAINTAINERS.md

8. Test Directory (TestDir)

9. Issue and Pull Request Templates

10. Security Policy (SECURITY.md)

11. Support (SUPPORT.md)

12. Accessibility Guidelines (ACCESSIBILITY.md)

13. Code Review Guidelines (CODE_REVIEW.md)

14. Governance Policy (GOVERNANCE.md)

15. Meeting Notes and Transparency (MEETINGS.md)

16. Community Acknowledgment (CREDIT.md)

17. Localization Guidelines (LOCALIZATION.md)

18. Funding and Sponsorship Transparency (FUNDING.md)

19. Adopters and User Stories (Adopters.md)

Conclusion

1. README

Why It's Important

The README is your project's front door. It orients newcomers to the mission, scope, and how to get started. A thorough, inclusive README also highlights who the project serves and how coders and non-coders can contribute.

History Behind It

- Roots in UNIX: The concept of "README" stems from early documentation conventions in the 1970s.

- GitHub Enhancement: Markdown rendering in GitHub turned READMEs into visually appealing mini-websites by 2010.

Risks of Not Having It

- Contributor Confusion: Prospective contributors cannot gauge whether the project aligns with their skills or interests.

- Poor User Adoption: If users can't see quick general information about what the project is about and how to install or use the project, they move on.

- Missed Nontechnical Contributions: Designers, translators, or event organizers may not realize there's a place for them.

Labeling and Ethics Behind It

- Recognizing Non-code Tasks: The README can name doc writers, outreach leads, or user-research champions.

- Equal Footing: By stating that non-code roles are vital, you respect the "invisible labor" that keeps a project healthy.

Checklist: README

- [ ] Project Overview
    - [ ] Summarize: Name, short description, main goal, relevant links.
    - [ ] Show a quickstart or installation instructions.
- [ ] Open Design Section
    - [ ] Briefly describe any user research, design sketches, or accessible features.
    - [ ] Invite nontechnical roles: "We welcome testers, translators, marketing folks—here's how to get involved."

[ ]   Link Key Documents

    [ ]   Code of Conduct, License, Contributing, etc.

    [ ]   Be explicit about how the community organizes itself and meets: Is it a forum, a message, or a social media app providing details for how contributors and users can contact the community.

Example of how your document can look like:

"This project aims to solve _____ for _____ audience."

"Our open design philosophy encourages contributions from _____ and focuses on _____."

2. Binaries (Security Rule)

Why It's Important

A fundamental pillar of project security is preventing sensitive files—executables, passwords, private keys—from slipping into your repository. By disallowing binary files, you reduce the attack surface, keep your repo's version history clean, and protect contributor privacy. This measure also conveys a sense of professionalism to prospective contributors, signaling that your team takes security and user trust seriously.

History Behind It

Before Git and distributed version control, developers commonly archived binaries into source tarballs—compressed packages that bundled together both human-readable source code and compiled programs (binaries) that computers could actually run—for distribution. This approach made sense when sharing software meant physically mailing diskettes or posting files on bulletin boards. Over time, however, these bundled packages became unwieldy: they were large, difficult to inspect (since you couldn't easily separate the readable code from the executable files), and made collaboration challenging when multiple developers needed to track changes. As continuous integration (CI) pipelines and automated builds became the norm—systems that could automatically compile source code into binaries whenever needed—storing pre-compiled binaries in version control became both inefficient and risky. Simultaneously, the rise of package managers—specialized systems like npm, pip, Maven, and others that handle the distribution and installation of software—provided dedicated channels for sharing compiled programs, eliminating the need to include binaries in source repositories altogether. Tools like .gitignore files emerged to tell version control systems which files to exclude, completing the separation between managing source code (what developers write) and distributing finished software (what users install).

Risks of Not Having It

- Security Vulnerabilities: Leaked passwords or tokens can compromise user data, brand reputation, and even personal safety.

- Repository Bloat: Binaries can quickly inflate repository size, making it hard to clone, browse, or contribute.

- Compliance Issues: Certain binaries might contain copyrighted or restricted materials, leading to legal complications.

Labeling and Ethics Behind It

- Transparency: Ensuring no secret files are stored fosters trust among all contributors—particularly those who do not have direct oversight of the repository.

- OCEAN Labeling: Label tasks like "security review," "repo audit," or "cleanup" to credit those who quietly keep the project safe.

Checklist: Binaries and Security Rule

[ ]   Create or Update .gitignore

    [ ]   Add lines for executables, .exe, .dll, .so, .bin, etc.

    [ ]   Add environment-specific artifacts (like .DS_ Store for macOS or Thumbs.db for Windows).

[ ]   Scan Your Repo

    [ ]   Use automated security scanning tools to detect any hidden credentials.

[ ]   Periodically check commit history for overlooked large files or sensitive data.

[ ]   Clarify Policy

    [ ]   In your README or CONTRIBUTING file, clarify that no binaries or secrets should be committed.

    [ ]   Indicate steps for contributors who accidentally commit sensitive items.

Your CONTRIBUTING.md file can resemble something like this:

"Our project excludes binaries by using _____ tool or _____ strategy."

"If a contributor finds a stored binary, they should contact _____ or follow _____ procedure."

3. Code of Conduct

Why It's Important

A Code of Conduct (CoC) anchors your project's commitment to respectful collaboration. It defines acceptable behavior and sets forth conflict-resolution processes. Rather than punitive "enforcement," I advocate for nonviolent language usage and a restorative justice-inspired approach—focusing on mediation, growth, and conflict de-escalation to help mitigate systemic issues that truly benefit the whole community and heal the individuals involved.

History Behind It

Early open source communities such as Linux Kernel and BSD often lacked explicit behavioral guidelines, which sometimes led to toxic interactions.

In 2014, Coraline Ada Ehmke created the Contributor Covenant, which became a landmark CoC, adopted by big communities like Kubernetes, Ruby on Rails, and Node.js, spurring a shift toward more inclusive open source cultures.

Risks of Not Having It

- Hostile Environment: Without a CoC, marginalized contributors can be driven away by bullying, racism, sexism, or other abuses.

- Reputation Damage: Sponsors or collaborators may be reluctant to invest in a project perceived as unsafe.

- Volunteer Burnout: Moderators bear the brunt of conflict without official backing.

Labeling and Ethics Behind It

- Maintaining Community Health: Moderators often do emotional and relational work behind the scenes. Label that work (e.g., "community management" or "conflict resolution") and celebrate it.

- Open Design: In a user-centric design context, CoCs create safe spaces that encourage a broader range of contributors, including end-users who might test or share feedback without fear of harassment.

Checklist: Code of Conduct

[ ]   Define Values and Expectations

    [ ]   Outline what respectful dialogue looks like; discourage harassment, hate speech, or disruptive behavior.

[ ]   Describe Reporting and Resolution

    [ ]   Provide multiple contact points for incident reporting (e.g., private email, forum form).

    [ ]   Emphasize restorative steps (apology, mediated conversation) before strict bans, where feasible.

    [ ]   Be clear about what happens when a report is received: what's the response time, what may happen to the person being reported, how you prioritize the reporter's safety and anonymity, etc.

[ ]   Credit Moderators

    [ ]   Publicly acknowledge the invisible labor of
        moderation.

    [ ]   Encourage a rotating moderation system to share
        the workload.

You can use the Contributor Covenant template to get started with your community code of conduct and shape it to your community needs (https://www.contributor-covenant.org/). I have created a code of conduct for OpenServ (https://docs.openserv.ai/resources/code_of_conduct) when working as a Developer Advocate for the company, simplifying the language and using nonviolent language avoiding, for example, the use of the work enforcement. IU can also recommend Mozilla's Community Participation (https://www.mozilla.org/en-US/about/governance/policies/participation/) as an inspiration.

4. License

Why It's Important

A software license clarifies who can use, redistribute, or modify the code—and under what conditions. This fosters collaboration, trust, and legal clarity, so no contributor inadvertently violates copyright laws.

History Behind It

The Free Software Foundation (FSF), founded by Richard Stallman in the 1980s, popularized copyleft licenses (GPL). In 1998, the Open Source Initiative (OSI) standardized definitions of open source licenses and validated permissive licenses like MIT and Apache.

Risks of Not Having It

- Legal Gray Zone: Without a license, the project is effectively proprietary by default.

- Blocked Adoption: Companies or other projects cannot legally integrate your code.

- Contributor Hesitation: Potential contributors may fear liability or IP entanglements.

Labeling and Ethics Behind It

- Minimizing Legal Risk: Nontechnical contributors (e.g., legal advisors and compliance checkers) deserve recognition for reading through dense legal text.

- Labeling: Tag tasks like "license compliance" or "legal review" so those who help finalize the license are recognized.

Checklist: License

- [ ]   Choose a license. Prefer a license that is well recognized and approved by the Free Software Foundation or Open Source Initiative. Note that specific licenses may have additional requirements (e.g., file naming conventions and mandatory license headers in source files).

- [ ]   Provide a rationale in the README for your choice.

[ ]   Add a LICENSE.md file.

   [ ]   Place it at the project root in a file named
          LICENSE or LICENSE.md.

   [ ]   Reference it in the README ("This project is
          licensed under the...license_____").

   [ ]   Verify Compliance Requirements. Research any
          additional steps your chosen license requires
          (headers, specific file names, attribution
          formats). Some licenses require additional steps
          and specific names for files (COPYING for GPL)
          or specific mentions of the license in every source
          code file.

[ ]   Acknowledge License Debates

   [ ]   If your community is uncertain, host an open
          design conversation or poll, ensuring all
          stakeholders can weigh the pros/cons.

An example of license acknowledgment:

"After community discussion, we've chosen the _____ license for
reasons of _____."

"To clarify any licensing concerns, email _____ or open an issue
labeled 'licensing.'"

4.1. License on Headers

Why It's Important

Placing a license notice at the top of each source file is an additional clarity
measure, ensuring that even if the file is taken or reused independently,
it's licensing is explicit. This also helps new contributors see usage
permissions without rummaging through the entire repo.

History Behind It

- Copyleft Approach: GPL historically recommended a notice in each file to preserve licensing obligations.

- Company Policy: Some organizations use header notices to meet internal legal guidelines.

Risks of Not Having It

- Ambiguity: Single-file consumers may be unsure about usage or compliance.

- Compliance Gaps: Inadvertent license violations can occur when code is snippet-copied.

- Underinformed Contributors: People modifying just one file might not realize the bigger licensing constraints.

Labeling and Ethics Behind It

- Minimizing Confusion: Non-lawyers or new contributors can see license clarity upfront.

- Tag tasks like "legal compliance" or "header maintenance" to credit the folks who systematically keep files up to date.

Checklist: License on Headers

[ ]   Choose a Notice Format

    [ ]   A short paragraph referencing the main LICENSE file.

    [ ]   Typically includes date and author names or project name.

[ ]   Automate

    [ ]   Tools like addlicense or license-checker can automatically insert or verify headers.

    [ ]   Provide instructions in CONTRIBUTING for how to add headers to new files.

[ ]   Keep It Brief

    [ ]   Avoid overly long boilerplate.

    [ ]   A simple line referencing the official license suffices for many projects.

Example of how your document can look like:

"Example header: // Copyright (C) 2023. This code is licensed under the MIT License. See LICENSE.md in project root."

"When creating new files, please add the license header referencing _____."

4.2. License Mention on README

Why It's Important

Even if you store a license in a separate file, referencing it in the README ensures high visibility. Many casual readers never scroll beyond the README, making it an ideal spot to reinforce usage terms.

Risks of Not Having It

- Hidden Terms: Users may not realize they have permission to reuse or modify the software.

- Frequent Queries: Maintainers get repeated questions about allowed usage.

- Legal Confusion: Downstream developers may only discover licensing constraints after major integration work.

Labeling and Ethics Behind It

- Inclusivity: Making the license easily readable respects users who are less familiar with software licensing norms.

Checklist: License Mention on README

[ ] Prominent Placement

    [ ] Include a short line near the top: "Licensed under...see LICENSE.md."

    [ ] Provide a rationale for why that license suits your project mission.

[ ] Optional Badges

    [ ] Tools like Shields.io allow adding a license badge at the top of your README for quick scanning.

[ ] Link to Further Info

    [ ] Provide a link to OSI or FSF pages if the license might be unknown or needs more explanation.

Example of how your document can look like:

"This project is released under the _____ license to reflect our core values of _____."

"Learn more about your usage rights in the LICENSE file or at _____."

5. Changelog and Semver

Why It's Important

A CHANGELOG.md helps users and contributors track updates between releases, see the progress, and understand new features or bug fixes. It also fosters accountability for changes—particularly if you highlight who contributed to each piece. It's also important for

- Predictability: Users and contributors understand what kind of update they are getting.

- Dependency Management: Helps maintainers track compatible versions.

- Clear Communication: Avoids confusion about when breaking changes are introduced.

Semantic Versioning (SemVer) is a standardized versioning system used in software development to communicate the nature of changes between releases. If a project uses SemVer, the CHANGELOG.md should reflect version increments and describe what changed in each release. It follows a three-number format: MAJOR.MINOR.PATCH.

- MAJOR (X.0.0) → Introduces breaking changes that are not backward-compatible.

- MINOR (0.Y.0) → Adds new features but remains backward-compatible.

- PATCH (0.0.Z) → Fixes bugs without changing functionality.

Example Versions in SemVer:

Version	Change Type	Example Use Case
1.0.0	Initial release	First stable version
1.1.0	Minor update	Added a new API function
1.1.1	Patch	Fixed a security bug
2.0.0	Major update	Removed deprecated features, breaking compatibility

Risks of Not Having It

- Unclear Development and Production Risks: Users can't tell what's new or fixed, risking confusion and repeated issues. More critically, users may unknowingly upgrade to versions with breaking changes, potentially disrupting production systems or causing compatibility failures.

- Difficult Collaboration: Maintainers may lose track of who contributed what feature.

- Missed Celebration: Contributors (testers, doc writers) don't get recognized for each release.

Labeling and Ethics Behind It

- Visibility for All: The changelog can highlight behind-the-scenes roles (bug triage, user testing).

- Labeling: Tag each credited role (e.g., "design, docs, testing, security review") to show the full collaboration scope.

Checklist: Changelog

[ ] Structured Versioning

    [ ] Adopt SemVer or a simple numbering scheme.

    [ ] List each version with categories like Added, Changed, Fixed, Deprecated.

[ ] Credit Contributors

    [ ] Mention each contributor's handle or name, including those who tested or documented.

    [ ] Optionally link to PRs or commits.

[ ] Highlight Impact

    [ ] Summarize how changes affect end-users, referencing user stories or design updates if relevant.

Example of how your document can look like:

```
"All notable changes to this project will be documented
in this file. This project follows **[Semantic Versioning]
(https://semver.org/)**.
## [2.1.0] - 2025-02-16
### Added
- Introduced a new **user roles system** for better project
access management.
- Added support for **multi-language UI**, with initial
translations in Spanish and French (  **label: translation**).
### Changed
- Updated **authentication flow** to use OAuth 2.0 for improved
security.
```

- Enhanced **documentation on API endpoints** (🏷 **label: documentation**).
Fixed
- Resolved issue where **session tokens expired prematurely**.
- Fixed broken links in **README.md**.
---"

Automating Changelog Generation Using Git

Instead of manually maintaining a CHANGELOG.md, you can use Git-based automation tools to generate changelogs directly from commit messages, issue numbers, or pull request descriptions. There are different ways to do it, being the most common the git log.

````git log --pretty=format:"- %h %s (%an, %ad)" --date=short > CHANGELOG.md```

- %h → Short commit hash

- %s → Commit message

- %an → Author

- %ad → Date

6. Contributing Guidelines
Why It's Important

CONTRIBUTING.md sets forth how new ideas, bug reports, or code changes should be submitted. It clarifies the process from proposal to final merge, reducing friction and setting an inclusive tone.
````

History Behind It

- Linux Kernel: Known for rigorous patch submission guidelines through mailing lists.

- GitHub Adoption: Around 2014, GitHub added special recognition for CONTRIBUTING.md.

Risks of Not Having It

- Contributor Confusion: People may not know your entire contribution process—from setting up a development environment and understanding code style to navigating the review and approval workflow.

- High Overhead: Maintainers must repeatedly answer the same process questions.

- Exclusion of Non-coders: Without explicit mention, nontechnical folks might assume they have no role.

Labeling and Ethics Behind It

- Open Design: By specifying how design decisions get discussed, you bring more perspectives into the dev process.

- Label tasks like "community outreach," "mentoring," or "fundraising" so these contributions aren't overlooked.

Checklist: Contributing Guidelines

- [ ] Submission Process

    - [ ] Steps for forking, branching, running tests, and making pull requests.

    - [ ] Mention any code style or linting tools.

- [ ] Inclusive Pathways

    - [ ] Provide "first-timer-friendly" issues.

    - [ ] Encourage design suggestions, doc improvements, or event organizing.

- [ ] Open Design Framework

    - [ ] Clarify how contributors can propose user research or design prototypes.

    - [ ] Offer typical design sprint outlines or user feedback cycles, if relevant.

Example of how your document can look like:

"To propose a new feature, please open an Issue labeled _____ and describe _____."

"We welcome non-code contributions such as _____ or _____."

7. Ownership File or MAINTAINERS.md

Why It's Important

The document identifies who is responsible for technical decisions, merges, community management, and other decision types. It ensures accountability and smooth transitions when maintainers step down.

Advanced projects can implement a "Contributor Ladder"[1] that defines clear pathways for advancement through different levels of responsibility.

History Behind It

- Apache and Mozilla: Large foundations began clarifying roles to manage thousands of contributors.

- Forking Explosion: With software development popularity and ease of forking, the question of "Who's in charge?" became critical for project continuity.

- CNCF Evolution: The Cloud Native Computing Foundation developed contributor ladder templates that formalize advancement pathways, recognizing both technical and nontechnical contributions as routes to leadership.

Risks of Not Having It

- Repository Abandonment: If maintainers leave without notice, urgent issues go unattended.

- Undefined Authority: Contributors don't know whose approval is required for merges.

- Unclear Advancement: People want to take on more responsibility but don't know how to progress.

- Unfair Workloads: The same people get stuck with invisible tasks (community help) without recognized roles.

---

[1] https://github.com/cncf/project-template/blob/main/CONTRIBUTOR_
LADDER.md

Labeling and Ethics Behind It

- Equitable Governance: OCEAN research highlights the need for distributing power beyond code merges.

- Pathway Recognition: Contributor ladders explicitly acknowledge that non-coding work—documentation, event organizing, community management—can lead to leadership roles.

- Acknowledging Triage: If someone answers user queries daily, they deserve an official role as user-support or triage lead.

Checklist: Ownership

[ ]   Basic maintenance information:

    [ ]   List key roles: Primary Maintainer, Release Lead, Community Manager, etc.

    [ ]   Include contact info (email or any other community contact).

[ ]   Succession planning:

    [ ]   Outline how new maintainers are appointed.

    [ ]   Link to Contributing Guidelines for how interested parties can step up.

    [ ]   Define inactivity and emeritus processes. This respectful title or status can be given to someone who has stepped back from active involvement but is honored for past contributions. Having defined eligibility criteria or recognition mechanisms may be helpful for transparency.

[ ] Articulate, in advance, the consequences of harmful or unethical behavior, including a defined process for revoking maintainer status when warranted.

[ ] Define advancement pathways:

[ ] Consider implementing a contributor ladder with defined levels (Community Participant ➤ Contributor ➤ Organization Member ➤ Reviewer ➤ Maintainer).

[ ] Specify both coding and non-coding routes to leadership (documentation, community management, event organizing).

[ ] Outline clear requirements and responsibilities for each level.

[ ] Recognize diverse leadership:

[ ] Admin roles include financial oversight or documentation lead.

[ ] Possibly incorporate them into the commit or merge decision-making process.

[ ] Include roles like Documentation Maintainer, Community Manager, or Release Manager.

[ ] Integrate nontechnical leads into decision-making processes.

Example of how your document can look like:

"Our contributor ladder recognizes multiple pathways to leadership, including _____ (technical roles) and _____ (community roles)."

"To advance from Contributor to Organization Member, requirements include _____, which can be met through coding, documentation, community management, or event organizing."

8. Test Directory (TestDir)

Why It's Important

Reliable testing fosters user trust and developer confidence. A dedicated /tests folder can host unit, integration, or end-to-end tests to catch regressions early.

History Behind It

- Pioneers: Agile methodology (late 1990s) championed Test-Driven Development (TDD).

- Modern Norm: CI/CD tools now expect standardized test suites for automatic builds.

Risks of Not Having It

- Frequent Breaks: Unverified code merges can break existing features.

- User Frustration: Poor stability discourages adoption.

- Burnout: Manual testers or bug reporters become overworked.

Labeling and Ethics Behind It

- Valuing Testers: QA (Quality Assurance) and Software Development Engineers in Test are valuable professions sometimes used as a step to other types of software development. When these roles are treated as fundamental in open source contributions, they can become valuable entry points into the job market.

- Recognize them with "QA" or "Testing" labels.

- Frame tests around real user scenarios (accessibility and multilingual support), acknowledging that user experience is crucial.

Checklist: TestDir

[ ]   Establish Testing Strategy

    [ ]   Decide on frameworks: Jest, Mocha, Pytest, JUnit, etc.

    [ ]   Document test coverage goals (unit vs. integration).

[ ]   Organize and Label

    [ ]   Encourage contributors to label PRs with "test coverage" or "refactor testing."

    [ ]   Provide examples of typical test file naming (example.test.js or test_example.py).

[ ]   Encourage Collaboration

    [ ]   Invite non-code testers: "Report user experience bugs or usability issues."

    [ ]   Provide guidelines for test data or user journeys.

Example of how your document can look like:

"We use _____ as our primary test framework. Our coverage goal is _____%."

"If you find a bug, please open an issue labeled _____ for test improvement."

9. Issue and Pull Request Templates

Why It's Important

Templates are essential tools that minimize guesswork for contributors by guiding them to provide key information, such as steps to reproduce bugs, desired outcomes, and design rationale. They enhance project accessibility by creating a consistent format, making it easier for all contributors to engage and for reviewers to assess submissions.

Incorporating user story prompts and highlighting accessibility considerations within these templates encourages contributors to think critically about the user experience and understand the reasoning behind each issue. This structured approach improves the quality of contributions and fosters a more inclusive development environment.

History Behind It

- GitHub Innovation (2016): Introduced .github/ISSUE_TEMPLATE and .github/PULL_REQUEST_TEMPLATE, widely adopted to standardize submission info.

Risks of Not Having It

- Incomplete Submissions: Harder for maintainers to resolve issues or evaluate PRs if critical data is missing.

- Communication Friction: Repeated back-and-forth requests for logs, environment details, or test results can lead to frustration on both sides—maintainers must solicit missing information, while contributors may feel overwhelmed or discouraged by requests they weren't aware were necessary. This not only creates additional overhead for maintainers but can also frustrate contributors who may not have known what was required in the first place.

- Exclusion: Nontechnical folks may not know how to structure a feature request or user story.

Labeling and Ethics Behind It

- Relational Work: Writing and refining templates is often done by community organizers who rarely receive credit.

- Insert "role tags" for who might handle design, docs, or event-based tasks, acknowledging that non-code PRs matter just as much.

Checklist: Issue and PR Templates

- [ ] Bug Report Template
  - [ ] Fields for environment, steps to reproduce, expected/actual results, screenshots, logs.
  - [ ] Encourage labeling tasks: "Translation needed," "Design fix," "Doc request."
- [ ] Feature Request or Design Proposal
  - [ ] Prompt for user story: "As a _____, I want _____ so that _____."
  - [ ] Encourage links to mockups or user feedback.

[]   Pull Request Template

     []   Outline purpose, changes, how to test, and relevant issue references.

     []   Affirm code-of-conduct compliance or design alignment.

Example of how your document can look like:

"For new features, please provide user stories: _____."

"Label your issue with _____ to help us triage quickly."

10. Security Policy (SECURITY.md)

Why It's Important

SECURITY.md outlines how to report vulnerabilities and how the project addresses them. This fosters trust among users, especially those who rely on the software in critical settings.

History Behind It

- Professional Disclosure: Corporate software historically used private channels for vulnerability reporting.

- Open Source Shift: The push for transparency led to the practice of public security policies, especially as major projects faced security crises (e.g., Heartbleed in 2014).

Risks of Not Having It

- Delay in Reporting: Users may find security flaws but don't know whom to notify, so they remain unfixed.

- Public Exploits: Hackers exploit known vulnerabilities if the community lacks a formal disclosure path.

- Loss of Confidence: Larger organizations or governments avoid your software if they see no security policy.

Labeling and Ethics Behind It

- Vulnerability Triage: Recognize the behind-the-scenes labor of analyzing reported flaws.

- Mark tasks like "security oversight" or "vulnerability triage" so the community sees these as vital roles.

Checklist: Security Policy

[ ] Disclosure Path

   [ ] Provide an email or form for confidential vulnerability reports.

   [ ] Indicate response time frames (e.g., "We aim to respond within 72 hours.").

[ ] Embargo Policy

   [ ] Specify whether your project supports coordinated disclosure under embargo—i.e., a defined period during which disclosed vulnerabilities are shared privately with trusted users (especially corporate consumers) before public release.

[ ]   State how long embargoes typically last (e.g., 7–30 days) and under what circumstances they may be shortened or extended (e.g., severity, exploitability, affected user base).

[ ] Patch Cycle

[ ]   Outline how you roll out security fixes, verify them, and communicate to users.

[ ]   Describe how security fixes are developed, tested, and released.

[ ]   Reference where fixes will be communicated (e.g., changelog entries, release notes, security advisories).

[ ]   If applicable, explain how semantic versioning or patch-level increments indicate security relevance.

[ ] Acknowledging Security Contributors

[ ]   Reward or credit individuals who responsibly disclose vulnerabilities.

[ ]   Consider listing them in your repository, on your website, or awarding badges or other forms of visible recognition.

Example of how your document can look like:

"If you find a vulnerability, please email _____ or fill out _____ form. Response target: _____."

"We publicly disclose vulnerabilities after _____ days to allow for patch testing."

"If you discover a vulnerability, please report it by_____ or filling out the form at _____. We aim to respond within __ hours.

For projects with downstream users or corporate dependencies, we follow a coordinated disclosure process. Vulnerabilities may be disclosed privately under embargo for up to __ days before public disclosure, to allow time for patch development and rollout.

Security fixes are published in the changelog and released as patch-level version updates. Contributors who report valid issues may be acknowledged publicly or receive a security contributor badge."

11. Support (SUPPORT.md)

Why It's Important

A SUPPORT.md file clarifies how and where users can seek help. This fosters a welcoming culture, especially for novices who might feel intimidated or confused about the right channel—issues, forums, social media channels, or something else.

Risks of Not Having It

- Scattered Queries: Users post questions in random places (pull requests, closed issues), leading to frustration.

- Overworked Maintainers: Repeated basic questions because there's no documented Q&A structure.

- Exclusion: Non-English speakers or folks with less technical background might never find the correct help route.

Labeling and Ethics Behind It

- Communication Overhead: People who manage social media or forum moderation do vital, often unseen, tasks—label them.

- Label: "Support lead" or "user-liaison" roles underscore that conversation and triage are recognized contributions.

Checklist: Support

[ ]   Main Contact Points

    [ ]   Link official channels: Discussion boards, mailing lists, social media used by the community or message apps, etc.

    [ ]   If possible, mention typical response times.

[ ]   Scope of Support

    [ ]   Clarify "We offer best-effort support for X, Y, Z but cannot guarantee immediate help for third-party integrations."

    [ ]   Encourage user-to-user collaboration if resources are limited.

[ ]   Feedback mechanism

    [ ]   Welcome feedback on usability or accessibility.

    [ ]   Provide distinct channels for design/UX questions versus pure code issues.

Example of how your document can look like:

"For urgent issues, contact _____ in the channel or our forum at _____."

"We respond within _____ days, focusing on _____ areas primarily."

12. Accessibility Guidelines (ACCESSIBILITY.md)

Why It's Important

This document sets clear guidelines for contributors on how to make software, documentation, and communication channels more accessible to people of all abilities.

History Behind It

Accessibility in software has been an evolving concern, with legal requirements such as the Americans with Disabilities Act (ADA), The European Accessibility Act (EAA), and Web Content Accessibility Guidelines (WCAG) influencing best practices.

Risks of Not Having It

- Users and contributors with disabilities may be excluded.

- Compliance issues with accessibility regulations.

- Higher technical debt as retrofitting accessibility is costlier than designing it from the start.

Labeling and Ethics Behind It

- Labeling: Recognize roles such as "accessibility reviewer," "screen reader tester," and "documentation formatter."

- Ethical considerations: Promotes digital equity and allows more people to engage in open source.

Checklist

[ ] Document accessibility requirements (contrast, keyboard navigation, ARIA roles, etc.).

[ ] Define testing procedures for accessibility.

[ ] List contact points for accessibility-related feedback.

[ ] Reference existing accessibility standards (e.g., WCAG).

[ ] Invite people with disabilities to be part of the development process.

Example:

"Our project is committed to accessibility to ensure all users, regardless of ability, can engage with our software. We follow WCAG 2.1 standards and encourage contributors to use semantic HTML, ARIA attributes, and proper contrast ratios. Our accessibility reviewers (✎ **label: accessibility-review**) test new features with screen readers and report findings in GitHub issues. If you have expertise in accessibility, you can contribute by reviewing PRs labeled **"needs-a11y-review"** or testing the interface with assistive technology."

13. Code Review Guidelines (CODE_REVIEW.md)

Why It's Important

Establishes a standard process for reviewing contributions to maintain software quality and encourage constructive feedback.

Risks of Not Having It

- Increased technical debt due to poor-quality code.

- Exclusion of contributors unfamiliar with unwritten community norms.

- Bias and inconsistency in review processes.

- Reviewing code can be one of the most powerful tools to learn; embracing it may bring more contributors, unburden maintainers, and empower the community.

Labeling and Ethics Behind It

- Labeling: Recognize roles such as "reviewer," "mentor," and "educator."

- Ethical considerations: Encourages fair treatment and constructive feedback for all contributors.

Checklist

[ ] Define expectations for reviewers (response time, criteria).

[ ] Clarify how feedback should be given (e.g., constructive, respectful).

[ ]   Outline the process for resolving review disputes.

[ ]   Encourage pairing junior contributors with experienced reviewers.

Example:

"Code reviews in our project ensure maintainability and knowledge sharing. Reviewers (🏷 label: reviewer), mentors (🏷 label: mentoring), and documentation stewards (🏷 label: doc-review) work together to assess contributions. PR authors should describe why their changes matter in "Why Is This Needed?" sections. First-time contributors are paired with mentors for guidance, and feedback should always be constructive. Our golden rule: "Make suggestions, not demands.""

14. Governance Policy (GOVERNANCE.md)

Why It's Important

Defines decision-making structures, leadership roles, and community governance to prevent power imbalances. It helps exercise authority transparently and fairly, enabling long-term project health.

Establishing governance proactively—before conflicts arise or the project scales—creates a foundation of trust and clarity. Retrofitting governance after tensions emerge is often fraught, as stakeholders may already be entrenched in opposing positions, making consensus or procedural adoption much harder.

History Behind It

Governance in open source has evolved from centralized models (e.g., GNU, 1983; Linux, 1991) to structured, community-driven systems (e.g., Debian's technical committees, Apache's meritocratic model). As ecosystems matured, foundation-based models (e.g., The Linux Foundation, 2000; Eclipse Foundation, 2004) helped balance influence between corporate stakeholders and individual contributors.

Risks of Not Having It

- Power dynamics may favor established contributors over newcomers.

- Power may become concentrated among early or vocal contributors.

- Decision-making lacks transparency, leading to contributor attrition or stagnation.

- Disputes escalate without clear mechanisms for resolution.

- External stakeholders may hesitate to engage without visible accountability structures.

Labeling and Ethics Behind It

- Labeling: Credit roles like "policy maker," "community advocate," and "moderation lead."

- Ethical considerations: Encourages fair representation, particularly for historically marginalized contributors and the users and communities affected by the project.

Checklist

- [ ] Define leadership roles and decision-making processes.

- [ ] Describe how decisions are made (e.g., voting, consensus, lazy consensus).

- [ ] Outline processes for conflict resolution and mediation.

[ ]   Indicate how and when the governance model will be reviewed or updated. Governance policies should be revisited periodically.

[ ]   Encourage early contributor involvement in shaping governance documents.

Example:

"This project uses a consensus-based governance model to ensure fairness and transparency. Core maintainers (label: core-team) are responsible for release management and technical direction, while community stewards (label: community-management) focus on fostering a welcoming environment.

Elections for governance roles are held annually, with all contributors eligible to vote. Financial decisions are documented and made publicly available.

Governance discussions are open to all and tracked under issues labeled governance. We hold quarterly open meetings (label: meeting-notes) to revisit governance structures and community health.

This policy was defined early in the project's lifecycle to ensure clarity and shared expectations from the outset."

15. Meeting Notes and Transparency (MEETINGS.md)

Why It's Important

Keeping meeting notes ensures transparency, helps new contributors onboard, and provides historical context for decisions.

History Behind It

Organizations and community-driven projects have long documented meetings for accountability, but this has not been standardized in open source.

Risks of Not Having It

- Decisions may lack accountability or clear historical records.

- Contributors in different time zones miss important information.

- Reinforces existing power imbalances when only a few have access to decisions.

Labeling and Ethics Behind It

- Labeling: Recognize contributors maintaining meeting notes as "record keepers" or "documentation specialists."

- Ethical considerations: Helps distribute knowledge fairly across time zones and language barriers.

Checklist

- [ ] Assign a note-taker or rotate note-taking responsibilities.

- [ ] Publish meeting summaries in an accessible location.

- [ ] Ensure that meetings are recorded or summarized in multiple formats (e.g., transcripts).

- [ ] Include action items and decisions made in meeting notes.

Example:

"All project meetings are documented and made publicly available to maintain transparency. Meeting facilitators (✎ label: meeting-facilitator) take notes, and summaries are shared in the repository within 48 hours. If you miss a meeting, you can check the "meeting-records" folder or review key decisions under the "Decisions" heading in the latest summary. Contributors in different time zones can request asynchronous input via our discussion board (✎ label: async-participation)."

16. Community Acknowledgment (CREDIT.md)

Why It's Important

A structured credit file ensures recognition for all contributors, including those performing invisible, qualitative, and affective labor.

History Behind It

Traditional open source recognition systems favor code contributions. Models like All Contributors and CRediT introduced expanded recognition.

Risks of Not Having It

- Many contributors, especially non-coders, remain uncredited.

- Maintainers rely on ad-hoc acknowledgment, which is inconsistent and prone to bias.

- Discourages participation from those whose contributions don't fit conventional coding metrics.

Labeling and Ethics Behind It

- Labeling: Assign roles like "community manager," "event organizer," and "financial supporter."

- Ethical considerations: Prioritizes equitable recognition for all contributions.

Checklist

[ ] Include a structured format for acknowledging contributions.

[ ] Automate credit tracking where possible (e.g., All Contributors bot).

[ ] Regularly update credit files to reflect new contributions.

[ ] Provide pathways for contributors to self-report their contributions.

Example:

"Open source contributions extend beyond code. Our Contributor Credit Table ensures that designers (🏷 label: ux-design), translators (🏷 label: translation), documentation writers (🏷 label: documentation), and event organizers (🏷 label: outreach) receive equal recognition. If you contribute but don't see your name listed, open a "credit request" issue, and we'll update it. We follow the OCEAN taxonomy to ensure fair attribution."

17. Localization Guidelines (LOCALIZATION.md)

Why It's Important

Provides contributors with instructions for translating and localizing project materials, broadening the project's reach. But international accessibility is not just about translating text. Technical design must anticipate and accommodate different languages, scripts, formats, and cultural norms. Internationalization (i18n) lays the foundation that enables effective localization (l10n)—it must be considered early in the project lifecycle, not retrofitted after global interest emerges.

- Internationalization (i18n): The process of preparing code and content to support multiple languages and regional formats. This includes externalizing all user-facing strings, supporting character encodings like UTF-8, implementing locale-aware date and number formatting, accommodating right-to-left scripts, handling pluralization rules, and designing layouts that can adapt to text expansion. For instance, a button labeled "Save" in English may need to expand significantly in German ("Speichern"), which affects UI spacing. Similarly, address formats and names vary culturally and should not be hardcoded.

- Localization (l10n): The act of translating and culturally adapting content to suit a specific locale, including not only language but also idiomatic expressions, tone, measurement systems, and regional conventions. Localization is only effective if the underlying system has been properly internationalized.

History Behind It

Early open source projects were often English-centric. As their global user bases grew, many faced retrofitting challenges due to hardcoded strings or assumptions about locale. Initiatives like GNU gettext (1995), Mozilla's Pontoon (2011), and Weblate (2012) emerged to address both the tooling and workflows required for scalable i18n and l10n. Internationalization (i18n) and localization (l10n) became essential as open source projects aimed to serve global audiences.

Risks of Not Having It

- Poor accessibility for non-English speakers, leading to limited adoption outside of English-speaking communities.

- Technical debt from retroactive internationalization.

- Mismatches between UI behavior and user expectations across regions.

- Difficulty coordinating translations across multiple contributors, creating a fragmented contributor experience for translators.

Labeling and Ethics Behind It

- Labeling: Recognize "translator," "language lead," and "proofreader" roles.

- Use tags such as "i18n-ready," "translation," "language-lead," or "locale-review."

- Ethical considerations: Language inclusivity reduces barriers to participation and increases representation from underrepresented geographies and communities.

Checklist

Generic—general items applicable to both i18n and l10n coordination:

[ ]   Provide a list of languages currently supported.

[ ]   Outline translation workflows and tools (e.g., Weblate, Transifex, Pontoon).

[ ]   Establish a review process for translated content.

[ ]   Document best practices for ensuring culturally sensitive translations.

[ ]   Document how to extract and submit translatable strings.

[ ]   Ensure all user-facing text is externalized and not hardcoded.

[ ]   Use message formatting libraries (e.g., FormatJS, Fluent) to support flexible grammar and placeholders.

[ ]   Encourage community localization leads or regional coordinators to manage consistency.

[ ]   Provide visual context (e.g., screenshots) for translators to resolve ambiguity.

Internationalization (i18n)—technical underpinnings that make localization possible:

[ ]   Externalize all UI strings and avoid hardcoded text.

[ ]   Support Unicode and bidirectional text (e.g., Arabic, Hebrew).

[ ]   Abstract locale-specific formats (date/time, currency, pluralization).

[ ]   Provide fallback mechanisms for missing locales.

[ ]   Design UIs that adapt to text expansion or layout changes.

[ ]   Include locale-specific test cases (e.g., RTL rendering, number systems, addresses).

[ ]   Ensure accessibility tools (screen readers, alt text) are compatible with localized content.

Localization (l10n)—processes and community engagement for adapting content to specific languages and cultures:

[ ]   List currently supported languages.

[ ]   Describe the translation process and tooling (e.g., Weblate, Crowdin, POEditor).

[ ]   Establish review workflows involving native speakers.

[ ]   Document cultural considerations, tone, and terminology consistency.

[ ]   Set up issue labels for language-specific contributions (e.g., language:fr, translation-request).

[ ]   Credit translators, language reviewers, and localization leads in release notes or contributor listings.

[ ]   Publicly track prioritized languages or localization milestones (e.g., via a translation board).

Example:

"Our project is designed with internationalization in mind. All text is externalized and locale-aware, allowing for seamless localization. We use Weblate for managing translations, and contributors can join as translators (label: translation) or language reviewers (label: language-review).

Please check the translation-requests board to see which languages need attention. Before submitting, verify that plural forms, date/time formats, and cultural references align with the target locale.

We welcome contributions to the i18n infrastructure itself—whether it's fixing string keys, improving fallback logic, or optimizing the formatting library. If you'd like to propose a new language or suggest a workflow improvement, open an issue under the localization label."

18. Funding and Sponsorship Transparency (FUNDING.md)

Why It's Important

Transparency around funding ensures accountability and allows contributors to make informed decisions and the community to know how the fund is being allocated.

History Behind It

Projects like Open Collective and GitHub Sponsors have created avenues for financial contributions, but transparency remains inconsistent.

Risks of Not Having It

- Contributors may be unaware of funding sources and how funds are allocated.

- Unequal distribution of funds can create power imbalances.

- Potential for conflicts of interest without public disclosures.

Labeling and Ethics Behind It

- Labeling: Recognize roles such as "financial steward," "fundraiser," and "budget manager."

- Ethical considerations: Promotes financial transparency and community trust.

Checklist

[ ] List all sources of funding and sponsorships.

[ ] Clarify how funds are allocated and managed.

[ ] Provide information on how contributors can apply for funding.

[ ] Ensure sponsorship guidelines align with project ethics.

Example:

"Our project is supported through Open Collective and GitHub Sponsors. All funds are publicly tracked, and spending is documented quarterly. Financial stewards (💰 label: financial-management) ensure funds are used for hosting, community events, and contributor stipends. If you'd like to request financial support for a project-related initiative, submit a funding request labeled "funding-needed".

19. Adopters and User Stories (ADOPTERS.md)

Why It's Important

An ADOPTERS.md file documents organizations, projects, and individuals who actively use your software in production or meaningful contexts. This serves dual purposes: it provides social proof for prospective users while offering tangible validation to contributors who invest their labor—both visible and invisible—into the project's development.

243

History Behind It

The ADOPTERS.md convention is widely used within Cloud Native Computing Foundation (CNCF) projects, where adoption documentation helps users evaluate the production-readiness of emerging technologies. Projects like containerd[2] maintain adopter listings that demonstrate real-world usage across diverse organizational contexts. This documentation pattern serves dual needs: contributors appreciate tangible evidence that people actually use and adopt the projects they work on, providing validation for their labor, while prospective users (individuals and companies) gain confidence knowing that others have successfully deployed the software in production environments.

Risks of Not Having It

- Contributor Demoralization: Without visible evidence of real-world usage, contributors—particularly those performing maintenance, documentation, or community management—may question whether their efforts create meaningful impact.

- User Hesitation: Prospective adopters lack confidence indicators, potentially choosing more established alternatives even when your project better serves their technical requirements.

- Ecosystem Fragmentation: Related projects cannot identify potential collaboration opportunities or shared user bases, limiting cross-pollination of improvements and best practices.

---

[2] https://github.com/containerd/containerd/blob/main/ADOPTERS.md

Labeling and Ethics Behind It

- Validation of Invisible Labor: ADOPTERS.md provides concrete evidence that community-building activities, user support, and documentation efforts translate into real-world value—validating contributions often overlooked in traditional code-centric metrics.

- Democratizing Success Stories: Unlike corporate case studies that privilege enterprise users, community-maintained adoption documentation can highlight usage across diverse organizations, from grassroots initiatives to academic institutions to multinational corporations.

- OCEAN Labeling: Tag roles such as "adoption advocate," "case study coordinator," and "user liaison" to recognize contributors who facilitate relationships between the project and its adopter community.

Checklist

- [ ] Structured Adoption Format:

    - [ ] Organization name, size/context, and primary use case

    - [ ] Brief description of how the software addresses their specific needs

    - [ ] Optional contact information for users willing to serve as references

[ ] Include organizations across different sectors, geographies, and scales.

[ ] Highlight non-traditional use cases that demonstrate software versatility

[ ] Feature educational institutions, non-profits, and community organizations alongside commercial users

[ ] Contribution Recognition:

[ ] Acknowledge community members who facilitate adoption relationships

[ ] Credit those who help document case studies or coordinate user feedback

[ ] Link adopter feedback to specific improvements or feature developments

[ ] Privacy and Consent:

[ ] Establish clear guidelines for including organization information

[ ] Provide mechanisms for adopters to update or remove their listings

[ ] Respect confidentiality requirements while maximizing transparency

Example structure: "Our software serves diverse communities, from _____ using it for _____ to _____ leveraging it in _____ contexts." "If your organization uses this project and would like to be listed, please _____ or contact our adoption coordinator (**label: adoption**)."

Integration with Community Health: Link ADOPTERS.md to your broader community documentation by cross-referencing user stories in roadmap discussions, citing adoption patterns in governance decisions, and celebrating milestone adoptions through your standard communication channels. This transforms a simple listing into a living testament to your project's real-world impact and community vitality.

Why Does Clear Documentation Matter?

Open source best practices provide structure and sustainability in a development model that relies on distributed collaboration. Unlike proprietary software, which operates under the oversight of a single entity, open source projects depend on the collective effort of contributors across various backgrounds, locations, and skill levels. This decentralized nature introduces challenges, making shared guidelines necessary to maintain clarity, equity, and long-term viability. These practices extend technical concerns, shaping the ways communities interact, make decisions, and distribute responsibility.

Code quality and maintainability stand at the core of these practices. Open source projects involve multiple contributors working asynchronously, often with different levels of familiarity with the codebase. Even in the AI era that is helping onboard newcomers, without standardized documentation, formatting conventions, and contribution workflows, inconsistencies emerge, making projects difficult to navigate. Readme files, contribution guidelines, and structured issue trackers reduce friction, offering newcomers clear entry points. In the absence of these resources, projects become insular, favoring those with prior knowledge while discouraging broader participation.

Collaboration in open source depends on transparency, but openness alone does not guarantee accessibility. Projects that lack clear processes unintentionally create barriers, where only those with insider knowledge can meaningfully engage. Contribution guidelines set expectations for participation, outlining how to report issues, submit changes, and interact with maintainers. Public decision-making structures ensure that discussions remain visible rather than occurring in private channels.

Without these frameworks, projects risk being open in name only, leaving newcomers uncertain about how to contribute or whose voices carry influence.

Legal and security considerations further shape open source best practices. A project without a clearly defined license creates ambiguity regarding usage, modification, and redistribution, leaving contributors and users without legal clarity. Security policies play an equally important role, in establishing processes for reporting vulnerabilities and addressing risks. Without defined protocols, security flaws may remain unresolved, exposing users to harm. These considerations extend individual projects, influencing broader trust in open source software as a whole.

Governance emerges as a key factor in long-term sustainability. Many open source projects begin as personal initiatives but expand into widely used tools. As they grow, leadership structures shape decision-making, community health, and the distribution of responsibilities. Without documented governance models, projects often rely on a small group of maintainers, leading to burnout or stagnation when key individuals step away. Structured governance provides pathways for leadership transitions, conflict resolution, and inclusive participation, reducing the risks associated with power imbalances and knowledge silos.

Non-code contributions form another essential but often overlooked aspect of sustainability. The open source ecosystem has historically centered on software development while undervaluing roles such as documentation, community moderation, translation, and outreach. These contributions sustain projects in ways that code alone cannot. Moreover, maintainers often spend significant time on tasks outside their coding expertise—marketing, community management, or program coordination—that specialists could perform more effectively. By recognizing and delegating this work to people with deep expertise in these areas, projects become more efficient and sustainable for everyone, while allowing maintainers to focus on their core technical contributions. Evolving best practices recognize this work through systems like OCEAN labeling, which assigns roles to contributors based on a broad spectrum of activities, and CHAOSS metrics create metrics to measure qualitative work community health. A project that integrates these acknowledgments into its structure creates a more equitable environment, moving beyond the outdated technocratic view that only code commits define meaningful participation.

Sustainability in open source depends on more than ongoing contributions; retention, funding, and institutional memory also shape a project's longevity. Many initiatives launch with enthusiasm but struggle to maintain momentum over time. Without planning for funding mechanisms, mentorship programs, and leadership transitions, projects risk stagnation or abandonment. Documentation of roadmaps, community-driven decision-making, and financial transparency contribute to long-term resilience. Projects that fail to account for these needs often experience contributor fatigue, leaving users dependent on software that no longer receives active support.

Open source best practices should extend far beyond technical guidelines. They have the power to become standards that shape the ways projects remain accessible, govern themselves, address security, and acknowledge contributions. Without these shared principles, open source risks becoming fragmented, exclusive, or unsustainable. Instead of relying on informal networks or unspoken rules, documented best practices create structured environments where participation remains fair, transparent, and adaptable to future challenges.

Communication Best Practices: Minimizing Information Imbalance

Effective communication is the lifeblood of any thriving open source project. However, communication in distributed, asynchronous communities is inherently complex—messages are sent across various channels, languages, and cultural contexts. To foster equity and leave no one behind, projects can adopt comprehensive communication practices that I like to categorize as procedural, daily, and long-term scales. Below, we expand on each area with concrete organizational tasks and examples that explicitly address power imbalances, promote user-centricity, and prioritize community well-being.

1. Procedural Communication

Procedural communication is about, as the name says, the procedures, methods, and how to operate. It aims to establish a framework that finds ways for every contributor to have equal access to the project's processes and decision-making channels. Clear and consistent systems, like a shared public issue tracker, organized meeting agendas, and straightforward ways to provide feedback, contribute to keeping everyone informed. This approach helps prevent anyone from feeling left out, even those who aren't as involved. Overall, these tools create a more inclusive environment where all contributors can participate and feel valued. Examples of organizational tasks can be as follows.

Centralized Issue Tracking

To maintain clarity and organization, it's essential to use a single public issue tracker for logging all types of contributions—bugs, feature requests, community discussions, documentation efforts, and even event planning. While platforms like GitLab and GitHub have revolutionized open collaboration by offering version control and project management tooling, many projects still fragment their coordination across wikis, chats, and private notes. This decentralization obscures the bigger picture and complicates onboarding for new contributors.

A centralized tracker makes project governance more transparent, encouraging broader participation and distributing knowledge more evenly. Importantly, it also serves as a record of decision-making and historical context, which helps flatten hierarchies and allows asynchronous contributors to stay engaged.

Power Balance and User-Centric Approach

Centralizing issue tracking supports equity by providing a shared, accessible space where all contributors—regardless of technical background—can participate in the project's evolution. This is particularly important for surfacing non-code contributions that are often invisible in standard contribution graphs. For instance, in Kubernetes, contributor events are planned and tracked through GitHub issues, with documentation stored as Markdown files in the repo. Similarly, within the CHAOSS project, educational content creation is fully managed through issues: writing slide decks, coordinating video recordings, and developing curricula are all explicitly scoped as trackable work.

The PyLadies Berlin[3] has adopted GitHub not only as a platform for code but as a comprehensive tool for community governance and event coordination. Through a set of thoughtfully crafted issue templates and labels—such as the detailed new-event template that outlines responsibilities and communications from one month prior to the day of the event—the chapter enables asynchronous collaboration and radically transparent organizing. Tasks such as speaker coordination, food logistics, accessibility needs, and post-event feedback are distributed across contributors, documented in issues, and archived for future reference.

At the national level, PyLadies Germany[4] employs a similar GitHub-based model to manage a common fund established by the Python Software Verband. The PySV PyLadies Germany Fund repository serves as

---

[3] https://github.com/PyLadiesBerlin
[4] https://github.com/PyLadiesGermany/PySV_PyLadies_fund

a living governance document, tracking all financial requests, approvals, and reimbursements via GitHub Issues. Funding requests—whether for event food, travel support, or community infrastructure—are submitted using standardized issue templates. Decisions are made by a rotating group of representatives from different chapters, with every step, from approval to reimbursement, made publicly visible. This system offers not only financial transparency but also a replicable structure for other decentralized grassroots communities.

These practices not only legitimize diverse forms of labor but also create structures where recognition, responsibility, and accountability are distributed rather than centralized.

Organizational Task

- Maintain an Active and Holistic Issue Tracker: Use the issue tracker as the central space for coordinating both technical and nontechnical work—event planning, outreach, documentation, and design discussions. Label issues clearly (e.g., needs-feedback, community-priority, non-code) to make them discoverable and actionable across disciplines.

- Normalize Issue-Driven Collaboration Across All Roles: Encourage all contributors to file and track their work through issues, creating a transparent and searchable record of the project's evolution. Templates for recurring tasks (e.g., events) help standardize practices and ease onboarding.

- Distribute Responsibility via Rotating Roles: Assign a rotating "issue moderator" role distributing responsibility, reducing power concentration and enabling wider participation.

- Embed Reflection and Accountability: End major initiatives with a short retrospective captured in the issue thread. These reflections strengthen accountability, support continuous learning, and make invisible work visible.

Public Meeting Schedules and Recorded Sessions

Schedule regular meetings with agendas published in advance, and record the sessions for asynchronous review. Aim to accommodate a variety of time zones, or consider creating local chapters to facilitate discussions and decision-making in friendly time zones, which can help reduce the frequency of larger meetings.

Power Balance and User-Centric Approach: By publishing meeting details in advance and making recordings accessible, contributors who cannot attend live—due to time zone differences, work obligations, or accessibility needs—are not excluded.

Organizational Task

- Create a standardized template for meeting agendas and minutes.

- To democratize leadership, designate a "meeting facilitator" role that rotates among team members. Include action items and summaries that highlight decisions, keeping the non-attending community informed.

- Avoid finalizing decisions during live meetings. Instead, allow a feedback window post-meeting so that people in other time zones or with other commitments that prevent attendance have a voice in the decision. This window will also allow thoughtful reflection and may bring additional feedback or objections before a decision is final.

Formal Feedback Mechanisms

Set up channels (like discussion boards, surveys, issue tracker, or moderated forums) where community members can provide feedback on processes and decisions. Such channels will serve also as documentation for the decision-making process.

Power Balance and User-Centric Approach: Such channels allow for feedback that is not monopolized by the most vocal members and that quieter voices have space to contribute.

Organizational Task: Schedule periodic feedback sessions and document suggestions and action plans in a central repository (e.g., a dedicated "feedback" wiki page). Use labels such as "feedback-review" to tag and track responses.

2. Daily Communication

Daily communication is about the day-to-day aspects; it involves routine exchanges that keep the community connected and informed about the project's ongoing activities. It includes status updates, progress reports, how to submit issues, propose enhancements or new features, how to contribute, and so on. A consistent daily communication strategy reduces ambiguity and keeps everyone on the same page, thus reducing the cognitive load on maintainers who might otherwise repeatedly answer the same questions.

A clear, consistent communication strategy enables contributors to stay aligned without relying on insider knowledge or real-time presence. It also invites asynchronous participation, which is especially valuable for distributed teams.

Status Dashboards and Automated Notifications

Use tools to aggregate commit activity, issue updates, and meeting summaries into a centralized status dashboard. Dashboards that also surface roadmap activities (e.g., CNCF Contributor Roadmaps[5]) help new and returning contributors identify where help is needed.

Power Balance and User-Centric Approach: This approach helps contributors who are not directly involved in daily communications stay informed about project health and progress. For example, a community member may regularly review the dashboard to understand recent updates and decide where to contribute next.

Organizational Task: Automate notifications from relevant systems (CI, GitHub, and project boards) into channels like chat platforms or email digests. Assign a rotating "dashboard curator" to ensure the information remains up-to-date and accessible.

Real-Time Q&A Sessions

Real-time Q&A sessions serve as an open forum where contributors, maintainers, and community members engage in direct, unscripted conversations. These sessions provide immediate clarification on project workflows, technical issues, and governance decisions, fostering a more connected and collaborative open source environment. Beyond resolving questions, they serve as a communal space that strengthens relationships, promotes inclusivity, and improves the overall sustainability of the project. While asynchronous communication—through issue trackers, mailing lists, and documentation—is crucial for accessibility across time zones, real-time interactions offer an added layer of engagement. These sessions reduce friction for new contributors who might otherwise struggle to navigate written documentation or feel intimidated by lengthy issue

---

[5] https://contribute.cncf.io/maintainers/community/contributor-growth-framework/open-source-roadmaps/

discussions. They also help mitigate information asymmetry, ensuring that knowledge is not concentrated among a small group of core maintainers but is actively shared with the wider community.

Power Balance and User-Centric Approach: In traditional development models, access to maintainers can be limited, reinforcing hierarchical structures where only a select few influence decision-making. A transparent, recurring Q&A format allows maintainers to engage directly with contributors of all levels, fostering a more horizontal and participatory culture. Instead of reinforcing gatekeeping, these sessions offer an opportunity to demystify decision-making processes and open pathways for more diverse voices to shape the project.

Organizational Task: Schedule regular sessions and record them for later viewing. Use platforms that support live captioning and translations to address language barriers. Label sessions with tags like "live-help" or "office-hours" to highlight their importance.

The format of Q&A sessions can be tailored to the needs and scale of the community. Smaller, more intimate projects might opt for informal office hours, while larger projects might benefit from structured AMA (Ask Me Anything) formats with pre-submitted questions to ensure broad participation.

- **Open Office Hours:** Provide a consistent, low-pressure space for contributors to share questions, feedback, or ideas. Scheduled at regular intervals (e.g., weekly, biweekly, or monthly), they create a reliable point of access for maintainers. A rotating roster of facilitators helps distribute responsibility, preventing burnout and making leadership roles more accessible. Or leave it at the maintainer's discretion to keep an agenda link for users to freely schedule a time.

- **Live AMAs (Ask Me Anything):** Structured sessions with pre-submitted or live questions—via video, chat, or forums—encourage broad participation across time zones and experience levels. These are especially effective for larger projects or when engaging external stakeholders.

- **Topic-Specific Q&A Panels:** Focused Q&A sessions on areas like accessibility, governance, or security allow for deeper, more technical exchanges with relevant maintainers and guest experts.

- **Mentorship-Driven Q&A:** Some projects integrate Q&A sessions into their mentorship initiatives, pairing new contributors with experienced community members. These sessions emphasize hands-on learning, allowing participants to seek guidance on technical contributions, navigating community norms, decision-making structures, and non-code contributions.

Community Example: CHAOSS holds a biweekly Newcomer Hangout where anyone new to the project can drop in to ask questions or seek advice. Experienced community members attend regularly to guide participants toward meaningful contributions. This lightweight, consistent format has proven effective in lowering entry barriers and retaining contributors.

3. Long-Term Communication

Long-term communication involves preserving and disseminating the historical context, strategic vision, and documented evolution of the project. This form of communication is essential for onboarding new contributors, maintaining institutional memory, and guiding future developments. It ensures continuity and transparency over the lifespan of the project. Examples of organizational tasks can be as follows.

Comprehensive Project Documentation

Maintain a well-organized documentation repository that includes the project's mission statement, goals, roadmaps, and historical decision logs.

Power Balance and User-Centric Approach: Detailed documentation allows every community member, regardless of their background or when they join, to understand the project's evolution and strategic direction.

Organizational Task: Create sections in a central wiki for mission statements, detailed roadmaps, and archival notes. Label documents with version information and maintain an "update log" that credits contributors, having roles like "documentation lead" or "historian" recognized.

Archival of Meeting Minutes and Decisions

Keep a permanent, searchable archive of all meeting minutes, recorded sessions, and major decisions.

Power Balance and User-Centric Approach: This archival process democratizes access to the project's history, ensuring that newcomers or remote contributors can catch up on past discussions without feeling isolated.

Organizational Task: Use a dedicated folder (e.g., "/archives/meetings") and enforce a standard format for meeting notes. Rotate the "record keeper" role and tag archived decisions with labels like "historical-decision" or "policy-update."

Strategic Roadmapping and Vision Workshops

Host regular (e.g., quarterly or biannual) workshops to collaboratively shape the project's long-term direction. These sessions make strategic decisions reflect diverse perspectives and foster a shared sense of ownership.

Power Balance and User-Centric Approach: Inclusive visioning processes reduce the risk of unilateral decision-making and affirm that contributors—especially those outside core roles—have a voice in setting priorities. It creates a sense of belonging for contributors, who feel that their perspectives are being considered.

Organizational Task: Use rotating facilitators, publish clear agendas, and label workshop outputs (e.g., vision-workshop and strategic-planning). Crucially, ensure that workshop outcomes are not siloed—integrate them into the project's roadmap and daily operations. This enables contributors to act on long-term goals through tangible tasks, aligning strategic intent with everyday project activity.

Debriefing: Historical Case Studies and Retrospectives

Periodically conduct retrospectives to evaluate what worked, what didn't, and why.

Power Balance and User-Centric Approach: These sessions are a learning tool and a method to recognize contributions that may have been overlooked. They help adjust processes to reduce future information imbalances.

Organizational Task: Document retrospective findings in a "Lessons Learned" section. Invite feedback from all community members and tag contributions to this process with "retrospective" or "improvement-suggestion" labels.

Additional Considerations for Minimizing Information Imbalance

Empowering Non-coding Contributions

- Recognize that contributions come in many forms—coding, documentation, design, user support, event organizing, translation, and more. Use open design principles in all communication tools by explicitly stating that all contributions are valued. For instance, when creating PR templates, include a section for describing non-code impacts (e.g., "User Experience Improvements" or "Community Outreach Efforts").

- Encourage a culture where tasks such as "community moderation" or "user research" are not only acknowledged but are also included in performance metrics and leadership evaluations.

Tools and Templates for Asynchronous Communication

- Automated Summaries: Use tools like meeting transcription services or automated summary generators to convert long meetings into digestible summaries.

- Multilingual Support: Ensure key documents and communications are available in multiple languages. Use collaborative translation platforms so that contributors can easily submit or review translated content.

- Role Rotation and Task Labeling: Apply labeling to assign roles such as "async coordinator" or "meeting archivist" to ensure that responsibilities are shared and recognized.

This explicit labeling also signals to the community that all forms of labor, even those not immediately visible in code commits, are integral to the project's health.

Addressing Power Imbalances

– Establish feedback loops where contributors can report if they feel excluded or if certain communications are consistently inaccessible.

– Implement a "diversity audit" periodically, assessing whether communication channels are meeting the needs of a diverse contributor base.

– Create mentoring programs that pair experienced members with newcomers, ensuring that institutional knowledge is shared and that no one is left behind because of language, technical expertise, or cultural differences.

Community Well-Being

• Regularly survey contributors about the clarity of communications and the accessibility of information.

• Create spaces for informal discussion and social interaction to build trust and mitigate the isolation that can come from asynchronous work.

• Offer training or resources on effective communication, particularly for contributors from diverse linguistic or cultural backgrounds.

Open source communities can greatly lessen the information imbalances that frequently prevent participation by implementing strong communication best practices. Daily communication keeps everyone informed and focused on the tasks at hand; long-term communication maintains the project's history and strategic goal; and procedural communication guarantees that all processes are open and transparent. In addition to streamlining operations, each of these characteristics aims to rectify power disparities, encourage non-code contributions, and advance community welfare. Open source projects may create spaces where each contributor feels appreciated and empowered by implementing intentional organizational chores like inclusive feedback channels, automated documentation tools, and rotating leadership roles. In the end, these methods create an environment that is more equal, diversified, and sustainable—one in which open source genuinely leaves no one behind.

Building an Ethical and Inclusive Open Source Future with Practical Standards

The intersection of increasingly dispersed collaboration, growing demands for equity, and the quick development of AI-assisted technologies have created a critical juncture for open source software development. This chapter has demonstrated how routine, file-level procedures, such as governance policies and CONTRIBUTING.md guidelines, can operate as the cornerstone for ethical supervision, historical reparations, and democratic engagement. However, a crucial question comes up: How can we make this theory establish itself in real-world, community-driven settings?

This concluding thought ties together the main idea of the chapter, which is that accountable open source standards can drive social transformation. In order to reduce obstacles to inclusive governance and accountability, we must look ahead at concrete steps for implementation tools that can facilitate such implementation. Automation frameworks, AI agents, and templates can assist in producing the necessary documentation. However, without incorporating the why behind the documentation and raising awareness and accountability among the community, changing the technocratic to a socio-technical focus, this will become like the open tab on your browser you will never read. By embracing both the micro-level details of equitable processes and the macro-level vision of a more just digital world, open source communities can reimagine technology itself as a catalyst for change. Ultimately, each small process improvement—labeling non-code contributions or embedding restorative principles in a Code of Conduct—represents another step toward a culture of shared responsibility and collective empowerment.

From Mechanistic Checklists to Cultural Shift

The prevailing argument here rests on the notion that "mundane" documentation is anything but mundane. Each set of guidelines—on code reviews, maintainers, or security—contains the seeds of a larger cultural reorientation. In conventional open source, success is often gauged by code velocity, star counts, or adherence to a license. While these criteria highlight certain project milestones, they shed little light on whether the community is equitably structured or if systemic imbalances remain unchallenged.

An inclusive approach, on the other hand, incorporates routine procedures—such as clear accessibility requirements and precise role recognition for all volunteers—into a governance model that expressly prioritizes intersectionality, democracy, and restorative ethics. According to this perspective, a code of conduct goes beyond politeness to become a proactive tool that recognizes the psychological and emotional security of all participants. Similarly, a special file on accessibility or community recognition lets all newcomers know that the project is based on reciprocity and empathy rather than simply technical skills.

Behind the many best practices explored in this chapter is a conviction that the smallest operational norms—a labeled pull request, a rotating moderation role, or a multi-lingual help channel—can gradually reshape the power dynamics of open source. Over time, these norms make the community accessible to those who may have been systematically sidelined. Culture evolves through recurring patterns, and these so-called "invisible" tasks, once formalized, establish precedents that extend outward, transforming open source from a simple coding activity into a framework for participatory governance and collective well-being.

Why It Matters: Linking Micro-level Documentation to Macro-level Change

A persistent objection arises whenever social or political values are mentioned in technical spheres such as software engineering: "Surely a well-designed README or Security Policy can't redress centuries of systemic inequity." If you have thought that, you are correct. Indeed, no single initiative or file can undo structural injustices. However, the sum total of day-to-day practices—when scaled across thousands of repositories—starts to rewrite the unwritten rules that govern who gets to contribute to, benefit from, and be affected by open source.

Imagine a repository that integrates the following: it provides a well-defined Code of Conduct informed by restorative principles, invests time in localizing documentation into multiple languages, and rotates ownership of core tasks to prevent gatekeeping by any single individual. Over time, this repository will attract contributors who historically avoid spaces where their labor is undervalued. It also mitigates turnover since folks find roles that match their interests and see real appreciation for both code-based and non-code labor.

As this becomes a standard, these small changes come together to create a larger movement toward open source that is more inclusive and ethically grounded. When stakeholders start to see the real advantages, such as having the project well sustained, robust, and user friendly, with strong adoption, they're likely to embrace these practices, not just out of kindness, but because they realize that such an environment leads to better, indeed innovative results. Writing code is a big part of open source. The other big part is all the others that make it adopted, improved, and become a tool that makes a difference in people's lives. In the end, open source is not an abstract thing; it is deeply connected to the people who create it and those who will be affected by it.

Measurable Impact: CHAOSS Project

Is it even possible to measure the success of inclusive or equity standards?

The CHAOSS Project was formed to address a fundamental gap in open source: how to measure, understand, and improve the health of communities that sustain free and open software. Despite the ubiquity of version control platforms like GitHub and GitLab, which readily track commits, issues, and pull requests, open source stakeholders historically lacked a unified toolkit and standardized metrics for assessing what really matters: the long-term vitality and inclusivity of their communities. In other words, everyone understood that "community health" was essential, but no one had a consensus blueprint for measuring it.

When CHAOSS began its journey around 2017, it set out to produce not only metrics but also the frameworks that would transform raw data into nuanced insights. From the start, the project recognized that community well-being is a multi-faceted concept spanning technical, social, and organizational dimensions. Instead of relying solely on surface-level data—like the number of commits or active contributors—CHAOSS steered the conversation toward deeper questions. Who is contributing, and does the project reflect a diversity of backgrounds? How effectively do maintainers respond to issues? What patterns of collaboration or potential burnout might be invisible in standard dashboards?

Early iterations of the CHAOSS metrics captured broad categories like growth, risk, diversity, and user support. Over time, the project matured, refining its definitions and adding specialized metrics for topics like event participation, leadership turnover, and documentation quality. These evolutions often emerged from real-world case studies, as open source foundations and companies began testing CHAOSS frameworks to answer practical questions. For instance, a corporate sponsor might want to know if a certain open source project is sustainable enough to justify long-term investment, while a community manager might search for indications of contributor burnout lurking beneath brisk commit activity. By systematically capturing and categorizing these data, CHAOSS laid the groundwork for a more realistic snapshot of community dynamics.

One of CHAOSS's signature achievements is its focus on building an inclusive ecosystem of tools that operationalize metrics in user-friendly ways. The project supports GrimoireLab, a data visualization and analytics platform that draws from multiple sources such as GitHub, GitLab, mailing lists, and discussion boards. GrimoireLab's customizable dashboards allow maintainers and analysts to spot trends in participation, highlight emergent conflicts, or identify maintainers who have taken on a disproportionate load of the work. Another key tool is Augur, which provides advanced analytics for repositories, focusing on items like code review patterns, pull request latency, and signals of community risk. Through the automation of data gathering and its connection to CHAOSS-defined metrics, tools such as GrimoireLab and Augur facilitate the extraction of significant findings from what may otherwise be a daunting amount of raw data for volunteers, project managers, and even outside academics.

In addition to the tools, CHAOSS has made significant contributions to the collaborative method used to produce its metrics. Initially, the project organized working groups around cross-cutting topics such as Diversity and Inclusion, Risk, Evolution, and Common Metrics, rather than making decisions from above. Contributors from open source communities, academia, and industry make up each working group. They look at the subtleties of measurements and the cultural settings that influence them —including the cultural and social dynamics often obscured by raw data. Participants in the Diversity and Inclusion working group, for instance, discuss both qualitative and quantitative issues since they are aware that simple statistics may mask complex power relationships. In a fast-changing digital market, these working groups work to be socially conscious by continuously reviewing and improving the metrics.

Over the past few years, however, CHAOSS has gradually shifted toward a context-based working group model. This newer approach emphasizes situating metrics within the environments where they are actually applied—such as OSPOs, academic research, scientific software, and non-profit infrastructure. These context groups enable practitioners working in similar domains to meet regularly, share use cases, and collaboratively adapt metrics to better fit their operational realities. This evolution reflects a growing recognition that metrics gain relevance and utility not just through technical rigor, but through deep alignment with the lived experiences and institutional goals of those who use them.

In practice, the CHAOSS framework challenges the community to think critically about what "health" entails. Rather than fixating on growth alone, maintainers might track how many first-time contributors return after their initial pull request. Rather than simply touting the total number of commits, they might explore whether those commits come from a small, overburdened set of developers. Similarly, they can measure the *Contributor Absence Factor*[6] scenarios by looking at code ownership or merge privileges. If a project's longevity hinges disproportionately on two or three people, the community can develop strategies to spread knowledge and reduce burnout, such as implementing rotating roles or mentorship pipelines.

---

[6] https://chaoss.community/kb/metric-contributor-absence-factor/

This perspective aligns closely with the standard proposed in the broader context of ethical, diversity-centered open source. The chapter's recommendations hinge on bringing typically invisible tasks—like conflict resolution, documentation, moderation, and translation—into formal recognition. CHAOSS metrics function as an indispensable layer that informs whether these tasks are tangibly improving community health. For instance, if a repository starts crediting translators in a CREDIT.md file, CHAOSS metrics can track if translation-related pull requests increase, and whether more individuals from non-English-speaking regions begin to engage in the project. Likewise, if a new Code of Conduct includes restorative justice mechanisms, community health dashboards built on CHAOSS data can detect changes in the frequency of negative interactions and see if those interactions are resolved more successfully over time.

When considering how this standard seeks to integrate democratic involvement in all facets of open source, the combination of the CHAOSS methodology and our approach of establishing a standard with organized governance and best practices is very significant. We can determine which governance reforms result in more equitable participation by examining how contributors interact and remain. For instance, CHAOSS measurements might be used to determine if the standard's recommendations for rotating lead maintainership or increasing diversity in core teams indeed lead to a more balanced amount of committed activity or a more healthy division of duties.

It also matters that CHAOSS is not simply a data project. It stands as a *community of practice and a living, iterative conversation* about what good metrics look like. This process-based orientation complements the chapter's central assertion that best practices must not be viewed as static. The standard for inclusive open source proposed here lives and breathes through continuous feedback loops. CHAOSS offers a mechanism to validate or challenge each new tactic introduced to strengthen a project's inclusivity, resilience, or accessibility. By aligning well-defined governance steps—like the use of a GOVERNANCE.md or a rotating conflict resolution panel—with CHAOSS dashboards, communities gain a rigorous basis for self-reflection and iterative refinement.

Recently, CHAOSS expanded this commitment by launching a *Practitioner Guide*[7] series, aimed at providing practical guidance to those seeking to apply metrics meaningfully within their organizational or community contexts. These guides—covering themes like Contributor Sustainability, Responsiveness, Organizational Participation, and Security—translate high-level metrics into concrete, actionable insights. They are designed especially for roles like maintainers, OSPO leads, and community managers, who often must navigate between abstract measurements and on-the-ground realities. With additional guides currently in development, this resource library reflects CHAOSS's evolving understanding that metrics must be interpreted in relation to the lived experiences of contributors and the governance structures that support them.

By integrating such interpretive tools with governance artifacts—like a clearly defined GOVERNANCE.md, a documented conflict resolution process, or rotating leadership roles—projects gain a robust foundation for self-reflection. CHAOSS dashboards, when read alongside these structural elements, provide both the data and the dialogic space necessary for adaptive governance. In other words, CHAOSS does not simply measure openness or inclusivity—it helps communities enact and re-enact these values over time.

The CHAOSS Project and its collection of tools contribute to this standard for they offer the trustworthy indicators required to assess if one's aspirational objectives are being realized. Encouraging equality, fairness, and historical reparations within an open source community is a potent idea, but it may be challenging to determine whether the community is actually changing in significant ways without continuous measurements. Widely validated measurements, well-defined definitions, and

---

[7] https://chaoss.community/about-chaoss-practitioner-guides/

comprehensive dashboards combine to create a valuable feedback loop. They enable maintainers to take action before issues become systemic crises by identifying early warning indicators, such as contributor turnover or an increasing backlog of unreviewed pull requests. They also point out positive aspects, such as spikes in the number of new contributors after an inclusive design workshop or a successful Code of Conduct launch.

CHAOSS Project stands at the intersection of data analytics and community well-being, facilitating a more thorough understanding of how code is produced and how people collaborate. Its evolution—from the early recognition that commits and stars were insufficient metrics to the sophisticated and ethically aware analytics of today—mirrors a broader shift in open source. As communities adopt the standard recommended in this chapter, which emphasizes intentionally inclusive processes, the metrics, and dashboards of CHAOSS become an essential mirror, reflecting back on whether those processes are leading to a healthier and more equitable environment. By tying measurement to action, CHAOSS not only diagnoses community health but also lights a path for progressive, data-informed improvements that align with the book's vision for a transformative, justice-driven open source ecosystem.

From Blueprint to Standard

Open source often prioritizes code commits and licenses while overlooking the "invisible labor" that keeps communities healthy. This chapter proposes transforming simple file-level best practices—like Code of Conducts or Ownership files—into robust moral and societal frameworks. By centering ethics, inclusion, and historical reparation, the aim is to catalyze cultural shifts and make open source more equitable.

A primary goal is to show how everyday documents (README, LICENSE, Code of Conduct) can fuse with macro-level governance structures to ensure that all contributions—whether documentation, moderation, or mentorship—are properly acknowledged and resourced. Simply having a license or code style guide does not guarantee balanced leadership or community well-being. Rather, projects need formal mechanisms that encourage restorative justice, recognize intangible tasks, and highlight democratic participation.

Crucially, missing files like an Ownership file leave direction unclear, while the absence of a Code of Conduct disempowers those facing hostility. Here, such documents become ethical and organizational signposts. Yet they only succeed if projects embed these signposts in a supportive, participatory governance model—one that accounts for behind-the-scenes labor and invests in historically marginalized voices.

This chapter contends that by reframing standards as social contracts, we can align day-to-day work with moral imperatives. Instead of treating open source purely as a technical endeavor, contributors and maintainers recognize that the technology they produce is political and can either perpetuate biases or challenge them.

Ultimately, the chapter sketches a roadmap for elevating local guidelines into widely embraced, democracy-anchored standards. This blueprint includes detailed documentation templates, strategies for acknowledging non-code work, and approaches to restorative conflict resolution, all in service of an inclusive environment where open source remains a force for collective empowerment rather than exclusion.

CHAPTER 5

Models for a Sustainable, Diverse Open Source

Open source has a bit of a contradiction problem, doesn't it? For all its democratic ideals and "free as in freedom" rhetoric, the community remains stubbornly homogeneous. We've spent the previous chapters dissecting why—peeling back layers of power dynamics, unpaid labor, and systemic exclusion that have calcified into what appears to be an immovable structure. We've proposed standards, guidelines, and governance models that might chip away at these foundations. But sometimes, to truly reimagine a space, we need to lift our eyes beyond the blueprint and witness transformation in action.

This chapter isn't about more theories or frameworks—it's about the dreamers and doers who refused to wait for permission to create change. It's about the rebels, the visionaries, and sometimes the quiet revolutionaries who looked at the status quo and simply asked, "What if?" What if we built a tech academy specifically for people never given a chance? What if we created a fellowship that valued design thinking as much as code commits? What if we structured an entire company like a pirate crew, distributing wealth based on contribution rather than position?

P. Oliveira, *Diversifying Open Source*, https://doi.org/10.1007/979-8-8688-0769-5_5

I've had the privilege of interviewing founders, participants, and architects of these alternative models—some operating within corporate behemoths, others building grassroots movements, a few inventing entirely new organizational structures. Their stories are not just inspiring; they're instructive. They show us that structural change in technology isn't theoretical—it's happening right now, led by people who might have been sitting next to you at the last conference you attended.

The journey through this chapter will take us from corporate initiatives that turned conventional hiring upside down to community-organized spaces that became lifelines for the marginalized. We'll explore a fellowship designed with transdisciplinary learning at its core, a "pirate organization" that distributes power in ways that would make traditional managers break out in hives and grassroots initiatives meant for liberation.

These disparate methods are united by the understanding that bringing about change necessitates actively creating opportunity compared to holding out hope. These are not "feel-good projects"; more so, they are calculated interventions that encourage the potential for breakthroughs while addressing social injustices. They are tests of what occurs when we completely renovate the dining room rather than only bringing in fresh perspectives.

Each model is unique—shaped by its founders, participants, sponsors, and historical moment. Some might work perfectly in a corporate setting but fail in a volunteer community. Others might thrive in certain cultural contexts but struggle to translate across borders. The goal isn't to provide a one-size-fits-all template but to expand your sense of what's possible— to provide a palette of options that might inspire your own revolutionary question: "What if we did things differently?"

Often, the most profound transformations begin with a single person asking precisely that question. Consider the developer who contests their company's homogeneous hiring model and proposes alternatives prioritizing diverse backgrounds. Or the community member who recognizes the isolation of remote work and establishes local meetups that become vibrant knowledge hubs. Or the employee who convinces their company to dedicate "Open Source Fridays," where team members contribute to the commons while being compensated for their time. These individual actions might seem small against the vast landscape of systemic inequality, but they are the seeds from which larger change grows.

In my own journey, I've witnessed how a single conversation can spiral into institutional transformation. The fellowship program I eventually built at Sauce Labs began as a persistent question that I refused to stop asking, even as it was initially dismissed as impractical or unnecessary. What came out was primarily a diversity program, yet what it was indeed was an exploration of how corporate resources could be redirected toward building more fair technological futures.

So pour yourself something delightful to sip, settle in, and prepare to be introduced to people who didn't just theorize about change—they built it, tested it, iterated on it, and now offer their experiences as both inspiration and practical blueprint. Their stories remind us that real change in tech culture rarely arises spontaneously from theoretical policies. It is born of people working collaboratively, of organizations willing to allocate money, time, and moral commitment, a symbiosis in which both sides have a strong value to offer and receive.

These initiatives collectively tell a powerful story: structural change in the technology industry needs more than token support for underestimated contributors. The way talent is identified, developed, honored, and integrated must be drastically reframed. We need new mental models to understand the world; we need to leave behind the old-fashioned self-destructive exploitation approaches we've repeatedly brought to life in open source.

Are you ready to think bigger? To go beyond standards and guidelines toward reimagining the entire ecosystem? Let's begin.

Creating Alternative Pathways in Open Source: The Sauce Labs Fellowship Program

The Sauce Labs Open Source Community Fellowship Program emerged from my own experiences at the margins. As an intern in the Open Source Program Office and later a junior software developer in the Community Team, I carried with me a fundamental understanding that my presence in those spaces was itself the result of programs that extended opportunities to those without traditional credentials. My deep involvement with open source had always been accompanied by a critical awareness of its exclusionary dynamics—dynamics that privilege a pyramid of inherited advantage disguised as meritocracy.

For almost two years, I pitched, shaped, and reshaped this fellowship program, responding to feedback from different managers until finally discovering a viable institutional pathway. I wasn't interested in creating yet another initiative for those already positioned to succeed. I wanted to extend the same hand that had been extended to me—to create space for those whose lives hadn't afforded them birth privilege, elite education, or established professional networks. People who, like me, simply needed someone to give them a chance.

The program took shape as more than an act of charity—it became a philosophical inquiry into how corporate resources might be redirected toward creating more equitable technological futures. Drawing inspiration from established initiatives like Outreachy and Rail Girls Summer of Code, I envisioned something that would transcend traditional boundaries between disciplines, between learning and producing, between individual advancement and community transformation.

Program Overview

In practical terms, the Sauce Labs Open Source Community Fellowship Program was a six-month paid initiative that ran from December 2022 to May 2023, employing five fellows from diverse backgrounds to revitalize Elemental Selenium—a neglected educational resource with over 23,000 subscribers that had been acquired by Sauce Labs years earlier.

This program was deeply connected to Sauce Labs' origins and mission. Sauce Labs was founded by Jason Huggins, the same person who created Selenium, an automated testing framework that revolutionized web testing by allowing developers to automate browser interactions and verify functionality across multiple environments. Today, Selenium remains one of the most widely used open source testing tools in software development, serving as critical infrastructure for countless companies. Sauce Labs emerged as a business model to provide cloud-based Selenium testing infrastructure, allowing companies to benefit from this powerful tool while creating a sustainable economic model around it.

The program ran with a total budget of $75,000, providing each fellow a monthly stipend of $2,300. Five fellows with varied backgrounds and skill sets worked remotely, supported by 23 mentors from across various departments at Sauce Labs, each dedicating approximately two hours weekly to mentorship.

The fellows were organized into five complementary roles: Content Creation (updating educational materials about Selenium), Design (conducting user research and designing new interfaces), Quality Assurance (developing testing protocols), Development (two positions implementing technical architecture), and it ended up with another role, Community Engagement, as one of the fellows, Janackeh Blackwell, is a natural community builder and found a true vocation during the program while testing different roles.

Core Objectives

The program was designed to achieve multiple interconnected goals: transform a neglected corporate asset (Elemental Selenium) into a maintained open source project; create pathways for underestimated individuals in technology; broaden the understanding of technology development beyond code-centrism; strengthen Sauce Labs' relationship with the Selenium community; and break down internal department silos through cross-department mentorship.

Additionally, the program addressed Sauce Labs' open source sustainability role by contributing back to the Selenium community. As a company founded on and profiting from Selenium, this reciprocal contribution was fundamental to avoid the "tragedy of the commons" scenario where companies extract value from open source without sustaining it.

The program also aimed to address open source sustainability more broadly by educating future technologists about its importance and preparing them to become the maintainers of tomorrow—understanding both the technical and community aspects of successful open source stewardship.

Key Outcomes

The program successfully revitalized and opened the Elemental Selenium project to the community, provided comprehensive professional development for five fellows from underestimated backgrounds, and created a replicable model for corporate investment in diversity and open source sustainability. It established cross-departmental connections that improved internal organizational communication while strengthening Sauce Labs' position within the Selenium ecosystem.

The program demonstrated that meaningful intervention in open source diversity doesn't require enormous resources or radical restructuring, but rather strategic vision, creative resource allocation, and thoughtful program design. It serves as a replicable model for how mid-sized companies can leverage existing assets to simultaneously serve business interests and advance social transformation—both sustaining the open source commons they rely upon and creating pathways for more diverse participation in technology creation.

Ripple Effect: How One Action Creates Waves of Change

The idea of "standing on the shoulders of giants"—realizing that our advancements are based on the contributions of our predecessors—is embodied in the open source foundation. Above code, this idea applies to the very human networks that create chances and provide access to others. The story of this fellowship is the living example of how individual choices can have far-reaching consequences that have the power to change people's lives.

In 2019, I walked into my first PyLadies Berlin meetup with shaky hands and a racing heart. In that room, I found more than just people learning Python—I discovered a safe space built by Meili Triantafyllidi years before I even knew I would need it. Jessica Greene, now a senior machine learning engineer and the beating heart of our vibrant PyLadies Berlin community, smiled warmly at newcomers while juggling her responsibilities as an organizer. Had Meili never created this space, had Jessica chosen Netflix over community organizing on countless Tuesday evenings—my story would have taken an entirely different turn.

The walls of that meetup room held whispered possibilities: announcements about Rail Girls Summer of Code and FrauenLoop that would become lifelines in my journey. Dr. Nakeema Stefflbauer's FrauenLoop wasn't just teaching women to code—it was arming us with industry survival skills through workshops on salary negotiation and interview preparation, acknowledging that technical skills alone wouldn't break through systemic barriers.

COVID-19 shattered my carefully constructed plans with Rail Girls Summer of Code. This was a global fellowship that provided three-month scholarships for women and non-binary coders to work on existing open source projects. This same program had given Jessica a chance to get her feet in the industry years earlier, and the cancellation of it made Jessica not just offer sympathetic words. Despite being a junior developer herself back then, she channeled her disappointment into creating Ecosia Summer of Code from scratch. She'd convinced her company to offer mentorship when they couldn't provide financial support. Would I be writing this book if she had simply said, "That's too bad" and moved on with her life?

I met Eli Flores organizing a workshop she offered at Pyladies. She was the first female software engineer hired by Sauce Labs in Germany and the one who referred me to Sauce Labs Open Source Program Office Internship. She recognized something in me that I couldn't yet see in myself. When my internship was ending and my future felt uncertain, she gathered evidence of my value like precious stones, presenting them to leadership with unwavering conviction. The safety net she wove beneath me wasn't in her job description—it came from a place of profound humanity.

And then there was Christian Bromann, creator of WebdriverIO and a fierce advocate for open source standards, sustainability, and diversity. Christian didn't just mentor me technically; he invited me into spaces I never thought I'd belong. I still remember the flutter of disbelief when he casually mentioned, "You should join this foundation call," as if my presence in such spaces was the most natural thing in the world. He unapologetically placed a chair at the company's table for me, integrating me into conversations where decisions were made. His unwavering belief that I belonged transformed my relationship with technology itself.

These heroes in my story likely don't recognize the magnitude of their impact. Christian probably doesn't realize how his casual invitation to join foundation work fundamentally reshaped my understanding of belonging in tech. Jessica likely can't see how her emergency creation of Ecosia Summer of Code demonstrated that institutional constraints can be reimagined through creative determination.

As I settled into my role bridging the Open Source Program Office and Community departments at Sauce Labs, their collective influence crystallized into a vision. I needed to find a model that made sense for a for-profit company while honoring the spirit of open access that had carried me forward. The key insight came from recognizing what companies and open source projects have in common: humans—messy, complex, generous humans who can transform systems from within.

My vision wasn't abstract. I could still feel the sting of rejection from competitive programs that required months of unpaid work prior to application—a luxury many couldn't afford. I wanted to create accessible pathways for aspiring local technologists that didn't demand privilege as an entry fee. I believed that by creating several small local initiatives, lowering the barriers to entry by not being so competitive, and making the application process easier would bring in more diverse contributors— especially those who couldn't commit unpaid labor on the promise of future opportunity.

What emerged was more than a program; it was a love letter to everyone who had held space for me. At its core, the fellowship represents the transformative potential of institutional "plumbing"—redirecting resources within existing structures to create more equitable futures. The program demonstrates how one person's experience of being supported can catalyze a chain reaction that extends opportunities to others, perpetuating the cycle of "standing on the shoulders of giants."

Sometimes late at night, I trace the invisible lines connecting these moments and people: If Meili had never founded PyLadies... if Jessica had chosen a quiet evening at home instead of organizing... if Eli had never seen potential in me... if Christian hadn't casually invited me into spaces of influence. Each decision—seemingly small in isolation—formed a constellation that guided me toward creating opportunities for others.

This is the profound truth I carry forward: we never know what will bloom from the seeds we plant. The seemingly small act of inviting someone to a meetup, advocating for a colleague's promotion, or creating an emergency program during crisis might eventually transform into opportunities for people we'll never even meet. Like code contributions that become part of systems we couldn't imagine when writing them, our actions of inclusion ripple outward in ways we cannot predict.

As you read about the fellowship program in the coming pages, remember the invisible network that made it possible—a living example of how open source principles manifest in human relationships. We truly stand on the shoulders of giants, not just through the code we inherit but through the doors opened by those who believed in creating space for others before knowing who would fill it.

Mapping Strategic Opportunities: Finding Your Organization's Elemental Selenium

The fellowship's material foundation came from an unexpected source: Elemental Selenium, a collection of educational materials designed to help users learn automated web testing with Selenium. Sauce Labs had acquired this resource years earlier, but it languished without clear ownership or maintenance for more than five years. With over 23,000 subscribers to its newsletter, this valuable marketing asset represented both untapped potential and a bridge to the broader Selenium community.

I recognized in this neglected resource what Adrienne Maree Brown might call *an emergent strategy*—the possibility of transforming available materials into something that could serve multiple purposes simultaneously (Brown, 2017). By focusing fellows' efforts on revitalizing Elemental Selenium, we could align corporate interests in maintaining a valuable asset with the ethical imperative to create meaningful learning opportunities for aspiring technologists from underrepresented groups.

The total investment I proposed was $75,000, which was based on Outreachy program grant. I have multiplied the grant value for five fellows over six months, which represented a fraction of the asset's original acquisition cost while potentially delivering significant value through its revitalization. This financial architecture created a pocket of different values operating within capitalist institutions. We weren't asking for charity; we were offering a strategic investment that served both business and social goals.

The material basis of the fellowship was grounded in a recognition often sidelined by conventional business logic: investing in the open source technologies that products depend on can generate long-term value across multiple layers—technical, social, and strategic. These contributions, though frequently invisible in quarterly metrics, reverberate through the ecosystems they support. When an organization chooses to support the technologies it relies on, the benefits often reach its users long before they're reflected in internal dashboards.

Take security, for instance. Supporting the frameworks that underpin authentication or encryption protocols is not just a question of meeting compliance checklists. It's a way of actively participating in the care and protection of user data and digital trust. An organization that helps maintain a widely used login library isn't just solving its own problem—it's reinforcing the very structures that countless people depend on every day, often invisibly.

The same logic applies to stability. Contributions aimed at fixing bugs, improving test coverage, better observability tools, or optimizing performance often result in services that are less prone to failure and more responsive in practice. The impact is most clearly felt by end users, who might never know that the platform they rely on is smoother and more reliable thanks to upstream contributions. A research institute that helps sustain a scientific computing tool, for example, creates conditions where researchers can work with fewer interruptions, deepening the institution's credibility through technical stewardship.

And when it comes to performance, improvements made to open libraries ripple outward, shaping the pace and fluidity of countless interactions. An education platform that enhances a rendering engine might notice students spending more time engaged with materials, not because content has changed, but because the experience of accessing it has become less frustrating. In a healthcare system, a faster database query can be the difference between a timely diagnosis and a missed opportunity.

How can you find opportunities in your own organization? How can you strategically map opportunities to run a fellowship you can call your own?

For technology companies, examine your dependencies on open source infrastructure with particular attention to how improvements cascade to customer experience. Which critical projects do your products rely upon that could benefit from performance optimization, security hardening, or accessibility improvements? Are there components of your proprietary technology that could be beneficially opened to the community while retaining your competitive advantage? A fintech company might identify opportunities in authentication libraries that simultaneously enhance security compliance and reduce login friction for users, creating a competitive advantage through superior user experience while contributing to the commons.

For research institutes, consider knowledge translation opportunities. Are there valuable research findings languishing in technical papers that could be transformed into accessible educational resources? A climate research institute might contribute to visualization libraries that make complex climate data more interpretable for both researchers and public audiences, enhancing both scientific collaboration and public engagement.

For educational organizations, examine curriculum gaps at the intersection of theory and practice. Are there pedagogical resources that could simultaneously serve students while addressing industry needs? A university might identify opportunities to revitalize outdated engineering curricula by connecting students with industry practitioners through collaborative open educational resource development. Could contributions to accessibility frameworks make learning materials more inclusive? A university might contribute to learning management systems that better serve students with disabilities, creating a more equitable educational environment while establishing the institution as a leader in inclusive design.

For non-profits, assess underutilized communication channels or community resources. Could outreach infrastructure or valuable content be repurposed to open up new avenues for community engagement? An underutilized database of health resources may be found by a health advocacy group and turned into a community-maintained knowledge base.

The most promising opportunities typically address multiple organizational needs simultaneously:

- Unlock value from neglected assets such as communication channels, community ties, or intellectual property.

- Attend to the needs of internal organizational development (such as departmental silos being broken down or mentorship opportunities).

- Support larger community or social change objectives (establishing avenues for marginalized communities or adding to resources based on the commons).

- Comply with the company's primary mission or goals (building new capabilities, promoting reputation, or improving product quality).

The key insight from my experience with Elemental Selenium is that the most sustainable initiatives don't require manufacturing entirely new programs from scratch—they identify existing resources flowing through the organization that can be redirected toward more equitable and generative ends.

When mapping your own organization for such opportunities, look especially at the edges—projects that fall between departmental responsibilities, resources acquired during organizational transitions, or initiatives championed by individuals who have since moved on. These liminal spaces often contain the seeds of possibility, waiting for strategic vision to transform them from organizational loose ends into foundations for meaningful change.

Navigating Institutional Plumbing

The fellowship's material reality required navigating complex financial and legal structures within a for-profit corporation. This process exemplified what Sara Ahmed calls "institutional plumbing"—understanding how resources and power flow through organizations and finding ways to redirect these flows toward more equitable ends (Ahmed, 2012).

The idea of institutional plumbing proved especially pertinent to my work on the fellowship program because it clarified how I needed to negotiate intricate organizational structures and find innovative ways to work within preexisting systems. Rather than calling for radical institutional change, which frequently encounters opposition, I found myself carefully examining existing "pipes" to identify where resources might flow differently.

Crucially, I discovered that distinguishing between a fellowship and an internship—a seemingly minor semantic difference—carried significant practical implications. In Germany and many other countries, internships often come with an unspoken promise and intrinsic legal requirements regarding potential employment, which would have necessitated securing budget approval for five full-time salaries for at least a year following the program. This would have increased our budget requirement from $75,000 to more than $500,000, making the proposal financially untenable.

Unlike a standard employment role, the fellowship was structured as a time-bound educational opportunity, allowing for a level of experimentation that might otherwise be limited by institutional frameworks. From the outset, the program sought to address imbalances in representation within open source communities. Its design followed in the spirit of *affirmative action*—not as an exclusionary measure, but as a deliberate commitment to equity, which we could call *equity-centered initiative*. Given the legal and political restrictions surrounding explicit affirmative action in some regions, the program addressed systemic barriers through strategic outreach, accessible application processes, and selection frameworks that valued diverse forms of expertise and experience, while remaining open to all. This careful calibration made it possible to uphold both fairness and legal integrity, while actively expanding participation.

Transdisciplinary Learning: Beyond Code-Centrism

From the beginning, I rejected the reductive framing of diversity initiatives as merely "bringing underrepresented people into tech." Instead, I wanted to explore how technological creation itself might be transformed through transdisciplinary approaches that value multiple forms of knowledge and contribution.

The five fellows selected for the inaugural program in December 2022—Danielle Madry, Django Skorupa, Esther Cotton, Janackeh Blackwell, and Rajene Harris—brought diverse backgrounds and experiences that transcended traditional pathways into technology. Each fellow took primary responsibility for a specific aspect of the project while also engaging with other dimensions:

- Content Creation: Updating and creating new educational material about Selenium

- Design: Conducting user research and creating new visual interfaces

- Quality Assurance: Developing testing protocols to ensure site stability

- Development: Implementing technical architecture for the revitalized site

- Community Engagement: Building relationships with Selenium users and contributors

This structure emerged from Donna Haraway's concept of "situated knowledge"—recognizing that all technological understanding emerges from particular embodied positions rather than abstract universality. When I designed these diverse roles, I was implicitly challenging what Haraway calls the "god trick"—the illusion of seeing everything from nowhere, the disembodied objectivity that characterizes much technological work. Through her critique of traditional epistemologies, Haraway reminds us that knowledge always materializes from particular embodied positions—positions historically excluded from technological creation (Haraway, 1988).

Haraway's idea that knowledge production is essentially relational rather than hierarchical was mirrored in the fellowship's organizational design. What she might refer to as a "diffractive" approach to technological creation—one that recognizes how various knowledges interact to create new possibilities rather than strictly mirroring existing power structures—was created by making room for multiple perspectives and forms of expertise to coexist and transform one another.

Django Skorupa, focusing primarily on design, described his process as such:

"The most challenging part has been narrowing the initial scope of the project. It's difficult to cull my dreams down to functional possibilities... The most fun part is when everything clicks and falls into place. I remember changing the footer I had previously designed and realizing that it made the website feel complete. It was like sitting in a perfect ergonomic chair" (Skorupa, 2023).

What Haraway theorizes—knowledge as embodied, partial, and tied to particular experiences rather than disembodied technical mastery—is exactly what their reflection expresses. Design work incorporates functional harmony and embodied experience in addition to aesthetic appeal. This comprehensive view contradicts reductive methods that isolate design from user research or technical implementation.

Esther Cotton's journey similarly illuminates the program's transdisciplinary character:

"I've always loved tech, but hesitated to turn my love for tech into a career. After my office closed during the pandemic, I decided it was time to do something scary and push past imposter syndrome, and dive into the tech industry...I was so excited and surprised when Paloma informed me that I had been accepted into the fellowship! To be a part of this program, being able to both learn and work, and have access to mentors and a great team of supportive fellowship members has been such an amazing experience" (Cotton, 2023).

Her experience reveals what philosopher Miranda Fricker identifies as "testimonial injustice"—the systematic devaluing of certain people's knowledge claims based on their social identity (Fricker, 2007). Imposter syndrome itself emerges not as a personal failing but as the internalization of systemic epistemic exclusion—the sense that one doesn't belong in spaces of technological creation. The fellowship created conditions where Cotton could find an authentic path and find a vocation in technical content that allowed her to be both expressive and creative, yet deeply technical challenging entrenched patterns of who counts as a knowledge creator in technological spaces. As an expressive and precise communicator, she carried almost alone the updating of the whole website content in five different programing languages, which also opened to her possibilities in quality assurance and support engineering careers. Following Cotton break her own barriers and flourishing in so many possibilities was one of the most rewarding aspects of this program.

This transdisciplinary approach recognized open source as a social practice that requires a variety of skills and knowledge, rather than just a technical one. Expanding our understanding of what makes a valuable contribution beyond coding enables us to create multiple entry points for people with a variety of interests and skill sets, changing not only who participates in open source but also how that participation manifests itself.

Although the idea of transdisciplinary learning is sound philosophically and ultimately beneficial, its implementation revealed certain discrepancy. The lived experience during the fellowship itself displayed tensions between theoretical ideals and embodied realities, even though post-program surveys showed positive results. The lack of didactic experience caused a gap between lofty learning objectives and real-world application, where fellows occasionally found it difficult to establish a firm foundation.

The simultaneous demands of learning across multiple domains while delivering a concrete product generated a tension that occasionally threatened to overwhelm rather than empower participants. Information cascaded faster than it could be metabolized, which created cognitive load—a mental effort required to process new information and integrate it into existing knowledge structures.

The very porousness of boundaries that makes holistic understanding possible can also dissolve the scaffolding that learners need, particularly those who are naturally specialists or who have defined focus. The absence of clearly demarcated territories—this is design, this is development, this is content—sometimes led to disorientation rather than liberation.

The pressure to deliver a revitalized product within six months further complicated the learning journey. While real-world constraints eventually proved valuable in focusing efforts, they initially generated anxiety about measuring up to imagined standards of productivity. This tension between learning and producing can also create a negative experience when the space doesn't feel safe enough to carry the emotional weight of constantly having to prove one's worth in an industry that has historically excluded them.

I still believe deeply in transdisciplinary approaches as fundamental to transforming technological creation. The holistic understanding they foster—seeing connections between user needs, technical implementation, documentation, and community building—remains essential for creating technologies that serve diverse communities. However, this experience taught me that such approaches require more intentional structuring than I initially provided—not to reinforce boundaries between disciplines but to create clearer pathways through their intersection.

A more effective approach might have established stronger rhythms between focused skill-building and integrated application, creating temporary supports that enable learners to accomplish tasks they couldn't manage independently.

The challenge lies not in choosing between structure and transdisciplinary exploration but in creating dynamic relationships between them—relationships that evolve as learners gain confidence and capacity.

Realities of Management: Juggling Autonomy and Structure

Overseeing the fellowship program exposed conflicts between academic principles and real-world limitations, between planned instruction and unstructured inquiry, and between personal development and collective agency. These tensions manifested as daily challenges requiring constant negotiation and adaptation.

The initial program months emphasized structured learning, with fellows participating in sessions led by mentors from various departments. However, this approach inadvertently reinforced what educational philosopher Paulo Freire calls the "banking model" of education—positioning fellows as passive recipients of knowledge rather than active co-creators (Freire, 1970).

A pivotal shift occurred with the intervention of Bee Sharwood, an agile coach who recognized that the fellows needed not just technical knowledge but a shift in mindset—from waiting to be told what to do to claiming ownership of their learning and contribution. Sharwood implemented a modified Scrum methodology with one-week review and planning cycles, creating structure that supported autonomy while providing necessary guidance.

This change is evident in a more active learning style that stresses the completeness of mentors and fellows, acknowledging that education is about transformation rather than just passing on information. The program encouraged a sense of agency that is frequently denied to junior positions in hierarchical organizational contexts, and by establishing an environment that allowed fellows to recognize their own questions and challenges.

This practice manifested in regular retrospectives where fellows and mentors reflected on what was working, what wasn't, and how processes might evolve.

Challenges and Continuity

Managing diverse expectations among fellows, mentors, and organizational stakeholders created significant complexity. Fellows often entered with high expectations for both structured learning and immediate impact, sometimes underestimating the time required to understand complex codebases or organizational contexts. Mentors faced the challenge of balancing regular work responsibilities with their commitment to supporting fellows.

When numerous mentors who supported the fellows were laid off across the company, these tensions were made worse. This event brought to light the weakness of programs that rely upon individual champions rather than deeply institutionalized commitments. We made sure fellows received the support and development opportunities promised by sticking to the six-month schedule in spite of the situation.

On May 25, 2023, as the fellowship drew to a close, the fellows publicly launched the revitalized Elemental Selenium, incorporating features based on feedback from over 100 users who had participated in surveys and interviews. As I described in our announcement:

"The new Elemental Selenium now belongs to the Selenium community. Its content has been completely updated, and it now looks forward to your contributions, dear reader, so that your experiences can benefit thousands of other people" (Oliveira, 2023).

With this public launch, a project was not only finished, but a corporate asset was turned into a community resource, transferring ownership from a single business to the larger ecosystem of Selenium contributors and users. Beyond the revitalized content and interface, we had created a meticulously architected open source project—complete with comprehensive contribution guidelines, governance documentation, and transparent development processes. A structure that actively invites engagement rather than just transparency. Fellows experienced firsthand the philosophical underpinnings of open source as they crafted documentation that acknowledged the often invisible labor of maintenance, established clear pathways for newcomers, and embedded values of reciprocity and transparency into both code and community practices. The project's structure became a tangible manifestation of open source ethics, teaching fellows not just about technical implementation but about the care, foresight, and relational thinking required to sustain technological commons. Through this process, Elemental Selenium evolved from a neglected resource into a living demonstration of how corporate assets might be reanimated as vital community infrastructure—owned by all and maintained through distributed stewardship rather than centralized control.

Outcomes and Impact

The fellowship program's impact manifested across multiple dimensions — technological, individual, organizational, and communal. On the technological level, the program successfully revitalized Elemental Selenium, transforming it from a neglected asset into an open source project with updated content and architecture. The project now incorporates clear contribution guidelines, making it accessible to future contributors regardless of their technical background.

On the individual level, fellows experienced profound personal and professional growth. As Danielle Madry reflected:

"I'm eager to expand my knowledge and skills, especially in regard to best practices in open source development. Although there's a lot of information to absorb, I've found the whole process to be incredibly rewarding. Being able to gain hands-on experience while learning has been amazing and I'm excited to continue growing as a developer" (Madry, 2023).

On the organizational level, the program fostered cross-departmental collaboration and knowledge sharing. The 23 mentors involved gained experience in teaching and supporting others—skills increasingly valued in technical contexts but rarely developed systematically.

At the community level, the initiative improved ties between Sauce Labs and the larger Selenium community. Beyond merely using open source software, the company showed its dedication by investing resources in reviving an educational resource that practitioners valued.

A Replicable Model

By design, the Sauce Labs Open Source Community Fellowship Program provides a replicable approach for companies looking to tackle their own diversity issues and the sustainability of open source while also dismantling internal organizational silos. This approach includes some procedures:

1. Strategic Opportunity Identification: Identify underutilized resources in your company, such as neglected codebases, documentation requirements, or community resources, that could be the basis for open source and diversity initiatives. Perhaps there is a chance to contribute it back to an open source library heavily used by a team and prevent your product from breaking.

2. Financial Aid: A stipend is essential because everyone needs to eat, most likely pay their rent, and use their time to concentrate on their work without worrying about how they will eat the next day. Six to twelve months is the recommended duration; any shorter time frame will not be a meaningful learning period and will frustrate both parties.

3. Transdisciplinary Structure: Design roles that span different aspects of a software product—content development, design, quality assurance, technical content, and community engagement are a few— while allowing fellows to collaborate across domains.

4. Cross-Departmental Mentorship Networks: To guarantee sustainability, bring in mentors from a variety of departments within the company, such as engineering, finance, and sales and marketing. Commitments should be kept to two hours per week. By fostering relationships between departments that might not otherwise interact, this method not only gives fellows a comprehensive understanding of the organization but also dismantles internal silos. In addition to giving fellows all-encompassing support, this will enhance the larger organizational culture and foster a sense of pride and belonging.

5. Get Ready for the Market: This should help people get started in the market, comprehend company structure, and learn how to deal with these dynamics that are not explicitly stated or learned. This will pave the way for them to succeed in their next position.

6. Work Transparently: Open-source approaches such as working in the open can help them become more confident about their own work by encouraging a collaborative atmosphere and assisting them in overcoming their fears.

7. Documentation and Knowledge Transfer: Thoroughly document the program's design, implementation difficulties, and lessons learned to give a chance for the program to continue, maintain, and modify it over time.

This replicable model demonstrates how corporate resources can be reallocated to improve access to technology and change internal organizational culture. When starting with concrete opportunities rather than ambiguous promises, engaging with diverse forms of knowledge and contribution, and building robust support systems that cross departmental boundaries, organizations can develop initiatives that promote both business interests and social transformation.

Corporate Models at Different Scales: A Comparative Reference

While the Sauce Labs Fellowship Program demonstrates how mid-sized companies can create meaningful change with targeted resources, it's worth briefly examining how similar principles manifest in larger corporate environments. The Delivery Hero Tech Academy provided an instructive contrast—operating at a significantly larger scale but addressing similar systemic challenges.

Launched in 2021, the Delivery Hero Tech Academy represented a comprehensive intervention by the global food delivery corporation to address both talent scarcity and systemic inequality in tech. The Academy offered a 9.5-month program focused on backend development using Java and Python—combining 7.5 months of intensive technical education with a 2 month practical internship within Delivery Hero's engineering teams in the city of Berlin. Developed in partnership with DCI Digital Career Institute, the program targets individuals with little to no prior coding experience, deliberately lowering traditional educational barriers that often exclude marginalized groups.

The Academy achieved remarkable diversity metrics in its initial cohort—75% female participation, representation from twelve nationalities, and an age range spanning from 23 to 41 years. This demographic composition directly confronts the stark gender disparities in Germany's tech landscape, where women constitute only about 17% of the technology workforce. As Felicitas Schneider, Delivery Hero's Director of Diversity and Inclusion emphasized, the Academy was conceived not as "a feel-good project" but as "a business imperative" connecting diversity to innovation potential.

Contrasting Approaches at Different Organizational Scales

Unlike the Sauce Labs program's $75,000 budget, Delivery Hero invested approximately €442,460 in their initiative (numbers taken from public sources)—nearly six times the investment—reflecting the expanded capabilities of a multinational corporation with over 41,000 employees (compared to Sauce Labs' approximately 300 employees at the time of our program).

The structural differences between the programs reveal how similar philosophical commitments manifest differently based on organizational scale and resource availability.

While the Sauce Labs Fellowship focused on revitalizing an existing open source asset through a six-month program, Delivery Hero developed a comprehensive curriculum managed by a third-party educational center. Both programs show how corporate resources can be redirected toward social transformation, but they do so through different temporal structures and engagement models.

The financial structure of the fellowships revealed not only differences in scale but also divergent approaches to economic equity. Sauce Labs implemented a standardized global model, providing each fellow with a monthly stipend of $2,300 regardless of location. Delivery Hero, conversely, offered approximately €1,647 monthly per participant plus a one-time €600 home office allowance, specifically calibrated to Berlin's cost of living.

This comparison illuminates a critical dimension of fellowship design: while Sauce Labs' uniform approach embodied administrative simplicity, it failed to address the significant disparities in living costs across different US cities where fellows resided. The flat-rate stipend barely met minimum wage thresholds in many locations, creating uneven economic security among participants. In contrast, Delivery Hero's Berlin-based stipend was deliberately aligned with local standards of dignified subsistence.

The disparity becomes particularly apparent when considering the diverse life circumstances of fellows—including one Sauce Labs fellow who was a single mother requiring additional economic stability. This experience suggests that truly equitable financial support requires responsiveness rather than uniformity—grounding stipends in the material realities of participants' geographic locations and individual circumstances. A more humanistic economic approach would recognize that equal stipends do not necessarily create equal opportunities when fellows face fundamentally different economic pressures.

Institutional Partnerships and Legal Frameworks

A critical difference between the two approaches emerges in their institutional structures and legal frameworks. The Sauce Labs Fellowship was conceived as an affirmative action initiative, but faced significant legal constraints when operating directly as a for-profit corporation. As noted earlier, we navigated these limitations through careful design of application processes and targeted community outreach rather than explicit selection criteria.

By contrast, Delivery Hero's strategic partnership with DCI (Digital Career Institute) enabled a more explicitly targeted approach to diversity. This partnership allowed them to operate within the educational exemption framework that permits affirmative action measures for training and educational purposes.

This distinction points out the substantial influence that institutional arrangements can have on a program's capacity to address systemic inequalities. While Delivery Hero's model displays how educational partnerships can provide more flexibility in pursuing equity goals, Sauce Labs' approach shows how businesses can work within current legal constraints through imaginative program design. Both strategies draw attention to how crucial it is to comprehend the institutional and legal framework when creating diversity programs.

Institutional Integration and Employment Pathways

The most significant difference appears in how each program approached employment pathways. The Sauce Labs Fellowship explicitly distinguished itself from an internship to create space for experimental learning without employment expectations. This distinction enabled the program to operate under a smaller budget while creating a meaningful educational opportunity.

In contrast, Delivery Hero's Academy was explicitly designed as a talent pipeline, with approximately 75% of graduates transitioning into full-time engineering roles at the company. This higher conversion rate reflects both the larger organization's capacity to absorb new talent and the program's specific design as a recruitment strategy rather than primarily a community contribution.

Both approaches have merit—one emphasizes community transformation through contribution without promises of employment, while the other directly addresses employment barriers through an explicit hiring pipeline. The difference illustrates that organizations can tailor their approach to both their resource capacity and strategic objectives.

What these contrasting models reveal is that the philosophical framework of redirecting corporate resources toward equity can operate effectively at multiple scales. Both programs demonstrate interventions that work within existing structures while creating spaces for transformative practices.

Organizations considering similar initiatives might examine these examples to determine which approach aligns with their specific context:

1. The Sauce Labs model shows how businesses with less funding can make a significant difference by strategically revitalizing their assets and giving back to the community.

2. The Delivery Hero model demonstrates how bigger companies can create all-encompassing talent pipelines that concurrently address business requirements and systemic exclusion.

3. Regardless of scale, both models place a strong emphasis on intentional pathway creation, mentorship networks, transdisciplinary learning, and living wages.

This comparative viewpoint supports the key takeaway from the Sauce Labs Fellowship Program: significant change doesn't necessitate massive budgets or drastic reorganization; rather, it calls for strategic vision, fostering relationships, and a dedication to establishing environments where a range of people can grow their abilities while working on worthwhile projects.

The Sauce Labs Open Source Community Fellowship Program demonstrates how mid-sized companies can redirect corporate resources toward creating equitable pathways in technology. By revitalizing Elemental Selenium—a neglected educational asset—the program created a strategic $75,000 investment that served both business goals and social transformation.

The fellowship rejected code-centrism in favor of a transdisciplinary approach that valued multiple forms of knowledge, carefully navigated institutional constraints through semantic distinctions between fellowships and internships, and created opportunities for five fellows from underrepresented backgrounds. By involving 23 mentors from across departments—from sales and marketing to engineering and finance—the program simultaneously broke down organizational silos while providing comprehensive support to fellows.

Despite implementation challenges balancing structure with autonomy, the program successfully transformed a corporate asset into community infrastructure while fostering fellows' personal and professional growth.

The experience offers a replicable model for organizations seeking to address open source sustainability through strategic opportunity identification, living-wage stipends, transdisciplinary learning, mentorship networks, and agile governance—proving that meaningful change requires strategic vision and relationship building rather than enormous budgets or radical restructuring.

The Pirate's Code: Coyotiv's Rebel Model

Conventional organizational structures manifest as soul-crushing vessels—rigid hierarchies that claim to foster creativity while systematically dismantling it. What might emerge if we turned toward an unexpected wellspring of organizational wisdom? Pirates—not the romanticized Hollywood version, but actual historical pirate crews—offer us a revolutionary alternative to the corporate architectures we've come to accept as inevitable.

When Armağan Amcalar founded Coyotiv, a software engineering academy and consultancy, he deliberately turned to pirate crews for inspiration.

"We are living in a traditional economy, but we have our own models of generating and sharing that value... it's designed after how pirates work and how pirates do value distribution."

—Amcalar in an interview for the author

This does not represent simply a wacky metaphor; more so, it represents a basic rethinking of how tech companies might organize themselves to actually promote diversity and inventiveness.

This "Coyotiv Model" is so intriguing because it reframes diversity as an economic necessity rather than as a moral checkbox. According to Amcalar's vision, diverse viewpoints are the very catalyst for innovation rather than something distinct from value creation that is overseen by HR. According to the model, maximizing the resources at hand necessitates a dynamic collaboration between individuals with diverse backgrounds, ideas, and abilities.

This section explores this revolutionary approach—examining how pirate-inspired organizational structures might offer us passage beyond both traditional corporate hierarchies and the well-intentioned but often superficial diversity initiatives that fail to address structural barriers to authentic participation. As we shall see, there's treasure to be found in these waters.

The Philosophy Behind Rebellious Ideals: Freedom Creates Value

The philosophical foundation of the Coyotiv Model begins with a radical premise that would make most corporate executives break out in hives: value creation emerges when people pursue what they feel most drawn to do at any given moment.

Wait—people should do what they feel like doing? Isn't that organizational chaos?

Well, yes—and that's precisely the point. But this isn't chaos as disorder; it's chaos as a natural ecosystem of human creativity and collaboration. The most innovative systems often operate at this edge where structure and flexibility coexist in dynamic tension.

Central to this philosophy is a deliciously subversive insight: traditional power structures in organizations are largely illusory. Control within typical corporate hierarchies represents a facade—a performance of power rather than its genuine expression. As Amcalar puts it with refreshing bluntness: "They're in control, but they don't have power. It's a fake representation of power. It's not real. It's not usable".

Sound familiar? Michel Foucault would be nodding vigorously. His analysis of power as circulating rather than possessed—not something wielded by individuals but distributed through networks of relationships— maps perfectly onto what Amcalar has discovered through practice. The *Coyotiv Model* makes room for more genuine, value-producing relationships by acknowledging the fictitious nature of hierarchical power.

Perhaps most importantly, this philosophy rejects the industrial-era understanding of knowledge work as labor. "We're not creating value through our labor," Amcalar observes. "We're creating value through our creativity and genius and the ability to create change... this is craftspersonship" (Amcalar, 2025).

This reconceptualization positions organizational management itself as a craft—requiring the nuance, adaptability, and deep understanding characteristic of artisanal practice rather than industrial production. The word "craft" comes from the Old English "cræft," connecting to both skill and strength—suggesting that true organizational power emerges from cultivated expertise rather than someone's position on an org chart.

In this philosophical framework, the organization exists not to satisfy egos or exert control but to create value—whether economic, social, or cultural. The practical implementation manifests in what Amcalar calls an "elastic organization based on purpose and people doing things," where hierarchy forms naturally based on contribution rather than being imposed artificially from above.

Organizational Architecture: The Elastic Crew

So what does a pirate-inspired organization actually look like in practice? First, throw out your org chart—you won't need it anymore. The *Coyotiv Model* eliminates rigid departments, fixed roles, and vertical hierarchies. Instead, it implements what we might call an "elastic crew" structure—a flexible, purpose-driven configuration that adapts to both the specific needs of projects and the strengths of individual contributors.

The design begins with a premise that would make Frederick Taylor roll over in his grave: "each cog in your system, each person in your team or in your company are autonomously exerting their own power," explains Amcalar. Rather than attempting to control these autonomous agents through traditional command structures, the *Coyotiv Model* seeks to "direct them like a magnet"—influencing their direction while preserving their intrinsic momentum.

Isn't that a beautiful metaphor? Leadership as magnetic field rather than direct force—creating conditions that naturally orient individual energy toward collective objectives without squashing individual autonomy. This approach has striking parallels to how complex adaptive systems function in nature, where local interactions produce emergent order without centralized control.

A distinctive feature of this organizational architecture is its rejection of rigid role definitions. The model embraces the possibility that teams can shape-shift, with groundbreaking ideas sometimes emerging from junior members who might drive critical business functions or execute specialized tasks.

This fluidity allows for expertise to emerge organically rather than being prescribed by position or title. Think about how this contrasts with typical organizations where your job title literally defines what you're allowed to contribute! The approach has fascinating connections to emergent design principles in architecture itself, where structure evolves in response to actual patterns of use rather than imposing predetermined functions on space.

The elastic crew architecture requires transparent, public communication as its foundation. Actual information transparency is achieved through open communication, decision-making, progress monitoring, and work organization.

"Have all your communication in public. Transparency of communication, transparency of chain of command, transparency of decision making, and transparency of progress and work."

—Amcalar in an interview for the author

Because of this transparency, information can freely flow, empowering independent agents to cooperate and make well-informed decisions. This kind of openness is a big change from traditional organizational information management, which treats knowledge as proprietary and distributes it based on hierarchical position rather than functional need. Elinor Ostrom's (1990) work on commons governance shows that this is a fundamentally restrictive approach.

Perhaps most significantly, the *Coyotiv Model* addresses a fundamental flaw in traditional organizational architecture that we've all experienced: the inability to gain leadership experience before receiving leadership titles. In conventional organizations, employees often become managers without knowing how to manage people because they've never had the opportunity to practice leadership before being assigned the role.

The Coyotiv Model facilitates the natural development of leadership skills across the organization by allowing for emergent leadership based on contribution rather than position. This is a far more logical strategy that is similar to the apprenticeship model of skill development, in which mastery develops through graduated practice rather than abrupt promotion.

Economic Model: Transparent Distribution

Let's talk about money—because ultimately, that's where organizational values either prove themselves or reveal their hypocrisy. The economic dimension of the *Coyotiv Model* is perhaps its most disruptive aspect. Rather than obscuring financial information and reinforcing hierarchical power dynamics, Coyotiv implements a transparent, algorithmic approach to distributing resources.

This economic model begins with radical financial transparency that would make most executives choke on their coffee: complete salary transparency for every member of the organization, including leadership. Directly quoting Amcalar:

"Everyone knows every cent the other person makes and I'm also included in that mechanism"

Yes, you read that correctly—complete salary transparency. But the transparency doesn't stop there; it extends to the methodology of compensation, which operates through a structured algorithm that allocates revenue according to multiple factors:

- A percentage reserved for organizational expenses
- A percentage distributed to project contributors based on their involvement
- A percentage shared across all organization members regardless of direct project involvement
- A percentage allocated to administrative support functions

Within this framework, individual compensation is determined through a sophisticated set of multipliers that consider the following:

- Project contribution (time allocation to specific projects)

- Contribution level (from replicable tasks to work requiring specialized expertise)

- Seniority and expertise

- Market realities for different specializations

- Geographic economic differences (using the Big Mac Index)

- Special contributions such as bringing in clients (earning ongoing commission)

Monthly income fluctuates with how much money the company makes collectively, creating an immediate link between individual contribution and shared prosperity. When your work generates additional revenue, you receive a percentage of that increase—a system that transforms personal effort into immediate reward, cultivating responsiveness and engagement that distant annual bonus cycles cannot sustain, while strengthening the collective foundation that sustains everyone's material wellbeing.

The Big Mac Index is a particularly brilliant aspect of this economic model. It creates equitable purchasing power across different economies by recognizing that numerical equality in compensation doesn't necessarily translate to experiential equality. The goal is for salaries to provide equivalent purchasing power across different economic contexts.

Think about how revolutionary this approach is compared to both traditional compensation systems and simplistic approaches to global pay equity. It acknowledges economic reality while ensuring fairness in a way that pure numerical equality simply can't achieve. Instead of concentrating only on numerical distributions, this capability approach to equality emphasizes what people can realistically afford and sustain within their economic circumstances.

This economic model applies game theory to organizational compensation, rejecting the adversarial dynamic where employees want to do the minimum work for maximum pay while companies want to pay the minimum for maximum output.

Instead, it creates a system where mutual benefit is mathematically structured—giving value to get more in return—resulting in higher per capita value creation over time. Principles for managing commons that stress proportional equivalency between benefits and costs are echoed by this alignment of individual and collective interests.

An important advancement in economic design is the use of compensation algorithms to mathematically express organizational values. The Coyotiv Model intentionally encodes its values in its distribution mechanisms, making the philosophical and the implicit explicit, rather than letting economic distribution develop as an afterthought or as a default to traditional patterns. As they say, money speaks, and in this instance, it's doing so in a language that is a revolutionary act.

Diversity As Value Creation Engine

Here's where things get really interesting. The Coyotiv Model reconceptualizes diversity initiatives by situating diversity as central to value creation rather than as a separate moral imperative. This approach stands in contrast to conventional diversity, equity, and inclusion (DEI) efforts that Amcalar critiques with refreshing honesty: "They see that bias, and they say, you have to work to remove this bias. Whereas what really happens is just like, naturally, you just have to focus on generating the biggest value".

In this framework, diversity becomes a pragmatic necessity rather than a moral obligation. According to Amcalar, organizations must leverage diverse perspectives and experiences because it creates the most value: "If everyone is the same, looks the same and thinks the same, you are very limited."

Doesn't that just make intuitive sense? And yet how many organizations still treat diversity as a box to check rather than a core business strategy?

This perspective transforms diversity from a deficit-oriented approach (addressing biases and gaps) to an asset-oriented approach (leveraging unique capabilities and perspectives). Just as biological ecosystems with greater genetic diversity demonstrate greater resilience and adaptability, organizational ecosystems with diverse cognitive approaches demonstrate superior problem-solving capabilities and innovative potential.

The Coyotiv Model places particular value on historically underestimated people—including junior developers and those from underrepresented backgrounds—recognizing their problem-solving abilities, resilience, and determination as valuable organizational assets. Amcalar explains why he prefers working with junior developers and people from underrepresented groups, as "they are better at problem solving, and they are way more resilient. They don't give up. And when given a chance, they try to make the most out of it".

The operationalization of diversity in organizations will be significantly impacted by this rethinking. The Coyotiv Model places more emphasis on fostering an environment where diverse people can contribute authentically, take responsibility for their work, and work well with others despite differences than it does on representation or bias mitigation. When establishing frameworks where diversity naturally arises as a value-generating dynamic, the emphasis moves from changing individuals to changing systems.

Leadership Methodology: Path Correction vs. Control

If there's one aspect of organizational life that's simultaneously overanalyzed and poorly understood, it's leadership. The leadership philosophy within the Coyotiv Model represents a fundamental departure from conventional management approaches. Instead of leading through control, authority, or directive management, the model advocates for leadership as "path correction."

Amcalar likens this approach to autonomous driving—vehicles (team members) navigate themselves, with leadership providing directional guidance and occasional corrections rather than constant control.

This approach rejects the metaphor of leadership as "dragging a sleigh" where without the leader's constant effort, progress ceases. Instead, it conceptualizes leadership as creating conditions where autonomous agents navigate toward shared objectives, with leaders providing guidance and course correction rather than force or control.

Isn't it fascinating how this conceptualization resonates with ancient Daoist concepts of leadership as "acting without doing" (wu wei)—where the most effective influence comes from working with rather than against the natural tendencies of people and situations? As Lao Tzu put it nearly 2,500 years ago, "The best leader is one whose existence is barely known".

The leadership approach of the Coyotiv Model prioritizes inspiration over authority. Inspiration and the capacity to unite individuals around a common goal are more important than strict hierarchical authority. Instead of upholding hierarchical distance, this orientation calls on leaders to build genuine human connections—a skill that conventional management structures frequently undercut, which makes the biggest failure of a leader that, as a manager or president of such an organization, you cannot really form bonds with people.

A critical component of this leadership methodology is the conscious relinquishment of ego and control. Leadership requires letting go of personal ego and encouraging others, especially senior team members, to adopt a common ground approach rather than asserting individual authority.

Think about how radical this is compared to traditional leadership approaches that often reinforce the leader's elevated status and decision-making authority. The approach instead positions leaders as facilitators of others' success rather than primary decision-makers.

Perhaps most significantly, the Coyotiv Model's leadership methodology creates space for leadership to emerge throughout the organization rather than being concentrated in designated positions. This distributed approach to leadership enables more effective decision-making, increases organizational adaptability, and cultivates leadership capabilities across the entire crew.

Amcalar uses a metaphorical tool analogy to describe effective management—just as different tools are needed to reach different parts of a cavity, different approaches are needed to bring out the best in each team member.

From positional authority to facilitative influence, from hierarchical control to path correction, and from ego-driven direction to purpose-driven guidance, this leadership philosophy is greater than a simple tactical approach; it is a fundamental reconceptualization of organizational power. Instead of leadership derived from management during the industrial era, it is leadership reimagined for the knowledge age.

Implementation Challenges: Navigating Resistance

Implementing something like the Coyotiv Model isn't easy. It inevitably encounters resistance, particularly from individuals accustomed to traditional organizational structures. The friction emerges not merely from procedural adjustments but from deep-seated psychological and cultural expectations about work itself.

The biggest challenge lies in overcoming traditional understandings of work. People who have spent their careers in conventional organizations arrive with implicit boundaries and expectations about being told what to do. This conditioning creates several specific forms of resistance: discomfort with autonomy emerges when people don't know what to do without explicit direction. The Coyotiv Model places responsibility on individuals to determine their own path within designated areas rather than waiting for instructions. This shift can be disorienting for those accustomed to hierarchical guidance.

Have you ever noticed this paradox? People simultaneously complain about micromanagement while feeling lost without explicit direction. This discomfort reveals how deeply dependency on hierarchical direction can become embedded in professional identity, creating what Erich Fromm identified as an "escape from freedom"—the tendency to prefer direction over autonomy when the latter creates existential uncertainty.

Difficulty receiving feedback in non-hierarchical contexts represents another challenge. When feedback comes outside traditional power structures, some interpret it as personal attack rather than professional guidance. This reaction demonstrates how feedback and correction become psychologically coded based on hierarchical position rather than substantive content—a coding that must be unlearned for effective non-hierarchical collaboration.

External pressure to conform to traditional management creates another implementation barrier. Friends and colleagues often advise more directive leadership while simultaneously advocating delegation. Catch that contradiction? It reveals the cultural ambivalence about leadership—simultaneously criticizing micromanagement while expecting visible control, an ambivalence that creates particular challenges for alternative organizational models.

Perhaps the most basic reason for opposition to the Coyotiv Model is a fear of losing control. Even though traditional power structures ultimately limit both individual and collective potential, they offer psychological security to those who are used to them. Institutional defense mechanisms that shield organizations from potentially dangerous information or change are one way that this fear shows up.

These difficulties demonstrate how deeply embedded conventional organizational paradigms are as well as how psychological adaptations are necessary to function well within the Coyotiv Model. In addition to structural adjustments, cultural change and mindset adjustments are also necessary for this model to be implemented successfully. The opposition seen demonstrates how organizational structures are internalized as psychological frameworks that influence identity, expectations, and behaviors in ways that go well beyond formal reporting relationships.

Implementation Guide: Building Your Pirate Crew

So you're convinced and want to try this pirate thing yourself? For organizations seeking to implement the Coyotiv Model, several practical steps emerge from Amcalar's experiences. These steps involve tactical adjustments and strategic reorientations toward more human-centered, value-generating organizational designs:

1.   Establish radical transparency: Begin with financial transparency, making compensation algorithms and individual earnings visible to all crew members. Extend transparency to communication (maintaining public channels), decision-making processes, and work progress. This transparency creates the conditions for informed autonomy and collaborative decision-making.

2.   Eliminate rigid roles and hierarchies: Replace fixed positions and departmental structures with purpose-driven, fluid arrangements that allow individuals to contribute according to their

capabilities rather than their titles. This fluidity enables expertise to emerge organically rather than being prescribed by position.

3. Implement equitable compensation algorithms: Develop transparent, algorithmic approaches to distributing resources that account for contribution, expertise, geographic differences, and market realities while ensuring everyone benefits from collective success. These algorithms make organizational values explicit through economic distribution.

4. Create space for autonomous contribution: Establish clear areas of responsibility without prescribing specific approaches, encouraging individuals to develop their own strategies and solutions within their domains. This autonomy fosters both innovation and ownership.

5. Develop path correction leadership: Train leaders to guide through influence rather than control, focusing on creating conditions for success rather than directing specific actions. This leadership approach maintains direction without undermining autonomy.

6. Cultivate authentic connections: Prioritize genuine human relationships throughout the organization, rejecting the notion that leadership requires emotional or professional distance. These connections create the trust necessary for fluid collaboration.

7. Address resistance constructively: Acknowledge the challenges of adapting to non-traditional structures and provide support for individuals navigating this transition, recognizing that previous organizational experiences create deeply ingrained expectations. This support facilitates the psychological transitions necessary for structural change.

8. Center value creation: Maintain focus on generating value rather than maintaining power structures, consistently evaluating organizational practices according to their contribution to purpose rather than their adherence to convention. This focus provides the ultimate criterion for organizational decisions.

Implementing the Coyotiv Model doesn't require wholesale transformation in a single moment. Organizations can begin with specific elements—perhaps implementing transparency before restructuring hierarchies, or experimenting with fluid roles within traditional departments. The key is consistent orientation toward the underlying philosophy while adapting specific practices to organizational context.

Broader Implications for Open Source

The Coyotiv Model, although deeply grounded in open source principles, also reflects back important lessons to open source communities grappling with challenges of diversity, sustainability, and governance.

Its emphasis on collective value creation over ego satisfaction offers a practical counterweight to some of the behaviors that have, over time, fragmented many open source ecosystems. As Amcalar, put it:

"They fork projects instead of contributing to them. Why the hell are you forking something that's super successful just because you have a marginally different understanding of what it should do? Just contribute to the main project".

This frustration resonates with many maintainers who have watched promising projects lose momentum due to unnecessary fragmentation. However, while Amcalar's frustration reflects the common concern, the reality of forking encompasses a spectrum of motivations and constraints. Many forks emerge not from preference but from necessity—when original projects maintain rigid contribution barriers, when corporate governance structures exclude certain types of improvements, or when fundamental philosophical differences about project direction create irreconcilable tensions. The technical ease of forking in distributed version control systems intersects with complex social and organizational dynamics: a contributor may prefer to contribute upstream but find themselves blocked by maintainer availability, review bottlenecks, or institutional policies that prevent meaningful collaboration. In these contexts, forking becomes less about ego and more about creating space for innovation that existing governance structures cannot accommodate.

Isn't that a perfect description of the fragmentation that plagues many open source ecosystems? The model promotes more cooperative, less fragmented open source development by placing more emphasis on group value creation than individual recognition.

Second, the economic dimensions of the Coyotiv Model offer alternatives to problematic funding mechanisms in open source. Rather than corporatized sponsorship that often distorts incentives, the transparent, equitable resource distribution of the Coyotiv Model could enable more sustainable funding that preserves open source's collaborative ethos while arranging for contributors to sustain their work.

This possibility addresses one of the most persistent challenges in open source development—reconciling the ideals of freely shared knowledge with the practical necessity of economic sustainability.

As Nadia Eghbal's research on open source sustainability demonstrates, finding economic models that support ongoing maintenance without corrupting community values remains one of the central challenges of digital commons (Eghbal, 2020).

Third, the model's approach to diversity as pragmatic value creation provides a compelling framework for increasing representation in open source without resorting to tokenism or superficial inclusion efforts. Open source communities can access the full range of human creativity and expertise by fostering an environment where diverse contributors can lead and participate completely.

This strategy provides a way to move past the performative nature of diversity initiatives that don't address systemic barriers to participation as well as the homogeneity that has defined many open source communities.

Finally, the Coyotiv Model's leadership philosophy offers a path beyond the "benevolent dictator" paradigm that has dominated many open source projects. By distributing leadership functions across the communities and emphasizing path correction over control, projects can become more adaptable, user centric, and resilient. It's a contemporary recognition that sustainable commons governance requires polycentric rather than monocentric authority structures.

Instead of offering a prescriptive solution, the Coyotiv Model offers a provocative alternative as open source communities navigate issues of sustainability, governance, and inclusion. It shows that it is possible to create technological communities that are more diverse, human, and economically viable than traditional models permit. "It's only through utilizing everyone that we can really prosper," Amcalar said, expressing his inspiration from Atatürk's modernization of Turkey.

The Coyotiv Model represents more than an organizational experiment or management technique—it offers a fundamental reconceptualization of how humans might collaborate to create technological value. Drawing inspiration from historical pirate crews and contemporary open source principles, this model challenges conventional assumptions about hierarchy, control, diversity, and value creation that have dominated organizational design for centuries.

What distinguishes this approach is its pragmatic rather than purely idealistic orientation. The Coyotiv Model doesn't emerge from abstract theory, it raises from practical necessity—the recognition that traditional organizational structures fundamentally limit the potential for human collaboration and evolution.

Isn't it time we admitted that most organizational structures weren't designed for knowledge work in the first place? They were designed for industrial production—for predictability, control, and standardization— precisely the opposite of what creative work requires. Reorienting around value creation rather than control, diversity rather than homogeneity, and distributed rather than concentrated leadership, the model offers a path toward more adaptive, equitable, and generative technological communities.

The challenges of implementing such revolutionary models shouldn't be underestimated. The resistance encountered reveals how deeply conventional organizational paradigms have shaped not only structures but psychologies—creating expectations, behaviors, and identities that can make alternative approaches initially disorienting. Yet these challenges shine some perspective on the transformative potential of such models, offering possibilities for professional relationships that are simultaneously more authentic, more equitable, and more productive than conventional hierarchies permit.

The model is a thought-provoking vision of alternative possibilities— not just different procedures, but fundamentally different relationships to power, value, and collaboration—as open source communities and technological organizations traverse an increasingly complex landscape. Such alternatives may prove not only desirable but also essential for tackling the complex challenges of technological development in various, international contexts in an era where traditional organizational structures are becoming more and more apparent for their shortcomings.

My favorite take is the model's reinterpretation of diversity—not as a problem of representation but as a source of value creation, and not as a moral obligation but as an economic necessity—may be this is its most significant contribution. The possibilities for technological communities to utilize the full range of human creativity and expertise are suggested by this reframing, which provides a way past the drawbacks of traditional hierarchies as well as the possible shallowness of traditional diversity initiatives.

In the final analysis, the Coyotiv Model invites us to imagine technological collaboration beyond hierarchical horizons—to envision communities of creation where value flows from authentic contribution rather than positional authority, where leadership emerges throughout rather than being imposed from above, and where diversity becomes not a problem to solve but the very engine of innovation itself.

Are we prepared to navigate these unknown waters? Those who dare to leave the comfortable confines of hierarchical organization will find the treasure of truly ecological-centered technological collaboration.

Creating Spaces of Liberation

The traditional narratives of open source transformation often center around technical innovations, licensing models, and governance structures. These frameworks, while necessary, prove insufficient for addressing the fundamental question of who creates, maintains, and ultimately benefits from open technological spaces. This section introduces a radical methodology for community-building that reconceptualizes privilege not as something to disavow but as a strategic resource to deploy toward its own dissolution.

The model presented here diverges sharply from commercial or business-oriented approaches to diversity. Rather than seeking to include marginalized voices within unchanged structures, it envisions the creation of autonomous spaces where those without traditional means can define technological futures on their own terms. This methodology recognizes that technological creation shapes our collective existence, making the participation of diverse voices necessary for an equitable future.

> *"What privileged people can do... is to create and imagine spaces where things can be different and then to also try to create space to empower others to take over those spaces."*

—Katharine Jarmul in an interview with the author

Katharine Jarmul

Katharine Jarmul approaches this work as a privacy activist and data scientist whose practice centers on security and privacy in artificial intelligence and machine learning systems. As author of Practical Data Privacy and founder of Kjamistan, she brings technical expertise coupled with radical political consciousness. Her international recognition stems from technical accomplishments to her sustained commitment to reimagining how technological communities organize themselves.

Jarmul's background proves particularly significant—her position as "an educated US American white woman in a world where that is generally very rewarded" provides both the privilege necessary to create institutional spaces and the critical awareness to recognize how those spaces must ultimately transform. This dual consciousness undergirds how she creates actions, spaces, and communities, allowing her to navigate the paradox of using privilege toward liberation rather than reinforcement.

Her formative intellectual influences emerge from Black feminist and anti-racist traditions, particularly the works of Audre Lorde, Angela Davis, Assata Shakur, bell hooks, and June Jordan. These revolutionary thinkers inform her understanding of how oppression operates through interlocking systems rather than isolated instances. Equally significant were her mentors at UC Santa Barbara, particularly Cedric Robinson—creator of Black Marxism—and his wife Elizabeth Robinson, who modeled alternative pedagogical approaches that centered marginalized knowledge.

This intellectual genealogy situates Jarmul's practical interventions within a broader tradition of liberatory thought. Rather than abstracting diversity from its political context, she grounds her work in radical traditions that understand liberation as collective rather than individual practice.

Theoretical Foundations: The Dialectics of Space-Making

The spatial politics of open source communities exist within broader structures of power and privilege that cannot be disentangled from histories of colonialism, racism, and patriarchy. It is necessary to address the flow of power through technological environments in order to create truly liberatory spaces, moving over representational politics.

In order for the space to realize its liberating potential, Jarmul's method reveals a dialectical process in which the very privileges that allow space-making must eventually be given up. This process is carried out by tangible organizational procedures that are specifically created to promote power transfer, not by impersonal dedication.

The proximity to power that privileged individuals experience creates responsibility rather than entitlement. For Jarmul, this responsibility manifests through intentional institutional design that creates conditions for others to flourish and eventually lead. The dual movement progresses through recognition of privilege, deployment of that privilege to create institutional structures enabling resource redistribution, and eventual evacuation of central authority.

The paradox of privilege is transformed from paralysis to praxis by this dialectical movement. Jarmul's approach aims to create spaces that contain the seeds of their own transformation within their design, in contrast to traditional diversity initiatives that diversify their appearance while maintaining existing power structures.

Case Study 1: PyLadies Origin

Jarmul's theoretical articulation of liberatory space-making takes tangible form in the founding of PyLadies, a community initiative that has become emblematic in the landscape of diversity efforts in tech. This origin story operates as more than a historical footnote—it serves as a practical case study of the paradoxes involved in using one's own privilege to dismantle exclusionary structures from within.

The PyLadies founders embodied the dialectical tension Jarmul identifies: they were insiders to a degree, positioned close enough to the centers of technological power in Los Angeles to leverage visibility, access, and legitimacy. Yet their objective was to construct a framework that could eventually function independently of their presence—making room for others who had long been excluded.

This dynamic reveals a deeper structural insight: the same privileges that make space-making possible can, if left unexamined, reinforce the hierarchies they initially sought to disrupt. The PyLadies founders navigated this contradiction by recognizing that real transformation requires a gradual decentering of the original actors. In doing so, they illustrate that liberatory design is not only about building new institutions, but about relinquishing ownership in favor of community governance.

In early 2010s Los Angeles, seven young female programmers found themselves at an unexpected inflection point: their informal Python meetups had ignited something that resonated far beyond their initial expectations. The sociopolitical background is crucial: it was a time when women made up less than 20% of technical positions, when Silicon Valley was dominated by "brogrammer" culture, and when women were often marginalized in technical communities.

Their events produced resources that needed to be managed, including community contributions, workshop fees, and sponsor donations. More importantly, they had a vision that needed institutional structure in order to succeed. In order to collect and distribute funds without being held personally liable, they decided to create a California nonprofit organization, a move that reflected both necessity and revolutionary potential.

Their ideals were quite precisely enacted by the institutional framework they created. Through facilitating leadership rotation with annual democratic elections, power concentration was prevented. Their financial strategy was inspired by Latin American alternative economies, which reimagine money not as abstract wealth to be accumulated, but as a communal resource that strengthens social bonds. This type of economy sees resources as community wealth that should be shared rather than hoarded.

Cryptocurrency is not the only alternative to institutionalized finance; communities around the world have long been weaving radical economic systems that challenge exploitative capitalism from its roots. In the sun-drenched barrios of Brazil's Fortaleza, residents created Banco Palmas[1] not from blockchain algorithms but from human relationships—a community bank where creditworthiness stems from a neighbor's word rather than a credit score, and where local currency circulates like blood through the neighborhood's economic body, refusing to drain away to distant financial centers. This stands as living proof that meaningful alternatives can emerge from collective wisdom rather than technological complexity.

Across Latin America, these community-powered economic experiments flourish in diverse forms. "El Túmin" is a peer to peer local Mexican value mostly used by farmers and indigenous people to stimulate

---

[1] Official website of the bank https://bancopalmas.com/

the agricultural economy. The Túmin—its colorful bills adorned with indigenous imagery—flows through twenty-four Mexican states, allowing small producers to bypass exploitative middlemen and trade directly with neighbors. When taxi drivers in San Cristobal offer change in Túmin and shopkeepers accept it for half a purchase, they participate in a quiet revolution that privileges relationship over extraction.

Meanwhile, in the steep hillsides of Caracas, where hyperinflation rendered national currency nearly worthless, communities created emergency currencies like the panal, demonstrating how economic sovereignty can be reclaimed even amid systemic collapse.

These systems don't promise overnight riches or disruptive innovation—they offer something more profound: economies rewoven into the fabric of community life, where currency serves as a tool for collective thriving opposed to individual accumulation. When a vegetable seller offers discounts for payment in community currency, or when interest-free loans fund local businesses, money transforms from master to servant, from mechanism of extraction to instrument of connection. Unlike crypto's often individualistic ethos, these community currencies embody a fundamentally different vision—economies built not on scarcity and competition, but on abundance, reciprocity, and the radical notion that finance should serve people, not the other way around.

With similar examples in mind, the group asks themselves: "What is it for us to charge 10 bucks a head for an all-day hackathon?" Jarmul asks. "It's nothing in Los Angeles, California, to then allow for that extra burden to be lowered. So how can we exploit the privileges of being in a wealthy city in the Global North for the benefit of the global community?" This question reveals how geographical privilege can become a resource for global redistribution rather than local accumulation.

Their first moment of critical self-reflection arrived quickly. Despite commitment to diversity, they recognized insufficient representation from Latinx communities, particularly Chicanos who form a significant part of LA's population landscape. Rather than tokenistic recruitment, they built partnerships with organizations like DIY Girls[2] led by Luz Rivas and Robert Hernandez's Hispanic Journalists of America. These collaborations exemplified their approach—creating bridges rather than competing for space, recognizing expertise already present in communities.

As their concept spread beyond LA, they developed the "open source PyLadies kit" with seed funding for new chapters. This kit embodied their most radical vision—that PyLadies would mean something different in Bangkok than in Berlin, something different in Nairobi than in New York. Their approach aimed for adaptation rather than replication, encouraging a variety of expressions as opposed to standardized forms.

As their resources grew, so did their dreams. They embraced revolutionary possibilities at a board retreat, moving above immediate practicalities. Christine Cheung proposed initiatives transforming their understanding of what PyLadies could become—leadership retreats bringing chapter organizers together across geographical boundaries, recovery spaces for PyLadies experiencing burnout, and scholarship funds for conference attendance.

These visions centered care explicitly within organizational purpose. In an industry glorifying exhaustion, they imagined spaces where restoration became revolutionary practice rather than productivity interruption. They conceived the idea for PyLadiesCon, which would be structurally different from Python's official conferences and would reflect their values in decision-making instead of copying the Python Software Foundation's "dude's club."

Their temporal context proves significant—this visioning occurred around 2012, contemporaneous with the founding of more commercially oriented organizations like Girls Who Code. What distinguished their approach was radical commitment to decentralization, open governance, and communal economics.

---

[2] DYI girls is still an active group, their website: https://diygirls.org/

Their story contains both inspiration and caution. Merely months after articulating expanded visions, internal conflicts coincided with complications from California regarding their nonprofit application. The Python Software Foundation subsequently assumed control of the PyLadies bank account, bringing the LA chapter's experimental governance to an end while the broader movement continued under different institutional arrangements.

Nevertheless, the PyLadies origin story sowed a remarkably potent seed that would grow all over the world in spite of these obstacles. The movement now has over 400 chapters worldwide, though exact numbers are still hard to monitor because chapters are independent and occasionally form without direct assistance from the main PyLadies governance board. For example, PyLadies Berlin helped me transition my career, which has enabled me to write this book, and gave me the vital support system I needed to settle in Germany. This global expansion serves as a powerful reminder that even initiatives with structural flaws can spark revolutionary communities when their fundamental principles strike a deep chord with people looking for camaraderie, education, and support.

Reflections from Afar in Time

PyLadies' origin history offers several crucial methodological insights for creating liberatory spaces in open source communities.

First, scale presents both opportunity and threat. Their rapid growth created possibilities for global impact but simultaneously introduced vulnerabilities to institutional capture. This suggests that liberatory spaces may require intentional scaling strategies that prioritize depth over breadth, relationship over reach.

Second, legal and bureaucratic structures create a complex terrain that liberation work must navigate strategically. Understanding the bureaucratic landscape we operate within is essential—not to be constrained by it, but to leverage it effectively. While their nonprofit status imposed administrative demands, it simultaneously provided the necessary infrastructure for resource redistribution. This suggests that liberatory spaces require neither blind compliance with nor wholesale rejection of institutional forms. Instead, they demand a sophisticated engagement—recognizing that we must function within the societal frameworks we inherit while creatively adapting these structures toward purposes they weren't designed to serve. Both procedural expertise and tactical inventiveness are needed for this strategy; one must be familiar enough with the rules to recognize areas of flexibility and dormant transformative potential.

Third, intentional institutional protections against the consolidation of power are vital for the preservation of open spaces. Their experience shows that, despite being consistent with liberatory ideals, an overabundance of openness paradoxically led to weaknesses that permitted power to consolidate without sufficient control. As stated in the interview, they required stronger checks and balances—systems to keep accountability distributed and stop unofficial hierarchies from becoming entrenched. Accordingly, liberatory spaces need protective structures commensurate with their revolutionary potential—not as obstacles to involvement, instead as barriers that keep them from being overtaken by personal interests or mission drift. Establishing these safeguards is necessary to maintain openness, not in opposition to it; it calls for constant attention to detail and systemic changes in lieu of just counting on well-meaning intentions.

Fourth, their history tells us how apparently innocent mundane administrative functions—controlling bank accounts, representing the organization to external bodies, making day-to-day operational decisions—constitute critical sites of power that profoundly shape the organization. These operational decisions are primary battlegrounds where the ideals can be either enacted or undermined. This implies that rather than treating these administrative domains as apolitical formalities, governance models should consciously address them by allocating authority over these routine but significant tasks. Power often resides in the everyday processes of organizational maintenance—the unglamorous work that determines who ultimately controls resources, sets priorities, and implements collective decisions.

Lastly, their experience shows how privilege can be strategically used by creating an institution that makes it easier for its own people to leave. This implies that in order to achieve emancipation, structural change that empowers marginalized communities to shape technological futures according to their own terms is just as important as diverse representation.

Case Study 2: Feminist.AI As Restorative Practice

A decade after PyLadies' formation, Jarmul found herself confronting a technological landscape simultaneously more inclusive and more oppressive. The crucial backdrop is the sociopolitical environment of 2023–2025, which includes resurgent far-right movements across the globe, restrictions on reproductive rights, declining gender parity, corporate control over democratic institutions, ongoing conflicts, and the quick adoption of AI systems that embed current power structures while claiming neutrality.

"I think what I noticed in myself and in others last year was a deep like depression," Jarmul recounts. "We had war, we had elections, we had misinformation, we had the rise of the far right... Plus, let's not even get started about AI is going to replace all the jobs and this and that, whatever. So there was a lot of bad news."

This collective despair prompted Jarmul to return to formative texts to guide her as a compass. "I can sit with those books as well as new books... I can sit with people whose very existence involves the forming liberation as a daily practice." A key realization emerged from this return to her traditions: imagination is a necessary political practice because the paralysis of despair itself supports oppressive structures.

This recognition gave rise to the Feminist.AI LAN Parties, which are places intended for collective imagination and restoration as well as technical skill development. These gatherings reject the false binary between technical competence and political consciousness, creating instead what Jarmul terms "little havens, like almost like a little pop-up swarm of recovery and imagination and love."

The methodology manifests through several interconnected practices:

First, creating physically separated spaces—temporarily disconnected from the public internet—where alternative technological futures can be imagined without constant intrusion of dominant narratives. These temporary autonomous zones allow participants to experience different relationships with technology, even if briefly.

Second, centering rest explicitly as revolutionary practice. "How do we create liberatory spaces for rest and for care?" Jarmul asks, recognizing that *"the people that are already in burnout or that are literally like in fear of their lives, their livelihoods, their families... they are not in a mental space to make that space, but they need to have that space so that they can survive."* This practice draws inspiration from the Nap Ministry,[3] Tracy Hershey's project framing rest as resistance to capitalist extraction.

The question of burnout in open source communities demands recognition that exhaustion itself functions as a political technology—one that transforms collaborative labor into an extractive mechanism. Burnout operates as both an individual crisis and a systemic architecture. The exhausted contributor becomes doubly marginalized depleted

---

[3] The Nap Ministry website: https://thenapministry.wordpress.com/

by the very systems meant to foster collaboration yet simultaneously expected to possess the energy necessary for their own restoration. The GitHub contribution graph, the perpetual issue tracker, the expectation of immediate response—these mechanisms fragment experience into measurable productivity units while colonizing the very rhythms of embodied existence.

Tracy Hershey's concept of rest as resistance, explored in *Rest Is Resistance (2022)*, provides crucial insight here. When she advocates for rest, she articulates what becomes, in the context of open source communities, a profound insurgency against the biopolitical regime of perpetual availability. The resting developer—the one who closes their laptop, who lets issues remain unresolved, who prioritizes sleep over code reviews—performs what Hershey identifies as radical refusal of capitalist extraction. This refusal becomes particularly transgressive within open source cultures that often celebrate "passion" and "dedication" in ways that obscure their participation in exploitative labor dynamics.

Adrienne Maree Brown's *Pleasure Activism: The Politics of Feeling Good* (2019) extends this framework by recognizing how pleasure itself creates "liberated zones" where different technological futurities become imaginable. The pleasured body, whether through rest, play, or genuine enjoyment of technical work, momentarily escapes what Foucault called the "political technology of the body." These states generate institutional anxiety precisely because they liberate the contributor from functioning as productive units and return them to existence as sensing beings.

When Hersey advocates for rest and Brown for pleasure, they articulate complementary insurgencies against this biopolitical regime. Biopolitics, a term coined by French philosopher Michel Foucault, means the administrative governance of biological life itself. The docile, productive body represents an economic asset and a political achievement, as institutions and discourses penetrate our very flesh, regulating when we sleep, how we feel pleasure, and which sensations we acknowledge as legitimate. The *body*, Foucault reminds us, "*is also directly involved in a political field; power relations have an immediate hold upon it; they invest it, mark it, train it, torture it, force it to carry out tasks, to perform ceremonies, to emit signs.[4]"*

The resting Black body under capitalism becomes doubly transgressive—first in its refusal of productivity, and second in its assertion of autonomy over the terms of its own existence. Similarly, the pleasured body (particularly marginalized bodies historically denied sovereignty) performs a radical dissolution of the disciplinary mechanisms that Foucault identified as controlling bodies through "an uninterrupted, constant coercion, supervising the processes of the activity rather than its result." Rest and pleasure converge here as experiential states that evade productionist capture, opening fissures in the seamless operation of power.

The emancipatory power of these practices emerges precisely because they reverse the flow of biopolitical control. While institutionalized power works by fragmenting experience into measurable units (work hours, productivity metrics, and optimized leisure), rest and pleasure reassert wholeness and presence. They constitute what Foucault might recognize as counter-conducts—practices that refuse normative ways of being governed. The resting body and the pleasured body both slip momentarily beyond surveillance, creating what Brown calls "liberated zones" where different futurities become imaginable. These states don't merely reject exploitation; they actively germinate alternative embodiments.

For communities whose bodies have been historically conscripted into systems of production—from plantations to factories to digital platforms—reclaiming rest and pleasure represents not simply self-care but ancestral healing. The unspoken wound within contemporary capitalism remains its genealogical continuity with explicitly racialized systems of bodily control.

---

[4] Foucault, Michel. 1977. *Discipline and Punish: The Birth of the Prison.* Translated by Alan Sheridan. New York: Pantheon Books, p. 25.

Foucault's analysis of biopower helps us recognize how "grind culture" and the denial of pleasure function as sophisticated techniques for managing populations by managing their embodied experience. Combining Hersey's and Brown's frameworks is to recognize that the intimate decisions about how and when we rest, find pleasure, and inhabit our bodies constitute political actions with profound collective implications.

This biopolitical reading reveals why practicing rest and pleasure generates such institutional anxiety—these states momentarily liberate the body from its function as productive unit and return it to its existence as sensing being. The sleeping body and the pleasured body both temporarily escape what Foucault called the "political technology of the body," where power operates by obtaining the exercise of power at the lowest possible cost...bringing the effects of this social power to their maximum intensity and ensuring their extension without failure or gap. In their deliberate nonproductivity and nonperformativity, rest and pleasure create precisely such "gaps"—spaces where different configurations of power, relationship, and embodiment become not just thinkable but tangible, breathing room for revolutionary reimagination.

The body that experiences pleasure rather than extraction, rest rather than optimization, becomes the primary site where alternative technological futures first materialize. This corporeal dimension remains crucial precisely because, as Foucault observed, biopower operates through "an anatomo-politics of the human body" that subjects our physical existence to "disciplinary methods" and "permanent controls." The unconference format itself—with its horizontal structure and emergent agenda—performed exactly the kind of institutional interruption that pleasure activism proposes.

What unfolds through this conceptual marriage of rest and pleasure is a methodology that refuses the false choice between technological engagement and embodied autonomy. Instead, it proposes what we might term a politics of technological embodiment—one where technical systems must adapt to human rhythms rather than human bodies

conforming to algorithmic demands. When participants encounter
these frameworks within technical spaces, the very parameters of what
constitutes "innovation" undergo quiet revolution. No longer measured
through efficiency metrics or scalability alone, technological progress
becomes evaluated through its capacity to facilitate rest, pleasure, and
collective flourishing.

This parenthesis leads us to the third finding, contesting dominant
technological narratives through collective imagination. The current
narrative is controlled by a fascism violent aesthetic made invisible by
the camouflage speeches, as Laura Summers revealed us in her talk "The
aesthetics of AI: From cyberpunk to fascism"[5] presented at the same
conference. This is what Jarmul emphasizes with FeministAI: "We need to
construct counter narratives. We need to own spaces where there can be
imagination for what should AI be". This practice recognizes that technical
systems always embed political values, making narrative contestation
essential to technical transformation.

Fourth, creating conditions for diverse expressions of technological
engagement rather than imposing standardized participation forms. The
Feminist.AI kits—covering data development, LLM hacking, hardware
setup, and zine-making—provide resources while avoiding prescriptive
approaches. Instead of using standardized inclusion metrics, this practice
acknowledges that diverse participation modalities are necessary for
liberation of us all.

Fifth, explicitly naming the revolutionary intention behind these
gatherings: "When you're done recharging after the Feminist AI land party,
then you can go spread the infection of feminist AI malware everywhere."
This framing transforms technical practice from individual skill to
collective resistance, recognizing that technological systems function
simultaneously as technical artifacts and political actors.

---

[5] Talk description https://pretalx.com/pyconde-pydata-2025/talk/933YXH/

The Feminist.AI approach illustrates evolution in Jarmul's methodology, responding to changing technological and political landscapes. Where PyLadies focused primarily on creating entry points for women in Python communities, Feminist.AI addresses the political dimensions of technological systems themselves. The evolution transpired not merely as strategic adaptation but through critical epistemological reflection on how naming practices themselves constitute political architectures of inclusion and exclusion.

Jarmul's realization emerged through witnessing how "Ladies" as signifier functioned simultaneously as invitation and boundary—drawing certain bodies into community while inadvertently establishing normative parameters around who properly belonged in these spaces. The word itself performed invisible labor, filtering participation through gendered expectations that contradicted the initiative's aspirations. Ironically, the nomenclature perpetuated the very divisions that its content aimed to eliminate.

This nominative reckoning signifies a profound ontological shift rather than a superficial rebranding, acknowledging that liberation necessitates challenging the very linguistic structures that we use to express community. When recognizing that emancipatory practice must start with the conceptual frameworks that determine who materializes as subject within technological discourse, the shift from "PyLadies" to "Feminist. AI" thus represents an intellectual leap beyond representational inclusion toward systemic transformation.

The evolution toward explicitly feminist framing creates space for bodies and knowledges traditionally excluded even from well-intentioned diversity initiatives—those existing at intersections of multiple marginalization, those whose gender expressions transcend binary categorization, those whose relationship to technology remains mediated through complex matrices of privilege and exclusion. Thus, this linguistic intervention opens up technological learning toward several liberating futures and is not just descriptive accuracy.

The outcome of that are participants describing feeling "a magnetic force that… put[s] people alike together," creating energizing connections rather than depleting extractions. This affective dimension reveals how liberation operates as embodied collective experience.

Creating a Methodology for Liberation Spaces

The experiences with PyLadies and Feminist.AI offer lots of inspiration which we can create methodological guidance for creating liberatory spaces in open source communities. This framework articulates twelve interconnected practices operating across cognitive, material, temporal, and social dimensions.

Cognitive Dimensions: Consciousness and Narrative

1. Critical Self-Reflection: Begin with explicit mapping of your position within systems of power and privilege. Identify with your privileged self-seeking recognition even within purportedly liberatory spaces—and actively work to counteract these tendencies.

2. Narrative Contestation: Explicitly challenge dominant technological narratives while constructing alternatives. Create spaces where marginalized communities articulate their own technological visions rather than responding to dominant frameworks.

3. Epistemic Openness: Recognize diverse ways of knowing and relating to technology. Value different approaches without hierarchizing them according to Western standards.

Material Dimensions: Resources and Structures

1. Institutional Design: Create formal structures explicitly designed to facilitate resource redistribution and prevent power consolidation. Establish governance mechanisms ensuring regular leadership rotation and democratic decision-making while maintaining organizational continuity.

2. Resource Redistribution: Explicitly acknowledge global and local power disparities and counteract them through material support for less priviledged communities. Direct resources toward autonomous community development rather than centralized control.

3. Spatial Justice: Recognize that open source spaces are not neutral but shaped by geographical, economic, and social disparities. Create conditions where diverse communities participate meaningfully regardless of geographical or economic position.

Temporal Dimensions: Process and Transition

1. Planned Obsolescence: Include explicit planning for leadership transitions from inception. Design institutional structures and cultural practices facilitating rather than obstructing leadership transitions.

2. Iterative Adaptation: Embrace ongoing evolution rather than fixed structures, recognizing liberation as process rather than destination. Regularly reassess organizational structures and practices to ascertain they continue serving liberatory purposes.

3. Restorative Temporality: Incorporate rest and restoration as essential aspects of liberation work, challenging productivist frameworks prioritizing constant activity. Create spaces where participants recharge and reflect, recognizing such restoration as necessary for sustained engagement.

Social Dimensions: Community and Coalition

1. Authentic Representation: Insist that communities reflect the diverse populations they exist within, moving beyond tokenistic inclusion to meaningful participation. As Jarmul articulates: "If the organization is not actually representative... in Berlin should be 30% Turkish German, right?... I'm not talking about quotas, but...you should actually at least minimally reflect."

2. Trust Building: Recognize that creating inclusive spaces requires building trust with marginalized communities over time. Engage sustainably, never superficially: "And that means like really doing the work, you have to go meet folks, you have to ask people how to meet folks, and then you have to give real power over and build trust. And that's not going to happen one meeting, two meetings, five meetings. Maybe it will happen after a year of knowing people."

3.   Coalition Formation: Build bridges with existing community organizations rather than competing with them or duplicating efforts. Engage in collaborative events and partnerships respecting others' autonomy and expertise while creating opportunities for mutual support.

Why This Methodology Matters

Based on Katharine Jarmul's experiences with PyLadies and Feminist. AI, this section offers a radical approach to establishing liberating spaces in open source communities. The method rethinks privilege as a tactical tool to be used in the pursuit of its own ultimate oblivion rather than as something to be denied.

This approach creates spaces for change, in contrast to traditional diversity initiatives that maintain current power structures while only diversifying their appearance. It offers specific advice for community organizers looking to go beyond tokenistic inclusion toward structural change through twelve interrelated practices that span cognitive, material, temporal, and social dimensions.

The approach offers a way to strategically use privilege for liberation rather than reinforcement, which is especially relevant for people in privileged positions within open source communities. By offering frameworks for establishing independent spaces where technological futures can be defined according to their own terms, it simultaneously speaks to members of marginalized communities.

Such a strategy provides crucial tools for contestation and reimagining in a technological environment increasingly characterized by AI systems that claim neutrality while embedding current power dynamics. It proves that open source liberation necessitates more than open code likewise open power—the conscious establishment of environments where technological know-how is shared rather than hoarded, where leadership is flexible rather than set, and where the future itself is a place of shared imagination rather than preset course.

When viewed in convergence, the methodologies articulated by the Sauce Labs Fellowship, Coyotiv's pirate-inspired organizational model, and Jarmul's liberation-centered framework reveal a layered topology of transformation, operating across individual, organizational, and systemic scales. While each initiative emerges from a distinct context, they are united by a shared commitment to redirecting existing power structures through intentional, situated acts of disruption. Their cumulative effect gestures beyond performative diversity, toward a more ambitious reconfiguration of the technological commons.

At the core of this convergence lies a strategic repurposing of existing resources. Whether drawing from corporate budgets, bureaucratic architectures, or social capital, each approach demonstrates how power, when critically reexamined, can be deployed against its own default trajectories. The Sauce Labs Fellowship, for instance, exemplified how even a relatively modest financial allocation—$75,000—could catalyze disproportionate impact when embedded within a thoughtful architecture of mentorship, cross-departmental collaboration, and structural accountability. Rather than positioning change as contingent upon large-scale investment or external overhaul, the program modeled a praxis of internal reengineering—where design, not dollars, served as the primary currency of transformation.

The logic underlying the model materializes in architectural structure in Coyotiv's model, where organizational infrastructure itself becomes a site of radical redistribution. Drawing inspiration from decentralized maritime economies, or, pirates, the model treats hierarchy as a resource to be disassembled and recomposed. Through transparent compensation algorithms and participatory governance mechanisms, Coyotiv reframes organizational coherence around equity rather than control. In encoding its values mathematically, it operationalizes inclusivity, making power legible and thus contestable. Value redistribution occurs not through goodwill or performative equity, but via structural mechanisms embedded in compensation systems and organizational logic.

Operating at another register, Jarmul's space-making methodology addresses the personal as political terrain, situating privilege as a strategic resource to be redirected toward its own obsolescence. Her approach reframes privilege not as a site of guilt or retreat, but as material for architectural use—a scaffolding for spaces that will, by design, outgrow their architects. This dialectical move—using power to erode the very conditions of its monopoly—demands intentionality ethos of planned irrelevance, where leadership is understood as transitory and legitimacy must be continually re-earned through accountability.

Across these interventions, transparency emerges as a catalytic mechanism—an epistemological commitment to the redistribution of knowledge, access, and authorship. Within Sauce Labs, process documentation functioned both as an internal accountability measure and as a knowledge commons for replication and critique. Failures were metabolized into shared learning, establishing a precedent for public-facing institutional memory.

Coyotiv's radical transparency, particularly in salary visibility and compensation logic, functions as a counterforce to managerial opacity. It challenges the logic of scarcity and competition that so often undergirds tech culture, suggesting instead that trust and clarity generate resilience. The act of revealing the economic schema shifts power away from arbiters of information and toward collective negotiation.

Jarmul's framework brings this principle into the realm of relational and political transparency, requiring that those engaged in space-making name the power they hold and design its eventual redistribution. In this schema, sustainability is inseparable from succession; without plans for exit and transference, liberation becomes performance.

What binds these methodologies is a shared expansion of what counts as contribution. Each challenges the primacy of code as the sole metric of value, insisting instead on a broader ecology of labor—content creation, design, documentation, community building, and emotional labor are not ancillary but constitutive. The Sauce Labs Fellowship formalized this recognition through its transdisciplinary structure and mentorship strategy, affirming the epistemic legitimacy of roles often rendered invisible in technical hierarchies.

Coyotiv institutionalized this principle through algorithmic means, embedding value pluralism into the very logic of remuneration. By factoring geographic diversity, role fluidity, and evolving contributions into its compensation model, it refuses the myth of meritocracy in favor of a model where equity is not presumed but calculated. Jarmul's framework advances this further still, constructing autonomous spaces where historically marginalized groups are not asked to integrate into existing models but to author new ones—spaces in which their knowledge traditions set the terms of engagement.

All three frameworks share a methodological humility—a recognition that transformation is never static, and that governance must be as dynamic as the communities it seeks to serve. Iteration replaces prescription. The Sauce Labs program demonstrated this through its pivot toward agile practices in response to participant feedback, prioritizing experiential learning over adherence to predefined curricula.

Coyotiv institutionalized fluidity in its design: roles are not fixed, but adaptive, and decision-making is collective and transparent by default. Its governance structure is less a hierarchy than a living membrane, continually adapting to the needs of its constituents. Jarmul's approach encodes this adaptability through mechanisms of planned obsolescence and feedback-driven evolution, ensuring that space-making is always a beginning, never an endpoint.

Together, these approaches articulate a multidimensional blueprint for open source transformation. They argue that meaningful change cannot occur through isolated interventions or symbolic gestures. Instead, transformation unfolds through cumulative, overlapping efforts—each grounded in an understanding that power must be named, redirected, and redistributed.

Their convergence suggests a series of enduring insights: that structural change requires more than representational fixes; that existing systems, if strategically engaged, can become sites of resistance; that transparency is not weakness but a precondition for solidarity; and that sustainability must be engineered from the outset, not retrofitted after the fact.

What is perhaps most striking is the ordinariness of their entry points—a fellowship, a payroll algorithm, a community gathering. These are not revolutions in the dramatic sense, but in the infrastructural one. Their power lies not in spectacle, but in scaffolding. They offer a quiet, deliberate form of resistance—one that builds the world otherwise, not by tearing down what exists, but by redirecting its flows, reauthoring its scripts, and imagining new terms of engagement.

In this light, the future of open source—as a set of practices, cultures, and possibilities—may depend not on charismatic interventions or capital influxes, but on the steady, strategic repurposing of what is already at hand. One fellowship, one compensation algorithm, one liberation space at a time.

CHAPTER 6

Weaving the Commons

Imagine walking through an ancient forest. Beneath your feet, fungi stretch their mycelial networks across vast distances, transmitting nutrients, warnings, and information between trees. These underground communication channels represent a form of distributed intelligence that predates human technology by millions of years. The forest operates through collaboration rather than competition, through plurality rather than hierarchy, through gift rather than extraction.

What if our technological systems could learn from these ancient forms of intelligence?

Throughout this book, we've explored the complex landscape of open source—its history, its contradictions, its failures, and its extraordinary potential. We've examined how standardization can either reinforce existing power structures or, when reimagined, help create pathways to more equitable technological futures. We've confronted hard truths about labor, exclusion, and the false promise of meritocracy. We've outlined practical frameworks for governance and contribution that honor the full spectrum of human participation.

As we arrive at this final juncture, our gaze shifts toward the horizon. In resonance with James Bridle's *Ways of Being*, open source emerges as a lens through which to rearticulate our relationship with technology—one that is not isolated from the living world, but embedded within it. This perspective is premised by posthumanist and decolonial approaches that challenge the centrality of the human and the extractive logics inherited from colonial infrastructures. Within such a paradigm, open source

© Paloma Oliveira 2025
P. Oliveira, *Diversifying Open Source*, https://doi.org/10.1007/979-8-8688-0769-5_6

becomes a space for experimenting with systems that are responsive, distributed, and interdependent—echoing the adaptive intelligence of fungal mycelia or the collaborative architectures of Indigenous knowledge and other cosmologies. It invites us to design technologies that participate in a wider ecology of care, that acknowledge cognition as plural and contextual. It offers us a chance to create tools that don't extract but regenerate, communities that don't exclude but embrace, and systems that recognize intelligence in all its diverse manifestations.

The revolution we need transcends questions of who writes code—it transforms what code does, how it's created, who it serves, and what values it embodies. By recognizing technology's deep entanglement with our social, political, and ecological systems, we shatter the myth of neutrality. Most importantly, we understand ourselves as active participants in shaping futures where we co-exist with all sorts of technological and ecological intelligences, rather than passive recipients of technological change.

As we stand at this crossroads, facing unprecedented ecological crisis, technological acceleration, and social fragmentation, open source offers us something precious: a living practice of solidarity, a commitment to the commons, and a reminder that other ways of being with technology alongside ecology are not only possible but already emerging around us.

The Journey Thus Far: Reclaiming Open Source's Revolutionary Potential

Our exploration began with a simple yet profound proposition: What if there existed a template that could be integrated into any open-source project that would bring more equity, awareness, and diversity? This question led us on a journey through the history, philosophy, and practical realities of open source software development, revealing both its transformative potential and its current limitations.

In Chapter 1, we established the fundamental connection between open source and broader social issues. We challenged the myth of technological neutrality, drawing on thinkers like Eugenio Tisselli, who remind us that technology is never just a tool but "a way of constructing order in the world" (Tisselli, 2016). Through the lens of Langdon Winner's question "Do Artifacts Have Politics?", we examined how technological choices—from nuclear power to solar energy—embed different political relationships into the fabric of our communities.

We explored Benjamin Bratton's concept of "The Stack"—the accidental megastructure of planetary computation that has reshaped political sovereignty, economic power, and social identity. This framework helped us understand how open source exists within larger technological systems that both influence and are influenced by societal structures. As Bratton reminds us, "The world itself is a model open to design and designation" (Bratton, 2018).

In Chapter 2, we broadened our understanding of what "open source" encompasses. Moving beyond code, we discovered open source as a cultural movement, an economic force, a philosophy of collaboration, and a practical tool against asymmetry. Through conversations with figures like Paulo Schor, Pedro Medeiros, and Luciano Ramalho, we witnessed how open principles transform fields from medicine to synthetic biology to education.

We saw how Brazil's early adoption of open source under Gilberto Gil's Ministry of Culture created pathways for digital inclusion and cultural expression that challenged global power dynamics. As Angelo Pixel recalled, these initiatives empowered communities by providing access to technology and knowledge previously inaccessible, demonstrating open source's potential for addressing systemic inequalities.

Chapter 3 confronted the uncomfortable realities of open source's current limitations. Drawing on theories of affective labor from Hochschild, Hardt, and Negri, we examined how open source often relies on unpaid emotional work that goes unrecognized and unrewarded.

We questioned the myth of meritocracy through Jo Littler and Daniel Markovits' critiques, revealing how supposed "neutral" evaluation systems actually reinforce existing power structures.

Through the work of Safiya Umoja Noble, Ruha Benjamin, and Caroline Criado Perez, we confronted the painful truth that technology—even open source technology—is never neutral but embeds and amplifies societal biases. As Noble demonstrates in *Algorithms of Oppression*, search engines replicate and reinforce racist hierarchies, while Criado Perez's *Invisible Women* reveals how data bias creates a world designed for men by default.

In Chapter 4, we shifted from critique to construction, offering a comprehensive blueprint for embedding ethics, inclusion, and democratic governance into open source projects. Through detailed templates for documentation—from READMEs to Codes of Conduct to Contributor Guidelines—we demonstrated how seemingly technical documents can become vehicles for transformative values.

Finally, in Chapter 5, we explored living examples of alternative models for open source. From the Sauce Labs Fellowship Program to Coyotiv's "Pirate Model" to Katharine Jarmul's creation of liberatory spaces, we witnessed how organizations and individuals are already reimagining open source practices to prioritize equity, inclusion, and collective well-being.

Throughout this journey, a central tension has emerged: open source exists simultaneously as a revolutionary practice with the potential to transform technological relationships and as a system that often reproduces the very power dynamics it claims to challenge. This tension is not unique to open source but reflects broader contradictions within technological systems.

Learning from More-Than-Human Intelligence

Bridle offers a reframing of intelligence and technology, challenging the human-centered, binary and quantitative computation-obsessed paradigm that dominates technological development. Bridle invites us to recognize intelligence as vastly more diverse than our narrow computational models suggest—existing in forests and fungi, in slime molds and cephalopods, in weather systems and rivers.

This perspective radically decenters the human in technological thinking, opening space for what Bridle calls "more-than-human" systems of knowledge and relation. Rather than seeing technology as an exclusively human domain that we impose upon a passive natural world, Bridle encourages us to understand technology as part of a broader ecology of intelligence in which humans are participants rather than masters.

"What we need," Bridle writes, "is not more powerful computational metaphors for nature, but more powerful natural metaphors for computation" (Bridle, 2022). This inversion challenges us to reimagine how we design, build, and relate to technology, drawing inspiration from the diverse intelligence systems that surround us.

What might an open source ecosystem look like if it were modeled not on factory production or market competition but on forest ecosystems or mycelial networks? How might governance structures change if they drew inspiration from the decentralized intelligence of slime molds, which solve complex problems without any central control?

In practical terms, this means moving away from code-centrism toward an understanding of open source as a holistic practice embedded in broader ecological and social systems. It means recognizing the diversity of contributions—from documentation to community care to artistic expression—as essential rather than peripheral. It means acknowledging that technology's impacts extend far beyond its intended functions, shaping environments, communities, and more-than-human beings in ways we often fail to recognize.

Bridle's work also challenges the binary logic that dominates computational thinking. "Binary thinking—the reduction of complex phenomena to simple yes/no decisions—is built into our computational systems," they write, "but it fails to capture the richness and ambiguity of the world" (Bridle, 2022). This binary reductionism limits what our computers can do and how we think about technology and its possibilities.

The open source revolution we need is one that resists this reductionism. It embraces messiness, contradiction, and plurality. It recognizes that software is never just software but an extension of human relationships, values, and ways of being in the world. Incorporating a more-than-human perspective, open source communities can further resist the binary logic that reduces technological development to a matter of efficiency, scale, or profit.

Solidarity As Technology: Reimagining Our Tools

If we take seriously Bridle's call to learn from more-than-human intelligence and Langdon Winner's awareness that artifacts have politics, we must reimagine, reorient who creates technology, the conditions, values, and worldviews that shape the technology itself; we must recreate the very nature of the tools we create.

Technology materializes relationships, encodes values, and reflects modes of existence that extend well beyond its functional capacities. For open source, the task is not limited to expanding access within established paradigms, but to cultivating practices and tools that make room for fundamentally different ways of relating—technologies that surface alternate imaginaries rather than reproduce inherited assumptions.

Consider tools designed for regeneration instead of extraction. Tools oriented toward care rather than surveillance. Tools built for distribution instead of centralization. Tools embracing complexity instead of binary reduction. Such tools would transcend technical problem-solving to create different relationships between humans, technologies, and the more-than-human world.

This reimagining flourishes in communities worldwide. The Digital Democracy Project co-designs mapping tools with Indigenous communities to support land sovereignty and ecological stewardship. These tools strengthen community relationships to land and traditional knowledge systems rather than extracting data from communities for external profit.

The Riseup Collective has spent decades building communication infrastructure prioritizing privacy, autonomy, and mutual aid instead of reinforcing surveillance and extraction. Their email, chat, and collaboration tools embody values of solidarity and collective care, demonstrating how digital technologies can support community autonomy.

These examples embody what I call "solidarity as technology"—a practice of tool-making that prioritizes relationship, reciprocity, and collective liberation. This approach recognizes that the technical and the social are never separate; they are always entangled, mutually constituting each other through their relationship.

For open source communities, this perspective suggests that technical decisions are always also social, political, and ecological decisions. The licensing models we choose, the governance structures we implement, the contribution pathways we create—all these shape relationships, communities, and possibilities for being.

Solidarity as technology also means recognizing the multiplicity of technological traditions that exist beyond dominant Western frameworks. Indigenous technological practices, for example, often embody deeply relational approaches to tool-making that prioritize sustainability, reciprocity, and community well-being.

Learning from these diverse technological traditions may guide open source communities to expand our understanding of what technology is and can be. We can move far away from the narrow confines of Silicon Valley innovation narratives toward a richer, more plural technological landscape that honors multiple ways of knowing and being.

The Impossible Gift: Derrida and the Paradox of Open Source

In a late-night conversation with my long-life partner Mateus Knelsen, who has followed the development of this book with the patience of someone who understands that ideas need time to ferment, he offered an observation that cut through months of theoretical wrestling: "You know," he said, "what you're describing about open source—this whole myth of altruistic giving—it's exactly what Derrida dismantled in his analysis of the gift." The statement hung in the air like a key finally finding its lock. It was a stroke of genius that connected philosophical insight to practical technological realities in ways I hadn't fully grasped.

Derrida's deconstruction of gift-giving, most fully articulated in his work *Given Time: I*,[1] reveals a fundamental impossibility at the heart of what we consider generosity. Building on Marcel Mauss's anthropological analysis of gift economies, Derrida identifies a temporal paradox: the moment a gift is recognized as a gift—by either giver or receiver—it enters into an economy of exchange that transforms it into something else entirely. The very consciousness of giving or receiving destroys the purity of the gift, binding it immediately into networks of obligation, gratitude, and future reciprocity. The pure gift—one given without expectation, without recognition, without any trace of reciprocity—would require

---

[1] Derrida, Jacques. *Given Time: I. Counterfeit Money.* Translated by Peggy Kamuf. Chicago: University of Chicago Press, 1992.

a giver so detached from social relations as to be almost mechanical, operating from a position of complete emotional and social neutrality that borders on the inhuman. In other words, the moment we acknowledge it—whether as giver or receiver—it slips into a system of exchange. Expectations creep in. Gratitude takes form. Debts (even emotional ones) begin to accumulate.

As Knelsen put it with characteristic precision, "For a true gift to exist, you would need to have zero feelings, zero motivations, zero expectations—you would essentially need to be a robot."

And yet, this strange, impossible ideal says a lot about the relationships we form around technology. Every time someone submits code to an open source project, there's an underlying current of expectation—however subtle. There's the dopamine of a merged pull request, the long-term benefit of building a public profile, the hope for recognition, or simply the satisfaction of solving a tough problem. These actions happen inside complex temporal and social ecosystems, not in some abstract void: from the immediate recognition of a merged pull request to the long-term career trajectories shaped by contribution histories, from the momentary satisfaction of solving a problem to the generational impacts of technological choices on communities and ecosystems.

But here's where it gets interesting: just because the pure gift is impossible doesn't mean giving loses its meaning. In fact, the impossibility opens up space for a different kind of generosity, "critical giving." This is giving that knows it's entangled in systems of exchange, and rather than pretending otherwise, it tries to work within those systems toward more just, more thoughtful arrangements. It's not naive altruism—it's what you might call a clear-eyed utopianism.

Consider the developer who releases their code as "open source." The rhetoric surrounding such acts invariably invokes language of gifts—"giving back to the community," "sharing freely," contributing without expectation of return. Yet embedded within every such act lies a sophisticated architecture of expectation and exchange that extends far beyond monetary transaction. The GitHub profile becomes a portfolio; the commit history transforms into social currency; the act of contribution positions one within networks of expertise and influence that carry tangible benefits in employment markets and professional communities. The very act of calling it "free" or "open" participates in a kind of collective pact. Both giver and receiver know it's not actually free, but we agree to call it free because there's something else operating there.

And that "something else" is where things get compelling. If you pull back the curtain on open source, you see a dense web of motivations: professional ambition, community recognition, career development, institutional prestige, academic credentials, personal satisfaction, ideological commitment, and yes, sometimes genuine care for collective well-being. But these motivations don't discredit the act of contributing. On the contrary—they show us just how rich and complex the open source ecosystem really is.

And it goes beyond human actors. Code relies on other code, which relies on servers, which rely on energy grids, which rely on resource extraction. Today's tech decisions ripple across time, infrastructure, and geography. They affect ecosystems, economies, and communities. This isn't about individual goodwill; it's a planetary, *more-than-human* story.

The insight becomes even more profound when we recognize that this deconstruction doesn't terminate in cynical dismissal but opens space for genuine transformation. Once we acknowledge that the "gift" isn't really a gift, we can engage in "critical giving"—a contribution that operates with full awareness of its embeddedness in complex economies while working to reshape those economies in more just directions. When you give a gift critically, and when someone receives a gift critically, you have a kind of game in motion where this giving and receiving, with each manifestation, gradually walks toward another place—and this other place is utopia.

What does critical giving look like in practice? It means implementing governance structures that explicitly acknowledge and redistribute the various forms of value—social, cultural, professional, and economic—that circulate through collaborative networks. It means creating recognition systems that honor the full spectrum of contributions: the documentation that makes code accessible, the community care that sustains participation, the emotional labor that mediates conflicts, the maintenance work that keeps systems functioning, and the advocacy that connects projects to broader social movements. Celebrating the work that often goes unseen is keeping it sustainable, as those are essential acts of care that hold everything together.

It means establishing resource-sharing mechanisms that support contributors who lack institutional backing or economic security—funding models that don't depend solely on corporate sponsorship, mentorship programs that transfer knowledge across hierarchies, and infrastructure that reduces barriers to participation.

This philosophical framework helps us understand how concepts like freedom, openness, democracy, and justice operate. These ideals gain their power not from being achievable in pure form but from functioning as "regulative ideals," sort of impossible perfections that nonetheless orient practice toward more ethical directions. Think about it as something impossible to fully achieve, but still shaping how we navigate. Perfect openness doesn't exist. Total inclusivity is unreachable. Absolute freedom is a myth. But striving for these things changes how we build our systems, how we govern our projects, and how we treat one another.

The templates, governance structures, and standards explored throughout this book operate within this tension between the impossible and the practical. They acknowledge that no project will achieve perfect inclusivity while establishing institutional arrangements that move toward rather than away from inclusive participation. They recognize that no license guarantees complete freedom while expanding access and reducing barriers to technological engagement. It's not about achieving some utopian endpoint, but about moving in a direction.

This perspective radically reframes how we understand the relationship between idealism and pragmatism in open source communities. Rather than opposing utopian aspirations to practical constraints, it positions utopian thinking as essential to effective practice—as the regulative ideals that prevent pragmatic accommodation from collapsing into mere reproduction of existing inequalities. The acknowledgment that pure democracy doesn't exist doesn't invalidate efforts to democratize technological governance; it clarifies what such efforts actually accomplish and why they matter. Utopian thinking becomes the engine of pragmatic action.

It also helps us see that decisions we often treat as purely technical—like what license to use, how to structure governance, who gets to merge a PR—are never just technical. They're social, economic, political, even ecological decisions. They carry histories, biases, and long shadows. When we examine what operates within open source economies of exchange, we discover forces that are much bigger than "just tech"—professional hierarchies, cultural capital, institutional power, geopolitical relations, ecological impacts, affective labor, care work, and complex webs of dependence and interdependence that extend across communities, continents, and ecosystems.

Every contribution—no matter how small—happens inside this web. The user, the contributor, the maintainer, and the sponsor—they're all embedded in networks of care, dependency, expectation, and power. None of them stands outside. None of them is "just" a giver or "just" a receiver.

And recognizing that complexity doesn't make things harder. It makes things clearer. It shows us that change isn't about sweeping transformations—it's about "patient intervention": the slow, deliberate shifts in how we work, how we recognize each other, how we share resources, and how we tell our stories. One step at a time.

Each implementation of more inclusive governance creates precedents that influence other projects; each recognition of care work makes such recognition more thinkable elsewhere; each experiment in resource-sharing demonstrates alternative economic arrangements that can be adapted and scaled. It means implementing governance structures that explicitly acknowledge and redistribute the various forms of value—social, cultural, professional, and economic—that circulate through collaborative networks. It means creating recognition systems that value diverse forms of contribution beyond code production. It means establishing resource-sharing mechanisms that support contributors who lack institutional backing or economic security. Most importantly, it means approaching open source development as an ongoing practice of world-making rather than a technical methodology.

Through this lens, open source isn't a finished alternative to proprietary technology. It's what we can call an "utopian tool," a practical way for organizing collective efforts while staying open to futures we can't yet imagine. The commons becomes an unfinished project, perpetually under construction through the concrete practices of communities that understand themselves as engaged in transformation rather than maintenance of existing systems. The commons isn't a thing we inherit— it's something we build, piece by piece, together.

That's why the binaries—commercial vs. non-commercial, individual vs. collective, and technical vs. social—don't hold up. They're not how open source really works. Open source is full of contradiction, tension, and overlap. And it's precisely in that messiness that we find the most room for creativity, transformation, and connection.

To borrow from Donna Haraway, what we need are "situated knowledges"[2]—ways of knowing that understand their own limits but still reach across differences. In open source, that means staying grounded in our specific contexts while building bridges toward broader, more inclusive futures.

---

[2] Haraway, Donna. "Situated Knowledges: The Science Question in Feminism and the Privilege of Partial Perspective." Feminist Studies 14, no. 3 (1988): 575-599.

Deconstructivists understand that words cannot be isolated from their contexts—that meaning emerges through relationships rather than existing as fixed essence. This is precisely what we're doing when we examine "free" and "open" in open source contexts. These terms don't carry stable, universal meanings but operate within specific economies of exchange, professional networks, and cultural arrangements. Rather than seeking universal solutions or neutral platforms, situated approaches to open source governance acknowledge that all technological development emerges from particular positions—geographical, cultural, institutional, and embodied—while creating conditions for these partial perspectives to connect, learn from each other, and coordinate action across differences.

This situatedness extends to recognizing diverse technological traditions that exist beyond dominant Western frameworks. Indigenous computational practices, for example, often embody deeply relational approaches to technology that prioritize sustainability, reciprocity, and collective well-being over efficiency, scale, or individual achievement. Feminist approaches to technology emphasize care, maintenance, and the politics of infrastructure over innovation narratives that privilege disruption and novelty. These alternative technological traditions offer resources for reimagining open source development in ways that honor multiple ways of knowing and being with technology.

What emerges is open source as a technology of approximation—a set of tools and practices for approaching impossible perfections through situated, concrete, and necessarily incomplete interventions. The value of such technologies lies not in their ability to achieve final solutions but in their capacity to open space for ongoing experimentation with alternative ways of organizing technological development and, through that development, social life itself.

AI and Open Source

The movement for open source AI represents one of the most important applications of open source principles today, in the time framed 2025 context. At this critical juncture in technological development, the accessibility of sophisticated AI models for research, adaptation, and public scrutiny has become essential for democratic technological futures. While proprietary systems consolidate power and reinforce existing inequalities, open source models create possibilities for collaborative examination and improvement—though the implementation of openness alone guarantees nothing.

Katharine Jarmul's work on critical AI offers crucial insights into what meaningful openness might entail. Far from resting on technical transparency alone, Jarmul's approach emphasizes models shaped by feminist ethics and critical interrogation rather than the violent, brutalist and alike fascist aesthetics that characterize many contemporary AI systems. Her work with Feminist.AI demonstrates how AI development can incorporate values of care, inclusion, and historical awareness from the ground up, rather than treating ethics as an afterthought to technical implementation.

The language models we build reflect the power structures we inhabit. When we fail to question those structures—when we accept the default parameters of how models are trained, what data they consume, and who gets to shape them—we reproduce technologies of control rather than liberation.

This critical orientation becomes especially urgent as AI outputs increasingly function as perceived truths in public discourse. The epistemological implications run deep—these systems, trained predominantly on texts that reflect existing power structures, now generate content that blurs ethical and moral boundaries while potentially erasing marginalized histories. While presenting as neutral information systems, they encode and amplify existing societal biases, often behind interfaces designed to obscure their constructedness and contingency.

The societal implications extend beyond epistemology into economic and social stratification. Building on Daniel Markovits' *The Meritocracy Trap*, AI technologies exponentially widen existing gaps in society. Those with access to these powerful tools—predominantly wealthy individuals and institutions—gain compounding advantages, while those without access face increasingly insurmountable barriers to participation in economic and social life. The meritocratic mechanisms that once promised mobility have become vehicles for inheritance, and AI threatens to accelerate this trend by automating professional work while concentrating the economic benefits among those who own and control the technology. This dynamic mirrors the broader patterns of technological development under capitalism, where innovations marketed as universally beneficial often deepen existing hierarchies.

Open source principles alone cannot address these structural dynamics. While technical openness creates necessary conditions for democratic oversight and participation, it must be accompanied by governance structures that actively redistribute power and resources. Models developed through feminist and decolonial methodologies, with explicit attention to who benefits and who bears the costs of AI development, offer pathways toward technologies that serve collective liberation rather than intensifying extraction.

This approach demands moving away simplistic understandings of bias and fairness toward deeper questions about what kinds of intelligence we wish to cultivate. Drawing inspiration from Bridle's more-than-human intelligence, we might imagine AI systems designed not to replicate human cognitive patterns but to allow its own intelligence to raise, guide them toward reciprocal relationships with each other and the living world. Such systems would prioritize contextual understanding over universal claims, relational knowledge over extractive data collection, and collective well-being over optimization metrics.

The stakes could hardly be higher. Without thoughtful intervention shaped by diverse voices and critical perspectives, AI systems risk amplifying existing biases, centralizing power, and accelerating extractive relationships with both human communities and ecological systems. Yet designed with care and governed democratically, these same technologies create possibilities for addressing complex social and ecological challenges, democratizing knowledge production, and cultivating more sustainable relationships with the living world.

This work represents not a peripheral concern but the very heart of open source's revolutionary potential in our time—a test of whether technological development can truly serve collective liberation or merely reproduce existing hierarchies in new forms.

Standards As Base for A New Narrative

Standards exist in that peculiar realm where intention meets invisibility— where what begins as explicit design gradually submerges into the taken-for-granted infrastructure of our lives. They shape our actions, define our possibilities, yet operate most powerfully when least noticed. As Georgina Voss demonstrates in *Systems Ultra*, the very systems that govern our technological lives achieve their greatest authority precisely when they fade from conscious awareness, when they become—to borrow Clifford Siskin's framing—the invisible architecture through which power flows.

Consider the ubiquitous QWERTY keyboard beneath your fingertips, a standard born from mechanical typewriter constraints that persists through digital transformation. Its arrangement shapes not merely how we type but how we conceptualize the relationship between thought and expression, between body and machine. The standard's power lies in its unremarkable presence, in the way it shapes behavior without announcing itself as a political or cultural intervention. The keyboard remains, while our awareness of its artifice recedes.

This quality of standards—their gradual disappearance into the background of everyday practice—offers profound possibilities for transformative change. Standards operate through habits, those embodied dispositions that structure how we perceive and respond to the world without conscious calculation. They work not through dramatic rupture but through the patient reconfiguration of what feels natural, what becomes automatic.

The standards proposed throughout this book aspire toward this quality of gentle enforcement. Far from imposing change through violence or mandate, they operate through representation in our collective imaginary—through subtle shifts in how we envision technological creation, what we value as contribution, and whose knowledge we recognize as legitimate. A README template that explicitly acknowledges affective labor doesn't merely document such work; it gradually reshapes what contributors understand as worthy of recognition. A governance structure that distributes decision-making power transforms not only who holds formal authority but also what forms of leadership become imaginable.

Standards possess a unique temporal dimension—they operate simultaneously in present practice and future possibility. The templates outlined in Chapter 4 function in immediate, pragmatic terms: they solve coordination problems, reduce friction, and clarify expectations. Yet they simultaneously encode aspirational futures, embedding within seemingly mundane documents the seeds of more equitable technological relations. Each time a contributor references the governance document or follows the contribution guidelines, they participate in performing both the present reality and the possible future the standard envisions.

The contemporary technological landscape remains deeply marked by persistent narratives about genius, innovation, and power. The figure of the individual (usually white, usually male) technical visionary continues to haunt our collective imagination. These narrative patterns run so deep they structure even counter-cultural technological movements, including many open source communities. When we are shaped by patterns we don't recognize, we might reproduce what we critique. Even those committed to technological democratization may unconsciously replicate hierarchical patterns that feel natural precisely because systems have rendered them invisible.

Standards offer one path through this predicament—not as universal solution but as grounded intervention. They operate within the tension between reification (turning abstract ideas into concrete forms) and participation (the social negotiation of meaning). Standards reify certain values—transparency, inclusion, and recognition of diverse labor— while simultaneously opening spaces for communities to participate in interpreting and adapting these values to local contexts.

The relationship between standards and narrative proves especially potent. Where dominant narratives about technology center individual brilliance, standards can foreground collective care. Where prevailing stories emphasize disruption and novelty, standards can illuminate continuity and maintenance. Where conventional accounts erase certain forms of labor and knowledge, standards can make these contributions visible and valued.

This narrative dimension matters profoundly because humans think primarily through frames and metaphors rather than isolated facts. The standards proposed throughout this book operate not merely as technical guidelines but as frames that shape how we perceive technological creation. They offer metaphors that transform how we understand the relationship between technology, society, and ecology.

Consider the standard practice of maintaining a CREDIT.md file that acknowledges diverse forms of contribution. Beyond its practical function, this document embodies a different metaphorical framing of technological creation—not as individual achievement but as ecological relationship, not as heroic invention but as collective stewardship. Each time a project updates this file, it subtly reinforces this alternative framing, making it more available for thinking and action.

Through this gentle, persistent reframing, standards gradually transform the cultural narratives that shape technological development. They work through recursive processes where classification systems interact with the entities they classify, changing how both are understood. The standards we adopt don't merely describe technological communities; they transform how those communities perceive themselves and their work.

The aspirational dimension of standards deserves particular emphasis. Standards function simultaneously as descriptive and prescriptive—they document existing practice while reaching toward possible futures. This temporal duality allows them to serve as bridges between current realities and imagined possibilities, creating "capabilities"—substantive freedoms to achieve various combinations of functions that constitute flourishing.

Within the specific context of open source, standards create capabilities for more equitable participation by establishing conditions where diverse contributors can meaningfully shape technological futures. They develop conceptual tools that help make sense of shared experiences, particularly those that dominant frameworks render illegible.

The standards proposed throughout this book thus represent material and affective frameworks that make certain forms of relation possible. They create conditions where care work becomes visible, where governance becomes participatory, and where technological creation becomes responsive to diverse needs and knowledges.

This transformative potential emerges not from the standards alone but from their embeddedness in living communities. Standards detached from practice quickly become empty formalism—bureaucratic exercises that reproduce the very hierarchies they ostensibly challenge. The templates in Chapter 4 achieve their transformative potential only when communities engage with them as living documents, adapting them to local contexts while maintaining their core commitments to equity, transparency, and shared governance.

364

Through this engaged adaptation, standards gradually modify our social imaginaries, the ways ordinary people imagine their social surroundings, often expressed in images, stories, and legends rather than theoretical terms. They transform what feels possible, natural, or inevitable in technological creation. The repeated practice of acknowledging affective labor, distributing decision-making power, or centering ecological relationships gradually makes these patterns feel normal rather than exceptional.

This normalizing function represents both the promise and the peril of standards. At their best, standards can normalize practices that foster more equitable and ecological technological relations. Yet this very power demands vigilance, as standards themselves can calcify into rigid forms that reproduce exclusion or exploitation in new guises. The templates offered throughout this book require continuous critical engagement, adaptation, and renewal to maintain their transformative potential.

The standards proposed throughout this book thus serve as base materials for new technological narratives—stories about how technologies emerge, who creates them, and what values they embody. By embedding different patterns of recognition, governance, and relation into everyday practice, they gradually transform distribution of the sensible, the system of divisions and boundaries that defines what is visible, audible, and ultimately possible within a shared social space.

Through this patient, persistent reconfiguration of technological practice, standards contribute to the pluriverse, a world where many worlds fit. They create conditions where technological creation can emerge from diverse knowledge systems, embody multiple values, and serve varied communities. Standards thus become not tools of homogenization but frameworks for plurality, not mechanisms of control but structures that enable flourishing across difference.

The work of standards remains necessarily incomplete, permanently unfinished. As Donna Haraway reminds us, we need technologies not of mastery but of partial perspective—situated knowledges that acknowledge their own partiality while creating possibilities for connection across difference. The templates offered throughout this book allows for this partiality, recognizing that no standard can encompass all contexts or anticipate all needs. Their transformative potential lies precisely in this openness to continuous adaptation, revision, and renewal.

In this sense, standards operate as tentative suggestions for how diverse worlds might temporarily coordinate without presuming final consensus. They create reflection spaces where communities can reflect on technological practices, consider their implications, and adapt them to serve multiple values and needs.

The transformative potential of standards thus emerges not from their authority but from their adaptability, not from their universality but from their situatedness, not from their permanence but from their continuous renewal. They mark an orientation, a coordination, and an opening toward technological futures yet to be crafted together.

The Ecosystem of Change: Individual, Collective, and Systemic Transformation

The challenges facing open source communities—from labor exploitation to exclusionary practices to binary thinking—cannot be addressed through individual action alone. They demand coordinated change across multiple scales: individual, collective, and systemic.

At the individual level, each person can examine their own relationship to technology and open source. We can interrogate our assumptions about merit, expertise, and contribution. We can amplify marginalized voices instead of speaking over them. We can practice forms of technological engagement that prioritize care, reciprocity, and collective well-being.

These individual practices create ripples that influence others and help shift cultural norms. Yet without collective organization to coordinate action, pool resources, and create structures for sustained change, they remain insufficient.

At the collective level, communities can implement the standards and governance models we've explored throughout this book. They can establish formal structures for recognizing diverse contributions, redistributing resources, and sharing decision-making power. They can build relationships of solidarity with other movements for social, economic, and ecological justice, recognizing that technological liberation intertwines with broader struggles for equity and sustainability.

These collective efforts create a common-pool of resources, shared resources that benefit all community members and are governed through collective decision-making, not by the common expected market competition or state control. Open source software itself represents such a commons, as do the knowledge, practices, and relationships that sustain open source communities.

Yet even robust community governance faces constraints from broader systemic conditions—from intellectual property laws that reinforce enclosure to economic systems that necessitate precarious labor to cultural narratives that privilege certain forms of expertise over others. Addressing these systemic factors requires engagement with policy, institutional change, and broader social movements.

At the systemic level, open source communities can advocate for policies supporting digital commons, from funding for public digital infrastructure to legal protections for community-governed technologies. They can build alliances with movements for labor rights, racial justice, disability justice, and environmental sustainability, recognizing the interconnectedness of these struggles.

This three-dimensional approach—individual, collective, and systemic—creates "stacked functions," a term borrowed from permaculture designers, where each element serves multiple purposes and reinforces other elements in the system. Individual changes in practice support collective governance intervention, which in turn create leverage points for systemic change.

When thinking ecologically about change, we move from linear, cause-effect models toward an understanding of social transformation as emergent, relational, and complex. This ecological thinking on a more-than-human perspective recognizes that technological change happens through intricate webs of relationship and interdependence, a refreshing approach to the old-fashioned and, honestly, boring, heroic innovation.

Seeds of Transformation: Stories from the Field

Throughout this book, we've encountered individuals and communities who are already practicing alternative ways of being with technology. These examples serve as seeds that can germinate in diverse contexts, adapting to local conditions while maintaining core principles of equity, sustainability, and shared governance.

In Chapter 5, we explored the Sauce Labs Fellowship Program, which created pathways for underrepresented and underestimated individuals in technology while addressing open source sustainability. This initiative demonstrated how corporate resources can be redirected toward equity when supported by intentional institutional design and clear ethical commitments.

We also examined Coyotiv's "Pirate Model," which reimagines organizational structure through decentralized authority, transparent compensation, and governance inspired by historical pirate crews. This experiment shows how alternative organizational forms can foster both innovation and equity, challenging conventional corporate hierarchies.

Katharine Jarmul's work creating liberatory spaces for feminist AI development offers another powerful example. By establishing temporary autonomous zones where different technological futures can be imagined and practiced, Jarmul demonstrates how intentional space-making can create conditions for technological sovereignty and collective imagination.

They are real examples of what Adrienne Maree Brown calls "emergent strategy"—approaches to change that recognize complexity, prioritize relationships, and embrace uncertainty. They start where they are, with the resources and communities available, rather than waiting for perfect conditions or universal solutions.

But these seeds need fertile soil to grow. They need supportive ecosystems of funding, mentorship, and institutional partnership. They need legal frameworks that protect commons-based approaches, and they need cultural narratives that value collective well-being over individual achievement or market growth.

Creating these supportive conditions requires economic practices that exist alongside, within, and against capitalist systems. From platform cooperatives to time banks to community land trusts, these diverse economies demonstrate that alternative ways of organizing resources and labor are not utopian fantasies; they are practical realities already emerging in communities around the world.

For open source, this means exploring funding models that are not solely reliant on corporate sponsorship or venture capital, governance structures beyond benevolent dictators or foundation control, and value metrics that consider qualitative and contextual interpretation. It means asking different questions that don't oversimplify or generalize it, as in "How can we sustain this project?" Instead, we could ask root questions such as "What kind of world is this project helping to create?"

The Living Practice of Open Source

As we've journeyed through this book, we've evolved from understanding open source as a method for producing software toward recognizing it as a living practice of relationship, collaboration, and collective imagination. This shift in perspective invites us to approach open source not as a fixed entity but as an evolving ecosystem of practices, values, and possibilities.

Seeing open source as a living practice means recognizing its contradictions rather than trying to resolve them into a single coherent narrative. It means acknowledging that open source simultaneously operates as a revolutionary force challenging proprietary models and as a system that often reproduces existing inequalities. It means understanding that these tensions aren't flaws to be eliminated but generative frictions that can drive transformation when engaged thoughtfully.

This living practice requires resisting both simplistic optimism and paralyzing pessimism in favor of response-able attention to complex realities, in Haraway's sense of remaining accountable within interdependent worlds. It means neither idealizing open source as a utopian solution nor dismissing it as irrevocably compromised, but rather committing to the ongoing work of making it more just, more inclusive, and more ecologically sustainable.

In practical terms, this commitment manifests in the continuous cycle of reflection and action that characterizes genuine transformative work. It means implementing the standards and governance models we've explored throughout this book, reflecting on their impacts, adapting based on feedback, and continuing the cycle of experimentation and learning.

This praxis isn't the responsibility of a few designated leaders or experts; it's the responsibility of all who participate, create, and consume it directly and indirectly. Each pull request, each code review, each documentation contribution becomes an opportunity to practice more equitable and ecological ways of creating technology. Each governance decision, each conflict resolution process, each resource allocation choice reflects and shapes community values.

Approaching open source as a living practice creates space for emergence—for new patterns, relationships, and possibilities that couldn't have been predicted or designed in advance. This emergent quality and natural self-organization of the commons is the process through which complex systems generate structures and behaviors without centralized control.

Self-organization doesn't mean abandoning intentionality or responsibility. On the contrary, it requires intentional adaptation—the deliberate cultivation of conditions that support desired emergent patterns. The standards, governance models, and practices we've explored throughout this book serve as these intentional adaptations, creating conditions where more equitable and ecological technological relationships can emerge.

An Ongoing Revolution

As we arrive at this moment of profound technological reorientation, open source returns as a critical force, and its principles resonating with renewed urgency. Yet for its potential to be fully realized, we must confront the contradictions and exclusions it has carried. What's needed now is not a finished program, but an ongoing, situated practice: one that embeds care, ecological consciousness, and plural ways of being into the very architecture of our tools. In reclaiming open source as a living, collective endeavor, we create space to reimagine how technology participates in shaping a world more attuned to interdependence, justice, and repair.

The future of open source isn't predetermined but continually created through our choices, relationships, and commitments. Each contribution, each governance decision, each standard implemented shapes not just software but the social and ecological systems in which that software is embedded. Each line of code carries within it particular ways of relating to the world—particular politics, ethics, and possibilities for being.

The seeming inevitability of current technological paradigms—surveillance capitalism, digital extraction, algorithmic control—is not a fact but a narrative that can be challenged and rewritten through collective action.

Open source offers us tools for this rewriting, and I am not talking about the technical tools; I mean the social ones, practices for cultivating the commons. Reimagining the tools is a fundamental part, for which we may use the lenses of more-than-human intelligence and solidarity, so we can transform open source from a method of software development into a catalyst for broader liberation.

This transformation begins with you—with your projects, your communities, your daily practices. It begins with implementing the standards we've explored throughout this book, with questioning assumptions about merit and contribution, with creating space for diverse forms of participation and knowledge.

But it doesn't end with you. It extends through networks of relationship, collaboration, and solidarity that span communities, movements, and ecosystems. It connects with broader struggles for social, economic, and ecological justice, recognizing that technological liberation is inseparable from other forms of liberation.

As you leave this book and return to your communities, I invite you to carry these questions with you:

- How can your open source practices foster relationships of reciprocity rather than extraction?

- Whose knowledge and labor are centered in your projects, and whose are marginalized?

- What forms of intelligence—human and more-than-human—might inform your technological practice?

- How can your governance structures distribute power rather than concentrating it?

- What worlds are your technologies helping to create, and are those the worlds you want to live in?

These questions have no simple answers, but the practice of asking them—of staying with the trouble—transforms both the asker and the technological systems they help create. It opens spaces for constellations of co-resistance, where diverse movements converge and strengthen each other through their relationship.

The revolution we need transcends the question of who writes code—it transforms what code does, how it's created, who it serves, and what values it embodies. By recognizing technology's deep entanglement with social, political, and ecological systems, we move beyond the myth of neutrality. Most importantly, we understand ourselves as active participants in shaping technological futures, rather than passive recipients of technological change.

As we stand at this crossroads, facing unprecedented ecological crisis, technological acceleration, and social fragmentation, open source offers us something precious: a living practice of solidarity, a commitment to the commons, and a reminder that other ways of being with technology are not only possible but already emerging around us.

The work continues. The revolution is ongoing. And you are invited to participate not as a consumer or user of technology but as a co-creator of technological futures that serve life, justice, and collective liberation.

Let us write the code that writes the world we wish to inhabit—together. And let us do so with full awareness of the paradox at the heart of this work: that every contribution, no matter how freely offered, is entangled in systems of recognition, reciprocity, and power. As Derrida reminds us, the pure gift may be impossible, but this impossibility is not a failure, it is an opening. It invites us into a practice of critical giving, one that does not deny its embeddedness in social and economic ecosystems, but seeks to navigate them with care, reflexivity, and a commitment to more just forms of exchange.

This is the horizon of open source as an impossible gift: not a naive offering beyond economy, but a conscious, situated act of giving that reshapes the very conditions under which giving and receiving occur. It is an invitation to build not only software, but new architectures of relation—where contribution becomes a practice of solidarity, and where every line of code might move us, however incrementally, toward worlds of reciprocity and equity.

Complete Bibliography by Chapter

General Works Referenced Throughout

Ahmed, Sara. *On Being Included: Racism and Diversity in Institutional Life.* Duke University Press, 2012.

Benjamin, Ruha. *Race After Technology: Abolitionist Tools for the New Jim Code.* Polity Press, 2019.

Benjamin, Ruha. *Viral Justice: How We Grow the World We Want.* Princeton University Press, 2022.

Bridle, James. *Ways of Being: Animals, Plants, Machines: The Search for a Planetary Intelligence.* Farrar, Straus and Giroux, 2022.

Brown, Adrienne Maree. *Emergent Strategy: Shaping Change, Changing Worlds.* AK Press, 2017.

Brown, Adrienne Maree. *Pleasure Activism: The Politics of Feeling Good.* AK Press, 2019.

Criado Perez, Caroline. *Invisible Women: Data Bias in a World Designed for Men.* Abrams Press, 2019.

Crenshaw, Kimberlé. "Demarginalizing the Intersection of Race and Sex: A Black Feminist Critique of Antidiscrimination Doctrine, Feminist Theory and Antiracist Politics." *University of Chicago Legal Forum* 1989, no. 1 (1989): 139–167.

Crenshaw, Kimberlé. "Mapping the Margins: Intersectionality, Identity Politics, and Violence Against Women of Color." *Stanford Law Review* 43, no. 6 (1991): 1241–1299.

Eghbal, Nadia. *Working in Public: The Making and Maintenance of Open Source Software*. Stripe Press, 2020.

Foucault, Michel. *Discipline and Punish: The Birth of the Prison*. Translated by Alan Sheridan. New York: Pantheon Books, 1977.

Haraway, Donna. "Situated Knowledges: The Science Question in Feminism and the Privilege of Partial Perspective." *Feminist Studies* 14, no. 3 (1988): 575–599.

Hardt, Michael, and Antonio Negri. *Empire*. Harvard University Press, 2000.

Hardt, Michael, and Antonio Negri. *Multitude: War and Democracy in the Age of Empire*. Penguin Press, 2004.

Hochschild, Arlie Russell. *The Managed Heart: Commercialization of Human Feeling*. University of California Press, 1983.

Littler, Jo. *Against Meritocracy: Culture, Power and Myths of Mobility*. Routledge, 2017.

Markovits, Daniel. *The Meritocracy Trap: How America's Foundational Myth Feeds Inequality, Dismantles the Middle Class, and Devours the Elite*. Penguin Press, 2019.

Noble, Safiya Umoja. *Algorithms of Oppression: How Search Engines Reinforce Racism*. NYU Press, 2018.

Ostrom, Elinor. *Governing the Commons: The Evolution of Institutions for Collective Action*. Cambridge University Press, 1990.

Siskin, Clifford. *System: The Shaping of Modern Knowledge*. MIT Press, 2016.

Voss, Georgina. *Systems Ultra: Decoding the Structures that Govern Our World*. Profile Books, 2023.

Winner, Langdon. "Do Artifacts Have Politics?" *Daedalus* 109, no. 1 (1980): 121–136.

Chapter 1: The Journey Begins

All references from general works plus:

Bratton, Benjamin H. *The Stack: On Software and Sovereignty.* MIT Press, 2015.

Delap, Lucy. *Feminisms: A Global History.* University of Chicago Press, 2020.

Federici, Silvia. *Caliban and the Witch: Women, the Body and Primitive Accumulation.* Autonomedia, 2004.

Gil, Gilberto. Various speeches and policy documents as Minister of Culture, Brazil, 2003–2008.

Robinson, Cedric J. *Black Marxism: The Making of the Black Radical Tradition.* 2nd ed. University of North Carolina Press, 2000.

Santa Cruz, Victoria. "Me Gritaron Negra." Performance poem. First performed 1960s, widely circulated from 1978.

Stallman, Richard. "The GNU Manifesto." 1985. `https://www.gnu.org/gnu/manifesto.html`

Tisselli, Eugenio, and Nadia Cortés. "Technological Rewriting." Presentation at inaugural technological rewriting meeting, Mexico City, 2016.

Chapter 2: Impressions of Open Source

Black Duck Software. "2025 Open Source Security and Risk Analysis Report." Synopsys, 2024. `https://www.blackduck.com/resources/analyst-reports/open-source-security-risk-analysis.html`

Davis, Angela. *Women, Race, and Class.* Vintage Books, 1983.

Ferguson, Kirby. *Everything is a Remix.* Web series, 2010–2012. Remastered 2015. `https://www.everythingisaremix.info/`

Fonseca, Felipe Schmidt. *Generous Cities: Alternative Approaches to Handling Excess Materials.* PhD thesis, 2024.

Free Software Foundation. "The Free Software Definition." Accessed January 2025. https://www.gnu.org/philosophy/free-sw.html

GNU Project. "What is Copyleft?" Accessed January 2025. https://www.gnu.org/licenses/copyleft.html

Haudenosaunee Confederacy. "Who We Are." Official website. https://www.haudenosauneeconfederacy.com/who-we-are/

hooks, bell. *Teaching to Transgress: Education as the Practice of Freedom.* Routledge, 1994.

Jordan, June. *Civil Wars.* Beacon Press, 1981.

Langel, Tobie. "1 Billion Dollars for Open Source Maintainers." State of Open Conference, London, February 2024. https://www.youtube.com/watch?v=oB-v2_YnrHk

Lopez de la Fuente, J. Manrique. "A Guide to Setting Up Your Open Source Program Office (OSPO) for Success." *Opensource.com*, 2020. https://opensource.com/article/20/5/open-source-program-office

Lorde, Audre. *Sister Outsider: Essays and Speeches.* Ten Speed Press, 1984.

Menotti, Gabriel. "Gambiarra And The Prototyping Perspective." Media Lab Matadero, Madrid. https://www.medialab-matadero.es/sites/default/files/import/ftp_medialab/5/5379/5379_4.pdfCreative Commons. "About CC." Accessed January 2025. https://creativecommons.org/about/

Omier, Emily. "What Is an Open Source Company?" Blog post. https://www.emilyomier.com/blog/what-is-an-open-source-company

Open Source Initiative. "The Open Source Definition." Accessed January 2025. https://opensource.org/osd

Peterson, Christine. "How I Coined the Term 'Open Source'." *Open Source Initiative*, February 19, 2018. https://opensource.com/article/18/2/coining-term-open-source-software

Surowiecki, James. *The Wisdom of Crowds.* Doubleday, 2004.

TODO Group. "Why Open Source Matters to Your Enterprise." Linux Foundation report, 2020. https://project.linuxfoundation.org/hubfs/Reports/Why-open-source-software-matters-to-your-enterprise_090820.pdf

TODO Group. "OSPO Definition." GitHub repository. https://github.com/todogroup/ospodefinition.org

Infrastructure, Governance, and Others

Cybersecurity & Infrastructure Security Agency. "Software Bill of Materials (SBOM)." https://www.cisa.gov/sbom

European Commission. "Joinup: Interoperability Solutions for Public Administrations." https://joinup.ec.europa.eu/

European Parliament Research Service. "Digital Sovereignty for Europe." Policy briefing, 2020. https://www.europarl.europa.eu/RegData/etudes/BRIE/2020/651992/EPRS_BRI(2020)651992_EN.pdf

European Union. "Cyber Resilience Act (CRA)." Legislative proposal. https://digital-strategy.ec.europa.eu/en/library/cyber-resilience-act

Kugler, Leonhard. "openDesk on openCode: Developing a Secure Office Suite and SDLC." FOSDEM 2025 Government Collaboration DevRoom. https://fosdem.org/2025/schedule/event/fosdem-2025-5572-opendesk-on-opencode-developing-a-secure-office-suite-and-sdlc/

National Security Agency. "Software Bill of Materials (SBOM) Requirements." Various policy documents.

Open Source Observatory (OSOR). "European Commission Open Source Strategy." Various documentation.

Sovereign Tech Agency. "Mission and Vision." https://sovereigntech/

Thévenet, Axel. "The Role of Open Source for an Interoperable Europe." FOSS-Backstage 2023. Video recording available.

United Nations World Summit on the Information Society. "Tunis Commitment." November 18, 2005. https://documents.un.org/doc/undoc/gen/n06/254/42/img/n0625442.pdf

White House. "Executive Order on Improving the Nation's Cybersecurity." May 12, 2021. https://www.whitehouse.gov/briefing-room/presidential-actions/2021/05/12/executive-order-on-improving-the-nations-cybersecurity/

Wired Magazine. "The Brazilian Minister Who's Freeing Culture." November 2004. https://www.wired.com/2004/11/linux-6/

Chapter 3: Unraveling Diversity and Labor Issues

All references from general works plus:

Benet, Jorge. "Cooperative Research: Technology Cooperatives Managing Digital Infrastructure." 2024. https://infraestructura.digital/index-en.html

Edwards, Paul N. *The Closed World: Computers and the Politics of Discourse in Cold War America.* MIT Press, 1996.

Freire, Paulo. *Pedagogy of the Oppressed.* Continuum International Publishing Group, 1970.

Gender Equity Policy Institute. "The Free-Time Gender Gap Report." October 2024. https://thegepi.org/the-free-time-gender-gap/

Gerson, Kathleen. *The Unfinished Revolution: Coming of Age in a New Era of Gender, Work, and Family.* Oxford University Press, 2010.

Global Slavery Index. "2023 Global Estimates of Modern Slavery." Walk Free Foundation, 2023. https://www.walkfree.org/

Hansen, Madeline Pendleton. Business model described in various interviews, 2023–2024.

Hershey, Traci. *Rest Is Resistance: A Manifesto.* Little, Brown Spark, 2022.

International Labour Organization. "Women in Labour Markets Report 2023." 2023.

International Monetary Fund. "Women, Work, and the Economy Report 2023." 2023.

Jones, Van. Comment on CNN. November 2024. https://youtu.be/mz_cPUwD2MU?si=RTMdq3nb8GccCdif

Oluo, Ijeoma. *So You Want to Talk About Race.* Seal Press, 2018.

Open Technology Fund. "FOSS Sustainability Fund Guidelines." 2024. https://www.opentech.fund/

Outreachy. "Program Information." Accessed 2025. https://www.outreachy.org/

Participatory Budgeting Project. "History of Participatory Budgeting in Porto Alegre." Various reports, 1989-present.

United Nations. "Gender Equity Report 2024." 2024.

White Swan Foundation. "Gender Norms and Unpaid Care Work Study." 2023.

Chapter 4: Making It a Standard

All references from general works plus:

All Contributors. "Recognition for Open Source Contributors." GitHub specification. https://allcontributors.org/

Casari, Alice, Katie McLaughlin, Matt Zampini Trujillo, et al. "Open Source Ecosystems Need Equitable Credit Across Contributions." *Nature Computational Science* 1, no. 2 (2021): 2. https://doi.org/10.1038/s43588-020-00011-w

CHAOSS Project. "Community Health Analytics Open Source Software." Metrics and guidelines. https://chaoss.community/

Contributor Covenant. "A Code of Conduct for Open Source Projects." https://www.contributor-covenant.org/

Ehmke, Coraline Ada. "Post-Meritocracy Manifesto." 2018. https://postmeritocracy.org/

Meluso, Julie, Alice Casari, Katie McLaughlin, Matt Zampini Trujillo. "Invisible Labor in Open Source Software Ecosystems." *arXiv preprint* arXiv:2401.06889v2 (2025). https://doi.org/10.48550/arXiv.2401.06889

Mozilla. "Community Participation Guidelines." https://www.mozilla.org/en-US/about/governance/policies/participation/

OCEAN Project. "Attributing Contributor Roles in Open Source Software." Vermont Complex Systems Center, University of Vermont, supported by Google Open Source Program Office.

OpenServ. "Code of Conduct." https://docs.openserv.ai/resources/code_of_conduct

Web Content Accessibility Guidelines (WCAG). "WCAG 2.1 Standards." W3C, 2018. https://www.w3.org/WAI/standards-guidelines/wcag/

Young, Jean-Gabriel, Alice Casari, Katie McLaughlin, Matt Zampini Trujillo, Laurent Hébert-Dufresne, James P. Bagrow. "Which Contributions Count? Analysis of Attribution in Open Source." *2021 IEEE/ACM 18th International Conference on Mining Software Repositories* (2021): 242-253. https://doi.org/10.1109/MSR52588.2021.00036

Chapter 5: Models for a Sustainable, Diverse Open Source

All references from general works plus:

Banco Palmas. "Community Banking Model." Fortaleza, Brazil. https://bancopalmas.com/

Cotton, Esther. "Meet the Fellows: Esther Cotton." *Sauce Labs Blog*, 2023. https://saucelabs.com/resources/blog/meet-the-fellows-esther-cotton

de Certeau, Michel. *The Practice of Everyday Life*. University of California Press, 1984.

DIY Girls. "Organization Mission and Programs." https://diygirls.org/

Escobar, Arturo. *Designs for the Pluriverse: Radical Interdependence, Autonomy, and the Making of Worlds*. Duke University Press, 2018.

Fricker, Miranda. *Epistemic Injustice: Power and the Ethics of Knowing*. Oxford University Press, 2007.

Gibson-Graham, J.K. *A Postcapitalist Politics*. University of Minnesota Press, 2006.

hooks, bell. *Teaching to Transgress: Education as the Practice of Freedom*. Routledge, 1994.

Ikegah, Ruth. Interview referenced in GitHub README stories. https://github.com/readme/stories/ruth-ikegah

Kanabar, Sandeep. "CNCF Deaf and Hard of Hearing Working Group Spotlight." *Kubernetes.dev*, September 30, 2024. https://www.kubernetes.dev/blog/2024/09/30/cncf-deaf-and-hard-of-hearing-working-group-spotlight/

Madry, Danielle. "Meet the Fellows: Danielle Madry." *Sauce Labs Blog*, 2023. https://saucelabs.com/resources/blog/meet-the-fellows-danielle-madry

Nap Ministry, The. "Rest as Resistance." https://thenapministry.wordpress.com/

Oliveira, Paloma. "The New and Improved Elemental Selenium is Here!" *Sauce Labs Blog*, 2023. https://saucelabs.com/resources/blog/the-new-and-improved-elemental-selenium-is-here

Paganini, Catherine. Work with CNCF Deaf and Hard of Hearing Working Group, 2023-2025.

Sauce Labs. "Announcing the Fellows in the Sauce Labs Open Source Community Fellowship Program." *Sauce Labs Blog*, 2022. https://saucelabs.com/resources/blog/announcing-sauce-labs-fellows-2022

Skorupa, Django. "From Dreams to Reality: The Challenges of Designing for Functionality." *Sauce Labs Blog*, 2023. `https://saucelabs.com/resources/blog/from-dreams-to-reality-the-challenges-of-designing-for-functionality`

Summers, Laura. "The Aesthetics of AI: From Cyberpunk to Fascism." Talk presented at PyCon DE & PyData Berlin 2025. `https://pretalx.com/pyconde-pydata-2025/talk/933YXH/`

Additional References

African American Policy Forum. "Intersectionality Matters!" Podcast. `https://www.aapf.org/intersectionality-matters`

Amnesty International. "Racial Bias in Facial Recognition Algorithms." `https://www.amnesty.ca/features/racial-bias-in-facial-recognition-algorithms/`

Amazônas. "Music Theatre in Three Parts." Collaboration between Laymert Garcia dos Santos and ZKM Center for Art and Media, 2010.

CHAOSS Community. "Diversity, Equity & Inclusion Working Group." Established 2017. `https://chaoss.community/`

Cloud Native Computing Foundation. "Deaf and Hard of Hearing Working Group." Various resources and meeting notes.

containerd. "ADOPTERS.md File." GitHub repository. `https://github.com/containerd/containerd/blob/main/ADOPTERS.md`

Crenshaw, Kimberlé, Neil Gotanda, Gary Peller, and Kendall Thomas, eds. *Critical Race Theory: The Key Writings That Formed the Movement.* The New Press, 1995.

Garay Ariza, Gloria, and Mara Viveros Vigoya, eds. *Cuerpo, Diferencias y Desigualdades.* Universidad Nacional de Colombia, Centro de Estudios Sociales, 1999.

Myers, Verna. *Moving Diversity Forward: How to Go From Well-Meaning to Well-Doing.* American Bar Association, 2011.

Salt of the Earth. Directed by Herbert J. Biberman. 1954.

Vice Media. "Amazon AI Recruitment Tool Gender Bias Investigation." 2018.

Chapter 6: Weaving the Commons

All references from general works plus:

Derrida, Jacques. *Given Time: I. Counterfeit Money.* Translated by Peggy Kamuf. Chicago: University of Chicago Press, 1992.

Haraway, Donna. *Staying with the Trouble: Making Kin in the Chthulucene.* Duke University Press, 2016.

Index

P, Q

GPSR Compliance
The European Union's (EU) General Product Safety Regulation (GPSR) is a set
of rules that requires consumer products to be safe and our obligations to
ensure this.

If you have any concerns about our products, you can contact us on

ProductSafety@springernature.com

In case Publisher is established outside the EU, the EU authorized
representative is:

Springer Nature Customer Service Center GmbH
Europaplatz 3
69115 Heidelberg, Germany